Wives for cattle

International Library of Anthropology

Editor: Adam Kuper, University of Leiden

Arbor Scientiae
Arbor Vitae

A catalogue of other Social Science books published by Routledge &
Kegan Paul will be found at the end of this volume.

Wives for cattle

Bridewealth and marriage in Southern Africa

Adam Kuper

Routledge & Kegan Paul

London, Boston, Melbourne and Henley

First published in 1982
by Routledge & Kegan Paul Ltd
39 Store Street,
London WC1E 7DD,
9 Park Street,
Boston, Mass. 02108, USA,
296 Beaconsfield Parade
Middle Park
Melbourne, 3206, Australia and
Broadway House,
Newtown Road,
Henley-on-Thames,
Oxon RG9 1EN
Set in 10 on 12 point Press Roman by
Hope Services, Abingdon, Oxon
and printed in Great Britain by
T. J. Press Ltd., Padstow, Cornwall

Library of Congress Cataloging in Publication Data

Kuper, Adam.
Wives for cattle.
(International library of anthropology)
Bibliography: p.
Includes index.
1. Bride price – Africa, Southern.
2. Marriage customs and rites – Africa,
Southern. 3. Africa, Southern – Social life
and customs. I. Title. II. Series.
GN656.K86 392'.5'0968 81-17872

ISBN 0-7100-0989-5 AACR2

For three fellow-tribesmen

Hilda Kuper (my FBW), who introduced me to the African cultures of Southern Africa, and to ethnographic fieldwork; Meyer Fortes, who encouraged me to reason about ethnographic materials; and Isaac Schapera, the master of Southern Bantu studies, who established standards of scholarship which inspire us all.

Contents

Illustrations

Maps

Preface

The present book ends a phase in a project which has occupied me for just over a decade. I began at Makerere University in Kampala by comparing my field materials on Kgalagari ward organization with the compilations of Isaac Schapera and others on Tswana, Southern Sotho and Pedi wards. After several weeks I told a friend I would abandon the attempt. It would take months to make sense of the resemblances and differences, and if I were to continue I would have to attack the kinship systems, richly documented but barely analysed. My friend, a sculptor, professionally reconciled to shaping recalcitrant materials, suggested that I persevere, and, although initially piqued by her lack of understanding, I did.

As the project developed it changed its form. Fresh problems were posed, requiring experiment with alternative methods and theoretical perspectives, which in turn were likely to suggest new approaches to the issues. Moreover, each successive analysis forced me to reconsider earlier hypotheses and models. Various papers published over the decade (and listed in the bibliography) record temporary syntheses, some since abandoned. I have no illusions that the present book represents a definitive statement, but further progress would probably involve either fresh field research or a shift to the study of other related themes, perhaps in neighbouring ethnographic areas, so this is a convenient moment to set out the analysis as far as it has been taken.

Over the past decade many people have commented on papers which I wrote as my research developed, and later on drafts of various chapters of this book. Isaac Schapera, David Schneider, Stephen Gudeman and Jessica Kuper read most or all of the chapters, sometimes in successive drafts, and made invaluable criticisms. Particular chapters were read by Hilda Kuper, Eileen Krige, Monica Wilson, Luc de Heusch, Patrick de Josselin de Jong, Arthur Goldberger, Maurice Bloch, Alan Barnard, Robert Ross, Jan Hultin, Paul Riesman, Bruce Kapferer, Amyra Grossbard and Jonathan Parry, and again each helped improve the argument.

My Leiden students, among them Chris Uhlenbeck, Kunnie Kooijman, Els Kocken, Cees Post, Trudeke Vuyk, Marja Molenaar and Marieke Boot kept up a lively flow of uninhibited criticism, and patiently listened to the most bizarre hypotheses. Franklin Tjon Sie Fat, also of Leiden, provided sophisticated criticisms, and he developed several of the diagrams used in this book. Els Kocken drew fair copies of most of the figures and prepared the bibliography. Dorothy Brothers, Liesbeth Zech and Ank Amesz typed the manuscript. My thanks to all.

Although I have published various papers which grew out of the present project, only three are incorporated in this book. The Venda chapter, Chapter 6, was published originally in *L'Homme*. Chapter 7, the Swazi case-study, appeared in a radically different form in *Man*, and Chapter 10, again somewhat altered since, first appeared in *Africa*. I am grateful to the editor of *L'Homme*, to the Royal Anthropological Institute and to the International African Institute for permission to republish these materials. The remainder of the chapters are published here for the first time.

This book was brought to completion at the Center for Advanced Study in the Behavioral Sciences, and my move to California for the purpose was facilitated by a grant-in-aid from the Wenner-Gren Foundation for Anthropological Research.

Palo Alto, California

Part one

The bridewealth system

1 Introduction

My central theme might be summed up in the Southern Bantu saying, 'Cattle beget children.' The exchange of cattle for wives, taking a variety of organizational, ideological and ritual forms, pervaded traditional social and cultural life in the region. It constituted one of those institutional complexes which seem to imprint a special character on a whole series of related cultures, like age-grade systems in part of Eastern Africa, or totemism in Australia, or the potlatch on the northwest coast of America. Despite long-term radical changes in the economy and the frontal assault of the missionaries, bridewealth institutions also proved to be extremely durable, adapting to varied and indeed revolutionary new circumstances.

My aim in writing about these bridewealth systems is two-fold. At an ethnographic level I wish to bring greater order to the scattered and often puzzling reports of traditional Southern Bantu marriage practices — an enterprise essential to the further understanding of these cultures. At the same time I shall broach the more general issue of institutional adaptation, which is not restricted to kinship studies or to the ethnography of any region.

In Southern Africa a family of bridewealth institutions developed which were adapted to a wide range of local conditions. These institutions performed a variety of functions, but evinced a marked degree of formal continuity with each other. They were, it seemed, not roughly cut into shape and hammered into place as circumstances demanded; rather, inherent potentialities were developed in a regular and systematic way. Consequently, while meeting the exigencies of different local organizations, the various bridewealth systems were linked to each other by a series of rule-governed transformations. These formal transformations are one of my main preoccupations in this study. I shall provide a 'reading' of Southern Bantu marriage practices which follows both a horizontal and a vertical path, moving within and between the cultures which participate in the Southern Bantu cultural tradition;

and this book is offered as a case-study of institutional transformations.

I use a method of structural comparison which focuses on a set of related cultures, in this case the Southern Bantu, and I hope the present book will bring the potential value of such an approach to the attention of more Africanists.[1] African anthropology passed through an early phase of diffusionist and 'culture area' studies. More recently, and partly in reaction, it has been dominated by the study of notionally isolated, bounded and timeless tribal cultures. African historians have corrected these biases to some degree, but only Luc de Heusch's study of Central African myth and ritual matches the structural comparisons which have been so successful elsewhere, from Radcliffe-Brown's Australian studies to Eggan's North American Indian work and Lévi-Strauss's massive analysis of Amazonian mythology. Yet the limitations of the conventional anthropological studies are evident, and a regional comparative approach allows one to escape many of the constraints imposed by such studies without running the risks which attend promiscuous cross-cultural comparison. The regional approach encourages the study of concomitant variation, structural transformation and historical change while imposing a sense of the context and meaning of cultural practices.

By good fortune an apprentice field study in western Botswana, which in fact stimulated me to move on to this comparative project, gave me privileged access to the ethnographic literature. Certainly if one is to judge by the most successful attempts, regional comparison benefits from the understanding and the impetus which comes from personal experience in the field.

The Southern Bantu area offers a particularly inviting stage for regional comparison. The published ethnographic materials are extremely rich, for obvious historical reasons. My main sources were classics in the field – the great studies of A. T. Bryant, Bishop Callaway, Eugène Casalis, Henri Junod, E. J. and J. D. Krige, Hilda Kuper, Isaac Schapera, J. H. Soga, N. J. van Warmelo and Monica Wilson (Hunter). Government commissions of enquiry in the nineteenth century and a succession of jurists, linguists, historians and anthropologists – so often missionaries – have added further detail and filled in many gaps. Recently N. J. van Warmelo's magnificent bibliography of ethnographic articles on the Southern Bantu (1977) has provided the student with yet another research tool to set beside the bibliographies of Schapera and others. In making comparisons one can be reasonably confident that on most subjects the important differences have been adequately documented. There certainly remain points on which little is known, and others (sometimes of great significance) on which the material is spotty. Conversely there are areas in which the ethnographic description is particularly rich. I have exploited the richest bodies of material as far as possible for my detailed case-studies, while attempting to cover the main variants.

The conventional classification of the traditional Southern Bantu cultures is based upon the established linguistic classification. The main sub-groups are the Nguni, Sotho-Tswana, Venda and Tsonga. These groupings, and the dialect clusters within them, are also on the whole geographically localized.[2] This is not to say that the Southern Bantu as a cluster or any of these sub-groupings constitutes a closed 'culture area', or represents a timeless organic unity. On the contrary, the history of the region is a history of continuous migration, local adaptation, borrowing and innovation. Indeed change — represented in the ethnographic reports mainly by way of local variation — is the basic condition of my method.

In positing a central cultural tradition I assume not the absence of significant change but rather a tendency for changes to take related forms throughout the region. The ethnographic materials published roughly in the century to 1940, which represent my main sources, bear witness to the cultural unity of the region throughout that time, despite profound political and economic changes resulting directly or indirectly from European colonial expansion. More radical discontinuities occurred with the incorporation of rural African communities in the modern political and economic system. External institutions began to play a critical role in determining the development of local communities. This process accelerated during the early twentieth century, reaching a critical point with the industrialization of South Africa in the 1930s and 1940s. My analysis is concerned with the pre-industrial period.

The geographical distribution of the cultural tradition I am content to leave unresolved. The fundamental similarity of the cultures discussed in this book is not open to serious question, but there may well prove to be further systematic relations with Bantu-speaking groups to the north and even with Khoi-speakers to the west. There is no reason to expect precisely defined boundaries. On the contrary, any apparently sharp discontinuity must be carefully scrutinized unless it clearly results from recent population movements.

The *Nguni* group, representing perhaps two-thirds of the total population, is sub-divided into: the Cape Nguni, largely Xhosa-speaking;

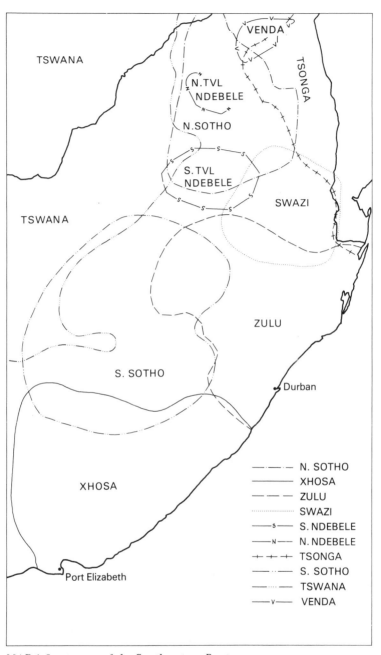

MAP 1 *Languages of the Southeastern Bantu*
Source: Van Warmelo (1952)
(Extract from Ethnological Publication, reproduced
under Copyright Authority 7666 of 15.5.81 of the
Government Printer of the Republic of South Africa)

the Zulu-speakers of Zululand and Natal; the Swazi, who live in and around Swaziland; the Transvaal Ndebele (of whom only the southern group retains a strong Nguni imprint); and the various military states established by marauding Zulu-speaking commanders in the mid-nineteenth century, of which the Ndebele of Zimbabwe is the most notable. The Cape Nguni (see map 2) may be sub-divided further into various historically related clusters, though cultural differences are minimal except in the case of the Fingo, loosely organized refugees from the Zulu kingdom.

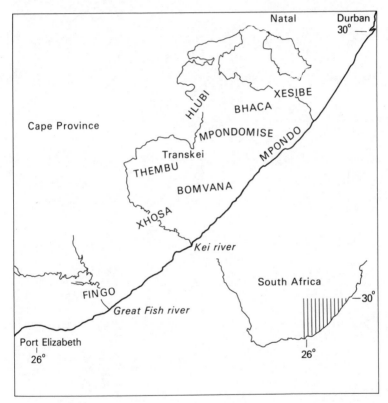

MAP 2 *The Cape Nguni*
  Source: *Shaw and Van Warmelo (1972)* (By permission of the authors)

The *Sotho-Tswana* are conventionally sub-divided into: the Southern Sotho or Basotho, living mainly in and around the kingdom of Lesotho;

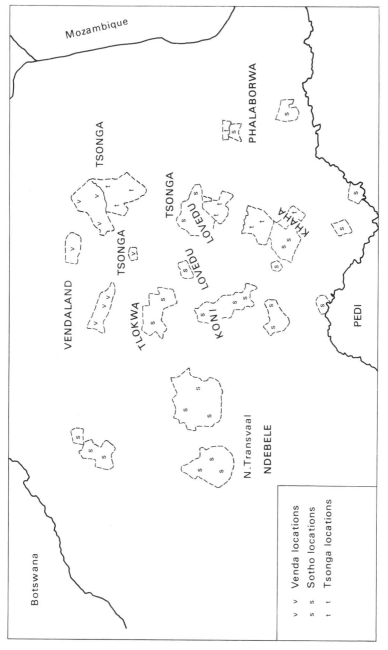

MAP 3 *Some ethnic groupings in the northeastern Transvaal Source: J. D. Krige (1937)*

the Tswana of Botswana and neighbouring areas; and various smaller groups in the Transvaal. The Pedi form an important cluster among the Northern Sotho, as do the Lovedu and their neighbours, further to the north. The *Venda*, from some points of view a distinct cluster, are closely related to the Sotho-Tswana in general and to the Lovedu in particular.

The *Tsonga*, who live in the eastern Transvaal and southern Mozambique, are again usually classified in various sub-groupings, of whom only the southern cluster, Junod's 'Ronga', are considered in detail here.

The organization of this book reflects the argument. In the following chapter, I discuss some of the main features of Southern Bantu thinking about men, women, cattle and fertility, ideas which form the intellectual base of the various local bridewealth systems. Chapter 3 sets out the common rules for the exchange of women and cattle, and defines the main variants. Part Two of the book then moves on to the political context of the bridewealth and marriage systems. Chapter 4 sets out the main characteristics of these political systems, and the remaining chapters of Part Two examine well-documented and important cases in detail, showing the adaptations in marriage practice. Part Three of the book is concerned with parallel ideological transformations. It deals with ways in which local realizations of the bridewealth and marriage system produce variations in wedding ceremonies and in the layout of the homestead.

I have tried to arrange the material in such a way that the ethnographic information is delivered in a cumulative fashion, without assuming any special prior knowledge.

Abbreviations

In describing kinship relations I shall often use the conventional abbreviations: B = brother, C = child, D = daughter, F = father, H = husband, M = mother, P = parent, S = son, W = wife and Z = sister, o/y = respectively older and younger, m.s./w.s. = respectively man-speaking and woman-speaking.

2 'Cattle beget children'[1]

The cattle-complex

In a paper published in 1925 the mother-figure of South African anthropology, Mrs A. W. Hoernlé, remarked: 'We can never hope to understand the real and original function of such customs as the *lobola* transfer of cattle for a bride, or the sacrifices to the dead, until we realize that we are in contact with ideas of cattle radically different from our own' (1925:482). In the following year Herskovits published a study, 'The cattle complex in East Africa,' in which he attempted to characterize these ideas and to map their distribution.[2] He later summed up his thesis in these terms:

> Cattle are found in many regions of Africa; but nowhere do they have a place in the life of the people in the manner which we find in East Africa. From the southern portion of the eastern coast to the Great Lakes and beyond they determine position and a man's prestige; they are utilized in ceremonials having to do with the great events in the life of the human being, birth, marriage, puberty and death, and their care is the privilege of their owner, who often knows each member of his herds by name. In the entire area, too, we find this cattle complex, as I have termed it, is superimposed on what appears to be an underlying agricultural culture which may have preceded it historically. Cattle, except for their milk, do not furnish food; they afford social position, and only as a ceremonial offering or through the death of the animals are they eaten. Food is obtained from the produce of the fields. And this, it should be noted, is obtained in the main by the work of the women, to whom in most of the area the care of the cattle is forbidden. (Herskovits, 1930:70)

Herskovits's historical speculations seem to be without foundation. The geographical distribution he suggested for the 'complex' had to be revised several times, and even the latest version is open to serious criticism. The debate he inspired about the economic rationality of East African pastoralists seems in retrospect misconceived and unproductive.[3] And yet the essential argument remains important. It is indeed the case that although agriculture is more important as a source of food than are pastoral activities in most Southern and East African societies, pastoralism is more prestigious and ceremonially important than agriculture. Moreover, pastoralism is the domain of men, agriculture of women. Indeed, among the Southern and Eastern Bantu women were traditionally regarded as a constant source of danger to cattle.

Paralleling Herskovits, one could pile up endless Southern Bantu examples of the central importance of cattle in ritual, their use in sacrifice and in bridewealth, the prestige lent by cattle-ownership, the celebration of cattle in idioms and songs.[4] The cultural bias is obvious. 'Do you prefer sons or daughters?', a witness was asked during the 1883 Commission of Enquiry. 'Both are good', he replied, 'the girls bring cattle and the boys look after them' (vol. II, part 1, p. 98).

The special male evaluation of cattle was brought home to me on an early field trip, listening to a village court session in the Kalahari. An old widow had brought a complaint that her field had been damaged by oxen. Although the right of women to present cases was not generally accepted, the members of the court were prepared to give the woman some informal help – but they felt definitely unhappy about the whole business. In the first place, here was a woman bringing a case against a man. That was bad enough. But to add insult to injury, she was defending agriculture against the depredations of pastoralism! The headman's son burst out: 'We should take care of fields. A lady likes her field . . . But the field is ploughed by cattle! We buy seeds at the shop with cattle! We buy clothes for our wives with cattle!' (A. Kuper, 1970a: 145-6).

The central role of cattle in ceremonial life, and the high value attached to cattle and cattle-keeping will be incidentally and unavoidably documented in a variety of contexts in this book. Equally, the association of men with cattle-keeping and of women with horticulture, corn and cooking[5] will keep recurring. This is a central theme of the culture – so pervasive, indeed, as almost to defy apt illustration. A single custom, for the moment, will stand for many.

Among the Tswana, the head of a family is buried in the cattle-byre, his wife beneath the threshing floor (Willoughby, 1923:65). The man's corpse is tied up in an ox-hide, and before burial an ox-bone is held towards the corpse and placed at his head in the grave. Then, in the same way, he is shown a milking-thong, the nose-cord of an ox and a milk bowl. Finally the peculiar whistle of the herd-boy is imitated, and some dry cow-dung thrown on the grave. In the case of a woman's burial, on the other hand, the corpse is presented with a pot, a spoon, a plate, a pronged porridge stick, a winnowing fan, a pestle from the corn mortar and a cracked pot, and then corn is scattered on the grave (Willoughby, 1905:308).

While the central features of Herskovits's 'cattle complex' are certainly characteristic of the Southern Bantu cultural tradition, one must enter some qualifications. For example, men may help to clear fields, and since the introduction of the plough they are usually responsible for ploughing with oxen. Conversely, although men are primarily responsible for cattle, and women are potentially dangerous to them, the absence of many able-bodied men as labour migrants has made it necessary in some areas for women also to play a part in cattle-husbandry. These are normally local and modern deviations, felt to be such by the people.

There are areas, however, where the boundary was traditionally less sharply drawn. Among the Lovedu, men used to join with women in hoeing, reaping and weeding, and women were not completely excluded from contact with cattle. Yet cattle remained important for bridewealth, and the introduction of ploughing with oxen in fact brought about a shift towards a more typical male–female division of labour, although the Lovedu persisted in looking down on Tsonga men, in part because they had never hoed or weeded. Among the Lovedu, too, cattle were not as relatively prestigious as elsewhere — 'A man will complain, not because he has no cattle, but because he cannot brew beer to maintain his prestige' (E. J. and J. D. Krige, 1943:40).

Another qualification worth noting — because it is so often forgotten — is that goats are also very important in many Eastern and Southern African societies, providing a major source of meat and milk. While they are not prestigious, they are in various contexts directly substitutable for cattle. As Monica Hunter reported for the Mpondo (1936:71): 'Goats are (and were) the poor man's cattle, supplying food and clothing, being a means of acquiring wives, and of establishing good relations with the ancestral spirits in exactly the same way as cattle, but always less efficaciously.'

More radical variations are to be found in some East African cultures, which fall beyond the scope of the present study. There is, for example, the tendency in stratified East African societies to oppose a category of high-status immigrant pastoralists and a category of low-status auto-chthonous agriculturalists. The pastoralists sometimes describe the whole agricultural stratum as 'female'. An extreme case is represented by the Hima pastoralist stratum in Ankole, which until very recently occupied a superior social and political position to the Iru agriculturalists. There were taboos against the mixing of milk and vegetable foods, and some groups of Hima men ate no vegetable foods at all. The division of labour between the two strata was in some places so strict that Hima women were banned from agricultural labour, effectively being put out of work by the Iru. In consequence the activity of the Hima woman was severely restricted, and in extreme cases she might hardly stray beyond her hut and yard (cf. Elam, 1973).

In some of these East African societies there is an even lower status category of hunters and gatherers. In areas of Southern Africa too, groups of Bushmen occupied a similar marginal and inferior position vis-à-vis Bantu-speakers. Within the Bantu-speaking communities themselves, however, hunting and gathering had a place, replicating at a 'natural' level the 'cultural' division of labour between male pastoralism and female horticulture.[6] While insignificant as a source of food except at times of crisis, hunting and gathering were of ritual importance. Hunting, a male activity, was a ritually heightened counterpart to pastoralism. It was not an important or regular source of food for most people, but large hunts were organized particularly at key moments in the social and natural cycles, marking initiation ceremonies, preparations for war, and the installation of rulers. Hunts might also be used to cause rain. Gathering, a female activity, was devalued as a source of food — it was the recourse of the pauper. Women had to gather firewood, however, and indeed the wife's duty to provide firewood was stressed in wedding ceremonies. Gathering was also a basic activity of medicine men, herbalists being essentially specialized gatherers of roots, and perhaps for this reason there is stereotypically some sexual ambiguity about male herbalists.

The basic division of labour (and a central part of Herskovits's thesis) can be summed up simply in a two-by-two table:

	MALE	*FEMALE*
CULTURE	PASTORALISM	AGRICULTURE
NATURE	HUNTING	GATHERING

Exchanges

Pastoral and agricultural products may be exchanged for each other: indeed, their exchange forms an integral feature of traditional ideas of social and economic organization.[7]

A Venda folk-tale tells the story of a monkey who owned cattle. Parties of young men went out to steal them, but the monkey shot the thieves with a bow and arrow. Finally a party of small boys said they would drive the cattle home themselves:

> The men of the kraal answered scornfully, 'You cannot do what your elders failed to do.' But the little boys went out without sticks, or bows and arrows, or spears; they took only a small hoe. They dug up sweet potatoes with the hoe and threw them one by one to the monkey, and, while he was busy eating the sweet potatoes, they drove the cattle home. (Stayt, 1931:345)

The appropriate exchange for cattle or cattle products is agricultural products — or, of course, women. The exchange of women for cattle is unquestionably seen as the central social exchange; and the direct exchanges of agricultural and pastoral products are themselves often associated with the relationship between affines. A man will always try to offer his wife's parents meat, and will expect to be offered beer and porridge by his wife's mother. Beer is also the appropriate payment for agricultural labour, but this is one of the duties a man owes his wife's parents.

The nexus of exchanges can be summed up simply:

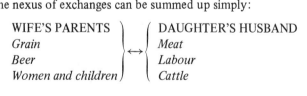

WIFE'S PARENTS 〉 〔 DAUGHTER'S HUSBAND
Grain   *Meat*
Beer   ↔   *Labour*
Women and children   *Cattle*

Hierarchical exchanges

These exchanges of pastoral and agricultural products between wife-givers and wife-takers provide only a part of the background necessary to understand the marriage exchanges. There are also crucial hierarchical exchanges, between ancestors and descendants, rulers and subjects, and household heads and their dependants; exchanges which are again bound up with marriage and bridewealth. In particular, these exchanges are the source of fertility. The superiors (ancestors, chiefs, fathers and husbands) provide cattle and fields, and make them fertile. The living, followers, children and wives give labour, meat and corn in return to the superiors.

The ultimate guarantors of welfare are the ancestors.[8] The national ancestors are responsible for rain, good harvests, victory in war, etc. They were also the original owners of the land, now held by the present ruler. Family ancestors are above all concerned with the health and fertility of the family. 'They have the power to send health to man and beast, to increase property, to ensure good crops' (Hunter, 1936:234). The Tsonga pray with striking directness, 'May the harvest be plentiful; may the cattle multiply; may all our wives become pregnant' (Junod, 1927, II:403). Cattle are, finally, the major goods handed down through inheritance from the ancestors, and a man's herd is regarded as the property of the family ancestors.

The tribal ancestors are approached by the ruler, and the family ancestors by the homestead head or his sister. Each also has specific responsibilities for the welfare of his people. The ruler provides land and, often, cattle. The land is distributed amongst his followers according to the number of wives they have. In theory, his followers have only the use of the land, but people are not ordinarily deprived of resources once granted.

Grants of cattle were the typical means of establishing political relationships. As Casalis described it (1861:155-6):

> Most of the flocks and herds captured in war become the property of the chief; and the subjects regard it as a favour to become the depositories and guardians of these new acquisitions. The milk belongs to them; they use the oxen as beast of burden, and, from time to time, obtain permission to kill an animal which is already old; but they must always hold themselves in readiness to present the flocks to their real owners when he wishes to inspect them. When this favour is once granted, the chief cannot withdraw it without good grounds for so doing. Such is, in fact, the great social bond of these tribes; the sovereigns, instead of being supported by the community, are the chief supporters of it . . . It is a fact, that since the natives have been able to obtain cattle by performing services for the colonists, the repressive power of the petty Caffre and Bechuana sovereigns has sensibly diminished.

The ruler was also expected to ensure that the land was fruitful.[9] This he was able to do by virtue of his special relationship to the tribal ancestors. He performed the first-fruit ceremony, ritually inaugurated the planting season, and above all he organized rituals to ensure that the rain fell.

In exchange for these services the ruler's subjects cultivated special fields for him and sent him tribute of beer and beef, and also trophies and meat from the hunt. Among the Zulu and Lovedu they also sent him wives.

Comparable hierarchical exchanges characterized the relationship of a homestead head and his dependants. He was the family intermediary to the ruler and to the family ancestors. He divided up the fields he received from the ruler and the cattle he inherited from the ancestors among the 'houses' of his wives. As husband and father he was also specifically responsible for making his wives pregnant, and this act was linked to more general notions of fertilization. Among the Tswana, for example, when a woman's family accepted a marriage proposal the suitor's party said, '"*Re nesa pula*" – "We cause it to rain for you"' (Schapera, 1938:131). Semen was directly associated with water and rain, and the fertilization of a woman might be compared with the fertilization of fields. As a Zulu rain-doctor put it: 'The husband fertilizes the wife. The fertilizer is the water. That is how it is with this thing of rain. It is the water of the sky which causes something to happen on the earth' (Berglund, 1976:62).

In return, the wives of the homestead head cultivated a special garden for him, provided him with corn and firewood, and cooked for him.

The relation between hierarchy and the provision of resources and fertility against a return of food and labour is therefore systematic and evident, and is repeated at three levels. It can be represented in a diagram (Figure 1).

Bridewealth payments of cattle must be set also in the context of this structure of transactions. Cattle and fertility (rain/seminal fluid) come ultimately from the ancestors and directly from the rulers and household heads who stand between the ancestors and their dependants. In some formulations the links of the chain may be conceptually elided. 'We cause it to rain for you,' the Tswana say when paying bridewealth. To the north, among the Shona, there is a story that when the creator spirit Mwari came to earth as a man and married a woman, he paid bridewealth in the form of rain. A Sotho folk-tale tells of a snake who married women and paid bridewealth in water (Murray, 1980:68–9).

Cattle are inherited from the ancestors, and people often talk as

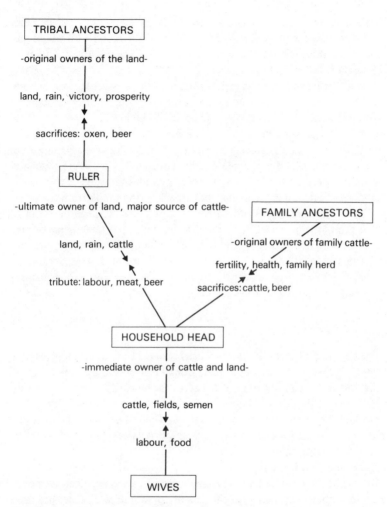

FIGURE 1 *Hierarchical transactions*

though the ancestors themselves pay and receive bridewealth. A woman's ancestors may even be said to withhold her fertility if the bridewealth is not paid in full. 'Cattle received as the *ikhazi* of a daughter are of special ritual importance . . . being given "in exchange for the blood of the family" . . . and conversely the passage of cattle put the girl received in exchange . . . in close relationship with the ancestral spirits of the family from which the cattle came' (Hunter, 1936:192). Conception itself may be represented as the work of the ancestors. Among the Zulu it is said that the woman's ancestors 'furnish the blood with which the shades of the male, in the male fluid, mould the child in the womb' (Berglund, 1975:207).

Another line of thought relates the milk of bridewealth cows and the substance of people. Among the Sotho-Tswana child betrothal is common, the girl being normally a close kinswoman. When she is engaged to be married her future husband may give a cow to provide milk for her while she grows up. Among the Cape Nguni the assumption is on the contrary that completely unrelated adult women are suddenly sent to marry particular men. These new brides are subject to various taboos at first, and in particular they may not drink milk from the cows of their husbands' herds until a special ceremony has been performed. This brings the new wife into a relationship with her husband's ancestors. It is as though the cool, 'white' milk of the family cows were equivalent to the semen of the 'white' ancestors which forms part of the bodily substance of their descendants. These notions of colour and 'coolness' are elaborated in the following section.

Hot and cool[10]

The payment of cattle for wives must be related both to the more general set of exchanges between the male domain of pastoral production and the female domain of agriculture, and to the series of exchanges of goods and services (basically the gift of fertility and the return of part of the product) between superiors and inferiors. There is also a third dimension to be taken into account: the opposition between 'hot' and 'cool' in Southern Bantu thinking.

On the one hand there are things and conditions which are 'cool' and 'white', such as water, rain, semen, etc. These are fertilizing agencies. On the other hand there are things and conditions which are 'hot' and 'red', such as lightning, fire and blood. These are dangerous and cause sterility and death. (In the colour system there is a third category of 'black' things, neither hot nor cool, associated with darkness, night, clouds, dry blood, bodily wastes, etc. 'Black' and 'white' may be opposed to 'red', or 'black' and 'red' to 'white'. 'Black' objects are especially important in medicine.)

There is a tendency for women and female sexuality to be regarded as 'hot' and dangerous: dangerous above all to men and cattle. The prototype of this danger is presented by witches, who are strongly contrasted to ancestors. Their 'preoccupation is to destroy fertility in men, beasts (particularly cattle) and fields' (Berglund, 1975:268). Witches are generally represented as women, and as women with perverted and insatiable sexual appetites. While ancestors 'like the cattle of the underworld, are thought to be white, a concept found generally on the African continent' (Berglund, 1975:371), female night-witches are black and fiery. They 'are born with an inherent quality of heat' (Mönnig, 1967:71); they are 'fires of the night' (Junod, 1927, II:507); their eyes 'are bright and shining like burning lumps of coal' (Stayt, 1931:274).

Ideas about conception bring this set of ideas into a sharp focus, and one particularly relevant to the argument of this chapter.[11] The menstrual blood of women is 'hot' and 'red', and is dangerous to men (and also to the fertility of cattle and of crops). Man's semen is like water, 'cool' and 'white' and fertilizing. The people believe that these two sorts of 'blood' (for both the woman's and the man's fluid is termed 'blood') fight each other in the womb. The child is itself a combination of the maternal blood, which provides its 'red' flesh and blood, and the paternal blood, which provides its 'white' bones and hair. A man should sleep with his wife for several nights in succession to ensure successful conception. If a miscarriage occurs this means that his 'blood' has been defeated, and a miscarriage is regarded as gravely polluting and dangerous, capable of causing drought and famine (Junod, 1910:139–40).

This 'hot'/'cool' opposition does not contrast male and female in simple terms. It classifies mainly states and conditions or phases rather than unchanging essences. Any man or woman may also become 'hot' through anger or jealousy — emotions which are believed to lead to sorcery — and must then be 'cooled down'. (In Zulu a 'red' temper, *inhiziyo ebomvu*, means a bad temper.) Men who have recently had sexual relations with women are 'hot', and women may be 'cool' before and after their phase of sexual maturity. Pre-pubescent girls, for instance, are favoured actors in some rain-making rituals. A mother's milk is also 'white' and 'cool', and a nursing mother must avoid sexual relations. A mother's milk cools her baby (Kidd, 1906:41–3), and a nursing mother working in a field has a positive influence on the crops (Berglund, 1975:340). 'When people are anxious to grow rich they wash themselves and their cattle with *intelezi*, or medicinal wash. The best form of wash for this purpose is made from the milk of a woman' (Kidd, 1906:40).

The opposition is between healing and fertilizing agents and dangerous and sterilizing forces. The 'cool' things heal or fertilize the 'hot', while the 'hot' endanger the 'cool'. The same word means 'to heal' and 'to cool' (*hola* in Tswana, *phola* in Zulu, etc.), and one word may mean to be hot and unhealthy (e.g. *shisa* in Zulu) or heat and fever (e.g. *mogote* in Tswana).

The central series of oppositions may be summed up as follows:

HOT (causing sickness and sterility)	COOL (causing health and fertility)
Red	White
Menstrual blood	Semen
Fire	Water, Ash
Lightning	Rain
Witches	Ancestors
Witches' familiars	Snakes, crocodiles

Cattle and cattle products are always cool, healing and fertilizing. The ox is 'the god with a wet nose'. Among the Cape Nguni particularly, men and women make necklaces from the hair of their family cattle to keep them healthy. Cattle dung is a cooling and healing agent, and the chyme and gall-bladder of a sacrificed beast have powerful beneficent properties. Like other cool agencies, cattle are also directly and positively associated with female fertility. They may even represent a superior source of fertility, as in the Zulu origin myth according to which the first men were 'belched up by a cow'. Callaway commented, 'It is a saying among the natives when they see an exquisitely handsome man, or when they wish to flatter a chief ... He was not born; he was belched up by a cow ...' (Callaway, 1870:34). Other Zulu reports show how these associations are played upon. 'A woman conceives and gives birth in the tenth month. So does a cow. It conceives and calves in the tenth month. So a cow is like a human' (Berglund, 1975:110). Cattle are at risk from 'hot' women, but the fertility of a girl brings cattle to her father: '... the private parts of a girl are often referred to as "father's cattle", in reference to the bride price he will secure for her' (E. J. Krige, 1968:177). The Venda say that when a young man marries, his bride should sleep with his father for the first few nights, since 'a child cannot open a cattle-kraal' (Van Warmelo and Phophi, 1948, I:209).

There are various rituals in which the positive relationship of cattle to female fertility is expressed. For example, if a Mpondo woman is having a difficult delivery the homestead head drives up his cattle to the hut in which she is lying.

Then he calls on the ancestral spirits, 'How is it that this my child is
like this? . . .' Then he calls the names of his ancestors, as at a ritual
killing. 'Then if one of the cattle passes water the child will be born,
unless the mother is being killed by a witch or sorcerer.' 'Sometimes
a beast goes up and licks the mother, and then a child is born.'
(Hunter, 1936:151)

The association of cattle and the ancestors is evident here, but the
cattle also intervene directly, and they act by passing water or licking,
i.e. by cooling.

The positive force for fertility represented by men and cattle, and
the danger to cattle and to human fertility represented by women are
brought out in a Thembu ceremony. When the bridewealth cattle are
delivered:

The boys and young men gather the cattle which have been hidden
some distance from the kraal and drive them in a stampede towards
the cattle-kraal. As the herd comes charging along, the wives of the
kraal form a line to obstruct their advance and prevent them from
entering the kraal. The boys and young men shout and urge the
cattle on. The wives wave and shout to drive the cattle back. The
young men, by smacking, hitting, pushing and shouting, at last
break the cordon of women, who fly in the face of the charging
herd, and drive the cattle into the kraal with great cries of excitement
and jubilation and shouts of *'Inkwenkwe! Inkwenkwe!'* (A son!
A son!) The natives claim that if the herd ignores the women and
rushes through them, scattering them as it enters the kraal, the
omen is good, for the bride will be fertile and bear a son. If the
women succeed in turning the herd, the omen is bad and the woman
will be sterile. (Laubscher, 1937:177)

Cattle and hoes

It is evident that the common Southern Bantu saying 'cattle beget
children' crystallizes a series of ideas. First there is the general opposition
of male pastoralism and female agriculture, in which the direct exchange
of women and children for cattle is one of a series of exchanges of
products from these two domains. Second, there is a system of hierarchical transactions in which ancestors, rulers and men enrich and
fertilize their descendants, subjects and wives. In this system cattle are
associated in a variety of ways with ancestors and with men, and so

with the life-giving and fertilizing powers. Third, there is a system of oppositions between the 'hot', dangerous and sterilizing and the 'cool', healing and fertilizing forces, and in this context cattle are 'cool', health-giving, and associated positively with female child-bearing. Finally, as the following chapter will show, the payment of bridewealth cattle gives the husband legal rights to the children his wife bears. As Jeffreys summed up the jural situation, '*Lobolo* is child-price' (1951). More precisely, the transfer of bridewealth cattle is necessary to the birth of a legitimate person. A person for whose mother no *lobolo* has been paid is not a full member of the community. Cattle transfers are therefore essential both to natural female fertility and to legitimate female fertility.

The use of cattle in bridewealth seems almost 'overdetermined'. And yet there are accounts among the Southern Bantu of bridewealth being paid not in cattle but on the contrary in agricultural implements and products — in hoes or grain. Some reports even mention the use of wild roots, or of copper, which is seen as red, hot and female. What is to be made of these anomalies?

It is worth paying attention to the terms in which these remarkable reversals are presented. In report after report the 'substitutes' are said to have been used in the more or less distant past, often in times of crisis resulting from war, cattle sickness and drought.[12] This may possibly be true, at least in some cases, but the vague terms in which the reports are couched, and the coincidence that in most cases an agricultural product or implement appears as the main substitute must suggest that these reports have another significance.

Moreover, during the rinderpest epidemic which wiped out huge herds of African cattle at the end of the last century these substitutes were not used. In 1897 Alfred Casalis, son of the famous Eugène, wrote from Leribe in Lesotho:

> Do you know what they are doing to-day? So-and-so approaches so-and-so to obtain his daughter . . . they proceed to the kraal. The kraal is empty and contains nothing but dry manure. That makes no difference. Into his kraal, the would-be husband brings a number of stones, let us say ten. These ten stones represent oxen, it is a debt of honour, it will be paid when the kraal fills with cattle again . . .
> (In Germond, 1967:472-3)

Reports of bridewealth being paid in hoes and grain and copper rings should probably not be read too literally. They suggest rather what people believed would happen in conditions which represented the antithesis of normality. The archetypal conditions were drought (equivalent to the failure of the ruler) and defeat in battle. In such a topsy-turvy world, men would pay bridewealth in female implements or products.

This interpretation is supported by a nice reversal which occurs in a Zulu story about the origin of mining and metal-working. 'The Zulus experimented with these metals, and found out that when heated red-hot they could be beaten into any shape required . . .' They introduced metal ornaments into *lobolo* payments. Then a calamity occurred. 'After these metal ornaments and implements had been in use for some years, a dreadful epidemic broke out and raged throughout the country. It was most contagious, and deadly, apparently a kind of cholera or fever which swept away whole kraals of people from one end of the country to the other.' The king summoned his diviners, and eventually the head diviner reports that 'the spirit said it was the use of metals which had brought this calamity upon them, which was proved by the fact that the skins of some of those who had died were found to have turned to a whitish colour before or after death.' The king ordered the burial of all the metal objects in the place where the metal itself had been mined, and blacksmiths had to abandon their business. The narrator says that strangely enough some people disobeyed and metal ornaments were worn as late as King Mpande's day, but the ornaments were clumsy and uncomfortable 'and on hot days water was poured over them to cool the arms' (Samuelson, 1930:50-3). In this version, then, it was not natural calamity that led to the temporary substitution of metal objects for bridewealth cattle but rather the introduction of metal objects which caused the calamity. In this story, the metal/cattle opposition also becomes a hot/cool opposition.

These hypothetical transformations of normality recall the reality represented by some of the Central African Bantu societies.[13] The traditional division of labour among the Central Bantu was concerned mainly with horticulture and *hunting*, respectively the characteristic work of women and of men. With the exception of the Ila-Tonga, the Central Bantu rarely kept cattle, and attached little importance to them. The Bemba, for example, 'used formerly to capture cattle from the surrounding tribes, and kept these sporadically, but . . . lack entirely the pastoral tradition' (Richards, 1939:18).

All these societies were matrilineal, but in some marriage was virilocal, and a husband gained considerable control of his wife's children. This was the case notably among the Ila-Tonga, the only societies in the group who traditionally valued pastoralism, and who paid bridewealth in cattle. Among all the other groups wives normally did not move to their husband's home on marriage, and men had little control of their children. And in these other societies bridewealth was paid in *hoes*.

The transformation of the Southern Bantu model is carried further into details of beliefs about conception. The Southern Bantu believed that a child was made up of 'red' elements, blood and flesh, which came from its mother, and 'white' elements, bone and hair, which came from its father. Among the matrilineal Central Bantu the father was thought to contribute the red 'shadow' while the mother contributed the white 'inner man' (Jacobson-Widding, 1979:304-24).

The Southwestern Bantu form an intriguing bridge between the matrilineal Central Bantu and the Southern Bantu. The Southwestern Bantu are conventionally characterized as exhibiting a system of double descent. There are matrilineal groupings, but residence is dominantly patrilocal. Most of these groups require heavy bridewealth payments in cattle, and Murdock observed that 'Patrilocal residence prevails in almost direct proportion to the importance of cattle' (1959:372). A further shift can be seen in the division of labour. Women are partly or primarily responsible for milking cattle. Otherwise the normal pattern is followed. 'The men hunt, herd, and clear new land. Both sexes fish, although women catch only small fry. Women gather and do most, but not all, of the field labour' (Murdock, 1959:371).

The point of this digression, however, is that just as the Central and Southwestern Bantu represent transformations of the Southern Bantu system in reality, so the reports of bridewealth payments with hoes in Southern Africa represent a conceptual transformation of the system, though in the form of a nightmare reversal of the normal conditions of life.

Other transformations are associated with recurrent anomalous situations, for example the death of unmarried men or the remarriage of widows. Among the Venda a young man who dies before he can be married may cause endless trouble to his family. To avert this danger the young man's spirit is presented with

an old used hoe handle . . . with a cotton string tied near the hole, to symbolise a wife, the string being her waistband and the hole the female genitalia. A girl, never the deceased man's sister, fixes this symbol at a fork in the path in a well cleared open space where the young man's spirit can clearly see it, with the handle pointing towards him as he approaches his old village. The handle is fixed with four pegs . . . and a woman of the headman's lineage . . . pours beer in the hole in the hoe saying 'Today we have found you a wife, the wife is here. Do not worry us any more.' (Stayt, 1931:241-2)

Here beer seals marriage to a hoe, where normally cattle seal marriage to a woman. The hoe itself becomes a symbol of sexual union, the 'male' handle penetrating the 'female' hole, an image used also in the rare but essentially similar rite used to placate the spirit of a girl who dies unmarried.

The idea that a man buys wives with cattle is reversed in some Sotho-Tswana rites of widowhood, in which a widow selects her new husband with beer. At the end of the mourning period widows are seated behind beer pots. Each widow sits with her hand covering the mouth of the pot. When a man acceptable to the widow is proposed as the levir, she signifies assent by lifting her hand from the beer pot. (See, e.g. Harries, 1929:48.)

If Herskovits intended to argue that the use of cattle in bridewealth was a consequence of the ideological value attached to cattle in a particular culture, then I would disagree. At the same time I would endorse Mrs Hoernlé's judgment that to understand Southern Bantu bridewealth institutions one must grasp their ideas about cattle. In this chapter I have tried to convey the meanings attached to bride-wealth payments, working through ideas about cattle and about men, women, fertility and hierarchy. These ideas inform every bridewealth payment: but they do not account for the presence of bridewealth institutions, or for the variations in bridewealth arrangements even within the Southern Bantu culture area. Those are different issues, to which I now turn.

3 The bridewealth account

Bridewealth: the basic rules

The fundamental bridewealth rule was that marital rights in a woman were transferred against the payment of cattle. The Southern Bantu emphasized particularly rights to a woman's children. Should a wife be childless, or should she die or desert her husband before bearing children, then either the bridewealth cattle had to be returned or her family had to replace her with another wife.

The transfer of rights in children was permanent. Children could not be claimed by the wife's relatives in the event of divorce or in any other circumstances. Moreover even after the death of the husband the widow was expected to bear children in his name, special leviratic or seed-raising arrangements being made for widows of child-bearing age.[1]

Normally the father was responsible for providing bridewealth to pay for the first wife of each of his sons, or at least the first wife of the oldest son of each of his 'houses'. He might be assisted by older brothers or other relatives, but this was essentially the father's responsibility. In exchange, the father could claim the bridewealth cattle paid for his son's first daughter.

In other circumstances a man might acquire a wife with the cattle he received from the marriage of a sister. Such arrangements normally held only between brothers and sisters of one house in a polygynous family. As will become evident, the sister would require an appropriate return. The 'cattle-linked' brother and sister were bound in a special relationship which generated a chain of individually marked ties with a 'linked' mother's brother, father's sister, sibling's child, etc.[2]

These two systems of raising bridewealth were commonly found in a single society. The first wife might be provided by the father while a second wife might be acquired with the proceeds of a sister's bridewealth. Sometimes only the bridewealth of the eldest son would be found by the father, younger sons marrying as and when their sisters married and brought in bridewealth.

There were alternatives, though some were not universally available. A man might own sufficient unencumbered cattle to be able to pay bridewealth from private resources, or he might earn cattle by trading grain or by hiring himself out as a herbalist or as some other sort of specialist. Increasingly in the latter part of the nineteenth century, he might earn the wherewithal to marry by working as a migrant labourer.[3]

Other relatives might also be involved. Most notably, the mother's brother was a major donor to the bridewealth of his nephew amongst the Sotho-Tswana. Consequently he was a major recipient of the bridewealth paid for his niece. Even non-relatives might provide part or all of the bridewealth a man required. In exchange the person who contributed to the bridewealth would have a claim on the first daughter of the marriage. This claim might be to the girl herself, as a future bride, or to an appropriate proportion of the bridewealth received for her when she married. The basic rule of reciprocity operated whoever raised the bridewealth, kinsman or patron, man or woman.

The transactions involved in raising bridewealth were strictly comparable to the great public transaction in which bridewealth was directly exchanged for a wife. All were governed by the same rule of reciprocity. The payment of bridewealth gave a claim to the wife. Each bridewealth payment consequently formed part of a chain of transactions, not only between the immediate 'wife-givers' and 'wife-takers' (however they might be defined) but between a series of debtors and creditors, related in a great many possible ways.

The house-property system

The parties to bridewealth transactions acted as members of 'houses', and to understand the bridewealth system it is necessary to grasp the basic principles of the 'house-property system' in which it was embedded.

The 'house-property system' or 'complex' has been the subject of a large body of legal literature,[4] for the very practical reason that it regulated the internal economic organization of the polygynous homestead, and ordered the transmission of office and property between generations. The system has also proved to be extremely enduring, perhaps in part as a consequence of legal codification. Even some modern Southern African legal systems retain the basic rules as though (to quote Hamnett's felicitous phrase) the customary law unions were still ideally polygamous, 'though it may be a case of "polygamy with one wife"' (Hamnett, 1975:149).

A 'house' was constituted by a major wife and her children, and each such house was allocated its own estate during the lifetime of the homestead head. As a magistrate told a commission of enquiry at the turn of the century, 'If a man had three wives he would have three separate estates' (quoted by Kerr, 1961:35). In addition to property allocated by the homestead head, a house had the right to the products of its gardens, to the calves and milk of its cows, to the earnings of the wife and her minor children, and, crucially for my present purposes, to the bridewealth received for its daughters.

If bridewealth for a daughter was used to acquire a wife for a man outside the 'house', then a debt was created. This was the case even if the cattle were used by the homestead head, either to acquire another wife for himself or to provide a wife for a son from a different house.[5]

Among the Cape Nguni all property was allocated to particular houses. There was no residue of 'estate' or 'kraal' property which the homestead head disposed of in his own right. Therefore among the Cape Nguni the second or right-hand house was always established with cattle taken from the first or great house. The great house could therefore claim the bridewealth of the first daughter of the right-hand house. And wherever a subordinate house was established by way of such a loan of cattle, the debt which resulted also established the relative rank of the subordinate house, and placed it in a special relationship to the providers of the bridewealth.

A detailed example of the importance of such considerations within a homestead was provided by Callaway's Zulu informant Mbanda (Callaway, 1868:262-4). Cattle of Uzita's great house were used to acquire a second wife for Uzita. The new wife duly bore a son and a daughter. Uzita announced that the son, Unsukuzonke, was next in line for the succession if the great house should fail to produce a male heir, as seemed possible. At the same time he expected that when Unsukuzonke's sister married, her bridewealth should be returned to the great house. However, when his sister married, Unsukuzonke turned difficult.

> Unsukuzonke objected, saying, 'shall a child of our house be eaten
> by another whilst I am living, I who was born of the same mother as
> she?' Uzita therefore wondered very much at Unsukuzonke, and said
> to him, 'If you try to eat the cattle of that child you will commit an
> offence, for your mother was taken to wife by the cattle of
> Ubalazeleni's house; this child belongs to his house; those who are

born after belong to you. Unsukuzonke refused, and said, 'Rather than that a child of our house should be eaten whilst I am alive, it is proper that I pay back those cattle, and I eat for myself.' Uzita would not agree, but said, 'If you take out those cattle of your own accord, you will take yourself out of the chief place; you shall no longer come next in order after Ubalazeleni; I will no longer know to what place you belong; you shall be a mere man without a name in this village. You have now taken yourself out for ever. I no longer know you for my part.'

Unsukuzonke did not repudiate the debt. He tried to redefine it. The great house had 'married' his mother, and so demanded her daughter. Unsukuzonke refused to render his sister, and tried to pretend that he was dealing with a mere loan of cattle. By so doing he was denying the special link which subordinated his house to the great house, and which (if accepted) might bring him the succession if the great house failed to produce an heir. Uzita threatened to follow through the implications of his son's action, and when the time came he excluded Unsukuzonke and his brother from the succession.

Ranking wives

As this case illustrates, the house-property system involved the ranking of the wives of a polygynist. Traditionally the eldest son of the great wife succeeded his father and inherited the lion's share of the family estate. If there was no son in the great house, then the son of the next wife became the heir. These matters were important not only for the individual women and their sons, but also for the relatives of the various wives. When a man succeeded to the leadership of a large homestead, let alone a district or tribe, his mother's relatives stood to gain by their influential connection.

Traditionally the critical test for the ranking of wives in a polygynous homestead was the source of the bridewealth paid for them. The simplest formula was that the wife provided by the father ranked first. Subsequent wives, for whom bridewealth was provided from house property (often the bridewealth payment given for a sister), ranked lower. With the codification of customary law another test became entrenched. This was that the first-married wife ranked highest. The assumption was, however, that the father provided the bridewealth for his son's first wife, who became his great wife.

The opposition between the great wife, provided by the father, and subsequent private wives was fundamental to household organization. As Casalis explained, writing particularly of the Southern Sotho:

> The marriage of all the wives is contracted in a similar manner; but a very marked distinction exists between the first and those who succeed her. The choice of the *great* wife (as she is always called) is generally made by the father, and is an event in which all the relations are interested. The others, who are designated by the name of *serete* (heels), because they must on all occasions hold an inferior position to the mistress of the house, are articles of luxury to which the parents are not obliged to contribute. (Casalis, 1861:186-7)

There might in addition be a third category of servant wives, attached to the more important wives. 'Her children are considered to be the legitimate offspring of her husband, they bear his name, and are treated as cadets of the house to which their mother was attached' (Ellenberger and MacGregor, 1912:279). They would typically be provided by the family of the major wife.

Among the Southern Sotho, and generally among the Sotho-Tswana, the important wives were ranked simply in order after the great wife. 'The first wife married is the "great wife" (*mosadi o mogolo*). The next wife is spoken of simply as the "second wife" (*mosadi wa bobedi*); then comes the "third wife" (*mosadi wa boraro*); and so on' (Schapera, 1938:14).

The Nguni arrangement was different. Generally only two or in rare instances three main wives were recognized. One was the great wife, the other was often termed the right-hand wife. Further wives were attached alternately to these two as subordinates, so that in the end there were two (or occasionally three) bevies of wives, each under the leadership of a main wife. Each bevy formed a unit for purposes of transmitting the succession. Only if all the wives attached to the great house failed to produce an heir would the succession pass to the right-hand house.

The Sotho-Tswana differed from the Nguni in another way as well. They preferred cousin marriage, and within the homestead a wife who was a mother's brother's daughter or a father's brother's daughter took precedence. A marriage with a cousin was normally arranged by a man's father, who would then provide the bridewealth. Such a wife was often betrothed in infancy, and indeed the Tswana formulation was that a matrilateral cross-cousin or a girl betrothed in infancy took precedence over other wives (Schapera, 1938:14n). Amongst the Lovedu the father did not normally provide sons with bridewealth cattle, and there 'the chief house of a polygynist is the house established by the cattle he received from the marriage of his sister; and at the same time the mistress of this house is his cattle-linked cross-cousin' (E. J. and J. D. Krige, 1943:99).

The normal traditional test is clear enough: the wife provided by the father ranks highest. Yet these subsidiary or alternative tests obviously introduced complications. The uncertainties permitted manipulation of the rules and tests to obtain political advantage.

In the case of a powerful man the choice of a wife for his oldest son was a matter of considerable political importance, particularly if that wife was to produce his son's heir. As Jones (1966:69) remarked for the Southern Sotho:

> a wealthy and powerful son could not marry anyone he pleased and make her his first wife. The marriage had to be sanctioned by the head of the house, that is, the marriage cattle had to belong to the head of the house, who was either his father or grandfather. This right to arrange the great marriages of his sons . . . gave a ruling chief considerable power over the succession.

But political circumstances could change: and there might be pressure later to nominate an alternative great wife. To put an end to the problems caused by such manipulation, the Laws of Lerotholi, compiled at the turn of the century, laid down that 'The heir in Basutoland shall be the first male child of the first married wife, and if there is no male in the first house then the first born male child of the next wife married in succession shall be the heir.' This immediately presented the problem of when a marriage was deemed to have been completed, necessitating a burgeoning series of subsidiary rules in an attempt to prevent political manipulation of the ranking of wives. (See Hamnett, 1975:41; Poulter, 1976:102–4.)

For Nguni aristocrats the opportunities to adjust the ranking of wives were even greater, since among the politically powerful the normal arrangements were inverted. A commoner Nguni polygynist married his first wife with cattle given by his father. She became his great wife and mother of his heir. He might then marry another woman using private resources and so establish another 'side' of his village. Once the two sides were established — as it were, the public and the private — subsequent wives might be attached to them.

The aristocratic pattern provided almost a mirror image of this.

A classic description was provided by Dugmore (1906:26-7) for the Xhosa:

> The first wife of a Kafir chief, 'the wife of his youth', is not un-frequently taken from amongst families of his own councillors. He is as yet 'unknown to fame'; his wealth is not so considerable as it *is* to be. After awhile his alliance becomes more worthy the attention of those of other tribes, whose daughters demand a higher dowry [i.e. bridewealth] than was required by the humbler parents of his first wife. Another and another are sent to him; for it must be borne in mind that a Kafir chief does not choose his own wives. He is surprised from time to time by the arrival of a bridal party, bringing with them as his offered bride some chief's daughter whom he has never seen before. The danger of refusing her is according to the rank and power of the family to which she belongs, for to refuse such an alliance is to offer a public insult to the whole tribe. The usual order of things, then, is that the chief grows older and richer, wives of higher rank are sent to him, and the reasons which operate against their refusal operate also against their having an inferior rank allotted to them in the successional distribution. The mother of him who is to be the 'great son' may thus be the last wife the chief has taken, which is in fact sometimes the case. (Cf. Kropf, 1848; Nicholson, 1888; Soga, 1931:36)

The aristocratic Swazi pattern was much the same, and Bryant (1923:47) recorded a similar system for Zulu nobles.

In the case of a major chief the great wife was paid for out of tribal resources, but she was chosen late. The options for adjusting political alliances through selecting the appropriate great wife were kept open as long as possible.

Customary law codes tried to reduce the uncertainty (see, e.g. Kerr, 1961:39-45), but the advantages were obvious enough. Not only could alliances be juggled, but, as Sir Theophilus Shepstone pointed out in his edivence to the 1883 Commission (vol. 11, p. 47), the system tended 'to prevent temptation to disputes about succession during the chief's life'.

The situation was further complicated, certainly in the Cape tribes, by the assumption that while the great house of a major chief would succeed to the chieftaincy, the right-hand house would not remain subordinate but would rather form the basis of a new tribe. Soga even suggested (1931:56) that 'the Right-Hand House has a semi-independent character and constitution, the object of whose existence is to spread

out the tribe on a two current basis.' (Cf. Hammond-Tooke, 1965.)
The relationship between the houses is referred back to an origin myth
which nicely illustrates the political implications of the ranking of wives:

> According to the story found in many vernacular traditions the
> Right-Hand House was founded in the time of Phalo, who reigned
> from ca. 1710 to ca. 1775. One day Phalo was embarrassed by the
> simultaneous arrival at his royal court of two princesses, one the
> daughter of the Mpondo Paramount and the other the daughter of
> the Thembu Paramount. He could make neither his Great Wife
> without offending the father of the other but his dilemma was
> solved by one Majeke, who asked: 'What is greater than the head
> of the Chief, and what is stronger than his right arm?' As a result
> one princess became the Great Wife and the other became the
> Right-Hand Wife. (Peires, 1975:114)

The sister's claim

If a woman's linked brother took the bridewealth cattle she brought in,
and used them to acquire a wife for himself, then he was placed in her
debt. She had given him a wife. In the view of the Lovedu:

> The house of the brother is thought to have been created by the
> sister whose cattle made the marriage possible. That is why, when he
> builds a new village, it is the sister who has to draw the magic circle
> of protection which renders it safe from witches. When the sister
> visits her old home, it is in the house of this wife that she will 'put
> her things' and make herself at home . . . The sister even wields a
> certain amount of authority in the house of her brother, as was well
> illustrated at a gathering we attended where the man of the house
> was quarrelling with his wife about an uninvited guest. In the midst
> of the uproar a voice was heard: 'This is my village which I have
> built. I will have no unseemly behaviour here.' It was the sister
> rebuking her brother, who subsided immediately and went on with
> the ceremonial as if nothing had happened. So strong is the interest
> of a sister in the house established by her cattle that she may on
> occasion even exercise some control in her brother's choice of a wife.
> (E. J. and J. D. Krige, 1943:75–6)

A similar pattern has been reported for Nguni groups. A woman
could help herself to the clothes and household utensils of her linked

brother's wife. Among the Mpondo she expected her younger brother's wife to wait on her, and to address her as 'female husband' (Hunter, 1936:33). 'The wives should appear glad', a writer on the Swazi commented, 'and only if articles of too great a value are removed may they complain against "the girl of the home"' (H. Kuper, 1950:99-100). An extreme situation has been reported for some Tsonga groups, where a woman descended on her brother's homestead when he died and demanded the goods of a house and even a wife and child (Earthy, 1933:14-18).

A woman did not rest content with her influence in the affairs of the house established with her bridewealth. She demanded a direct return from her brother. She had provided him with cattle which he had used to acquire a wife. In return she must be given a wife. She claimed a co-wife, to work as her subordinate in the homestead, and to bear children for her house; or alternatively a daughter-in-law to marry her son and to look after her. In the latter case the marriage would be a matrilateral cross-cousin marriage from the point of view of her son.

Once again the strongest statement of the claim was made by Lovedu women, whose jural position was exceptionally strong. The Lovedu recognized: 'the right, enforceable at law, of every woman to a daughter-in-law (to render services to her and marry her son) from the "house" of any woman who has been acquired by means of her own bridewealth, for, failing a son, the woman may marry the girl herself' (E. J. Krige, 1974:15). The legal status of this claim was exceptional, though among the Pedi too a woman would marry her brother's daughter herself if she had no son (Mönnig, 1967:206). Among all the Sotho-Tswana, and the Venda, however, matrilateral cross-cousin marriage was legitimated at least in part with reference to a woman's claim on her brother for a daughter-in-law in return for the bridewealth with which she had provided him.

Some Southern African societies prohibited mother's brother's daughter's marriage. Among the northern Nguni and the Tsonga the sister asked rather for a subordinate co-wife. From the point of view of her husband, this was a claim on a wife's younger sister or, failing her, on a wife's brother's daughter.[6]

This seems unreasonable: a man paid bridewealth once and demanded two wives in return. The equity of the claim arises from the fact that it lay with the sister rather than with her husband. As one report, on the Swazi, explained: 'The man's own wife is the proper person to go and woo a girl for him at her own kraal . . . It is more probable that if the husband takes his wife's sister as an *inhlant'i* and not another woman, it will be because his own wife wishes it' (Engelbrecht, 1930:6–7). Women favoured such marriages since 'Close relatives are considered useful allies as co-wives' (H. Kuper, 1950:94).

To sum up, among the Sotho-Tswana and the Venda a woman required that her brother's daughter be married to her son. Among the northern Nguni and Tsonga she claimed a sister to be a co-wife. In both cases these marriages repaid the debt owed by her brother, who had used her bridewealth to marry a wife.

The Cape Nguni diverged from the general pattern in an instructive way. The Xhosa prohibited mother's brother's daughter marriage and also marriage with a wife's sister during the wife's lifetime. Even if the wife died childless they did not normally expect her sister or brother's daughter to be provided as a substitute (van Tromp, 1948:37).

Did the Cape Nguni woman then enjoy no return on the bridewealth she earned for her family? The solution to this apparent inequity is to be found in two other institutions.

Firstly, the Cape Nguni emphasized the payment of a dowry in the strict sense of the term, a gift which accompanied the bride to her new home. The dowry was formally allocated to the husband, but he could alienate it only with the agreement of his wife. It might be considerable. Thus a Gaika elder, giving evidence to the 1883 Commission (vol. 11, 1, 82), remarked:

> We always provide our girls with things, and what we give is called *ikazi*. It often happens when a marriage is divorced (sic) that the dowry cattle [i.e. bridewealth] are not sent back by the father of the girl, because the cattle taken to the husband's kraal were equal in number . . . Among us, when an alliance is made between two rich men, the cattle pass each other, and the one family gets as much as the other.

Secondly, the Cape Nguni — alone in Southern Africa — insisted that the bridewealth paid for a woman should not normally be used by her father or brother to acquire a wife, but should rather be held in trust for her. Thus another Gaika elder told the 1883 Commission (p. 93):

> When a girl is married she goes from one family or tribe to another, and cattle are sent from the other family or tribe to show their recognition of her, and also to provide an asylum for her future, supposing she should come to need it; then the cattle are divided

among the father's family, so that if the father himself became poor, the girl in case of need could claim from others who had received *ikasi* cattle.

Soga (1931:277-8) summed up the general expert view when he argued that a woman's bridewealth:

never actually belongs to the bride's parents while she lives, though they often make use of the cattle. They sometimes even sell them to meet their own liabilities, but in such an event they should consult the person to whom they really belong, namely, their daughter. The latter always refers to these cattle as *'ikazi lam'* – 'my dowry'. In the case of a parent squandering his daughter's *ikazi* he becomes liable to her for its restoration . . . In theory it is unalienable until her death, when it reverts to her parents, but never to her own children.

Among the Cape Nguni (certainly the Xhosa), in short, crucial elements of the Northern Nguni system were altered. Here a man did not use his sister's bridewealth to marry, and consequently he owed her nothing in return. A woman's bridewealth went to her father, but he held it as a surety for her. Moreover he provided her house with dowry cattle. There remained no debts between brothers and sisters or fathers and daughters.

The short-circuiting of the exchange transaction occurred also at the level of the main bridewealth exchange, for bridewealth was more or less counterbalanced by a payment of dowry. Consequently relationships with the wife's family were truncated. The new Mpondo wife could henceforth drink sour milk only from her husband's herds and no longer from the cows of her father or brothers (Hunter, 1936:200). Her ties with her parents and brothers were sharply diminished, and her children's relationship with their mother's brothers were insignificant. Relationships seem to have been elaborated rather within the homestead, marked by the emphasis given to bridewealth debt relationships between the houses.

The mother's brother in South Africa

The claims of a woman on her brother had repercussions in turn for the relation between her son and her brother. This is the famous mother's brother/sister's son relationship. Radcliffe-Brown's paper (1924) dealt particularly with the Tsonga mother's brother, an extreme case as will become apparent. I begin with the Northern Nguni.

> Among the Swazi the fact that the father's sister bestowed benefits on the father through her marriage cattle entitles her, by Swazi standards, to make various demands on him, on his wives, and on the children of the union which she made possible. On the other hand, the maternal uncle receives advantages through the marriage of his sister, and she and her children may receive help from him. The *umalume* (MB) is always a great favourite; the *bashane* (ZS) may take beer from his hut without asking his permission, they bring him their troubles and seek his intervention in disputes with their own father. (H. Kuper, 1950:102-3)

But the mother's brother did not normally provide his sister's son with a wife, and he should not even offer to help him raise bridewealth, except with the permission of his father (Marwick, 1940:52; Engelbrecht, 1930:14).

Similarly among the Zulu, 'You may do anything you please at the *malume*'s kraal and demand anything you desire. You may not take your *malume*'s things without permission, but when you ask for anything he *must* give it to you if he possibly can' (E. J. Krige, 1936:26-7). As one informant explained, this was because 'It is through me that my mother has discharged the obligations (the bearing of children) for which her *lobola* cattle were paid. So my *malume* is pleased, for he holds the cattle' (*ibid.*). Again, among the Bomvana, 'A man is always kind to his sister's son . . . He cannot refuse food or aid . . . He treats him more kindly and generously than his own sons for "he ate his sister's *ikazi* cattle"' (Cook, 1931:36).

Elsewhere in the Cape there was a marked decline in the importance of relations with the mother's kin, including the mother's brother. The Mpondo recognized 'no special bond between a boy and the mother's brother who benefited from his mother's *ikhazi*. One's mother's relatives are likely to be friendly, and are therefore people from whom to ask gifts, but gifts are asked in the same way from friends or a chief' (Hunter, 1936:48). The Xhosa ethnography allots little space to the mother's brother.

Among the Sotho-speaking peoples and the Venda, relations with the mother's kin were intimate but the mother's brother was not the indulgent figure found among the Northern Nguni.

Casalis (1861:181) wrote that: 'Among the Basutos, the eldest brother of the mother (*malume*), also enjoys special rights over the children. He is understood to replace the mother, whose sex keeps her in a state of dependence. This is a counterbalance to the authority of the father and the eldest son . . .'

Brown (1926:53-4) even suggested that among the Tswana 'the individual whose power seems to be greatest over a child is neither the father nor the father's people, but the mother's eldest brother.' Where the Nguni argued that the mother's brother was indebted to his sister's son, the Tswana, according to Brown, took the view that 'The rights of a maternal uncle (*maloma*) to any of the possessions of the sister's son are based on the fact that the son has drawn his nourishment from that sister's breasts and so owes not only his life but its maintenance to his family.'

Schapera (1940:113), writing of the Kgatla, stressed particularly the relationship with the brother who received a share in the mother's bridewealth, the brother to whom she was 'linked' by their father. The 'linked' mother's brother:

> must be consulted on all matters specially affecting his sister's children; his opinion is so important when their marriages are being arranged that his veto is often decisive; he contributes towards the *bogadi* bridewealth given for the wives of his nephews, and shares in the *bogadi* received for his nieces; he helps with food and clothes when they are born, initiated, confirmed into church membership, or married; he takes a leading part in their funerals, being charged with the duty of preparing their corpses for burial, and receiving as his portion of their estate their clothes and other personal belongings; and exchanges of property are frequent between him and his nephews. (Cf. A. Kuper, 1970b.)

In sum, the outstanding characteristics of the avunculate among the Sotho-Tswana were that the mother's brother was a figure of semi-paternal authority, who could claim property belonging to his sister's son (particularly the first fruits of all his labours), and who provided his sister's son with either a wife or with bridewealth. (It seems that he would in fact contribute to the bridewealth only if his own daughter was not actually the bride − see, e.g. Mönnig, 1961:135, 199.) On all these points the relationship differed from the avunculate among the Northern and Southern Nguni and the Tsonga.

Among the Xhosa and Mpondo a woman was not seen as a creditor of her brother and father, and her son did not have a highly developed relationship with her family. Among the other Nguni a debt existed because her brother had married with the cattle earned by her marriage. Her brother returned a co-wife to her, but she and her son retained a claim on the house established with her bridewealth, and this was expressed by her son's claims on his mother's brother. These claims were taken to an extreme amongst the Tsonga, where the sister's son made 'joking' claims on the mother's brother's wives and food.[7]

Among the Sotho-Tswana and Venda the mother's brother reversed the gift in the following generation. This in turn placed the sister's son in his debt. The sister's son therefore paid bridewealth and served his mother's brother. The reciprocity was maintained from generation to generation. If it were for some reason interrupted, then a new cycle would be initiated. For example, among the Venda a man who did not marry his daughter to his linked sister's son was obliged to return to his sister his share in her daughter's bridewealth. This would be used to finance the nephew's marriage to another woman (Stayt, 1931:175). An even more complex rule was recorded for the Sotho Khaha by Junod (1927, I:293):

> Among the cattle which a Khaha pays for his wife, there is a cow called 'the cow used to nurse the child.' This cow is meant to provide milk for the girl 'begotten by the oxen' who is to become the wife of that man's son. When this son is grown up, he will have the right of claiming from his maternal uncle this special cow with all its offspring . . . and these cattle will form the nucleus of the herd which he must pay to obtain his cousin. Should the girl refuse her cousin, her parents will force her to consent . . . The *motsoala* [cross-cousin] is his wife! If her parents cannot overcome her resistance and she definitely refuses, the father of this boy will go to the Court and claim not only the cow to nurse the child, but all the cattle which he paid years ago to obtain her mother, and the chief will admit his claim.

Reciprocity and the time factor

The system of marriage and bridewealth rested on a simple and ineluctable principle of reciprocity. Cattle were exchanged for wives, wives for cattle. This rule applied not only as between a man and his wife's family, but at every step between those who contributed to bridewealth payments, and those who exchanged bridewealth directly for wives.

Reciprocity was direct, wives were always exchanged for cattle. Even where matrilateral cross-cousin marriage was preferred and statistically common, the ideological emphasis was not on 'generalized exchange' of wives, but on the direct exchange of women for cattle. Moreover, it would be misleading to say that men were exchanging women among themselves. Rather, men and women exchanged certain rights in women for cattle.

Anyone who contributed bridewealth had a claim on the 'house' established with it. Among the Venda, indeed, if a man's father provided him with the bridewealth to acquire a wife, she would at first be called the wife of his father (see below pp. 79–80). Generally the ultimate provider of the bridewealth could claim in return the right to dispose of the first daughter of the house in marriage, or at any rate to take the bridewealth she brought in.

The fundamental difference between the two main classes of Southern Bantu marriage systems lies in the time element. Among most of the Nguni and Tsonga, debts might be transmitted over the generations but ideally each transaction was discrete and settled within a generation. Among the Sotho-Tswana and Venda each gift necessitated a fresh counter-gift, the exchanges of wives-for-bridewealth-for-wives-for-bridewealth ideally stretching from generation to generation. This open-endedness was encoded also in preferential kin marriage rules. It crucially affected the structure of relationships generated by marriage and bridewealth, as will become more evident in later chapters.

Part two

Politics, alliance and bridewealth

4 States, clans, lineages and ruling lines

The myth of clans and lineages

The literature on traditional African political systems is largely shaped by two guiding concepts: 'divine kings' and 'clans'. Both have now gone a little out of fashion, but neither has really been discredited; and anthropologists in particular still tend to operate with a whole theoretical system of 'clans' and quasi-clans or 'lineages'.

This poses a problem for me. The second part of this book deals with the political implications of marriage in pre-industrial Southern Bantu societies. I shall not be writing about 'clans' or 'lineages', but spectral 'clans' and 'lineages' populate the literature on Africa so thickly that they cannot just be ignored. They must be exorcized.

On the other hand, this is not the place for a thorough historical critique of descent theory in its various ramifications. After all, elaborate models of 'clan' and 'lineage' systems are still being propagated by writers of diverse theoretical persuasions, including British structural-functionalists, 'alliance' theorists, and French Marxists. (A more detailed critique may be found in A. Kuper, 1982.) For present purposes it is perhaps enough to sketch the development of the model and to suggest why it cannot advance the analysis of traditional Southern Bantu political systems. I shall then introduce a more appropriate model, which will be applied in the case studies that follow.

Morgan is the most important ancestor of the modern orthodoxy. In *Ancient Society* he opposed two plans of government, 'gentile organization', based on personal kinship relations, and political society based upon territorial units. The gens, 'a body of consanguinei descended from the same common ancestor, distinguished by a gentile name, and bound together by affinities of blood' (Morgan, 1878:63), was originally matrilineal, later becoming patrilineal. It was also exogamous, so protecting its members from 'the evils of consanguine marriages' (p. 69, cf. pp. 74-5). Finally, the gens was totemic (p. 86) and functioned as a religious congregation.

The political system based on the gens was of a peculiarly natural and attractive kind. 'Liberty, equality, and fraternity, though never formulated, were cardinal principles of the gens' (p. 85). These principles were present also in the larger federations of gentes which were sometimes formed (rather like the American Union, perhaps). At each level the organization was governed by councils and elected sachems, members being bound by obligations of mutual help, defence and redress. This gentile system dominated the earlier history of mankind, being swept away only by the emergence of the state, private property, and a territorial form of organization.

Morgan's conjectural history (in some ways paralleling the ideas of Maine, whose direct influence on British anthropology was more immediate), was recast in modern Africanist theory with the publication in 1940 of *African Political Systems*, edited by Meyer Fortes and E. E. Evans-Pritchard. Invoking Maine rather than Morgan, the editors opposed two kinds of African polity: that based on the state, and that based either purely on kinship or on the clan and the lineage. 'Stateless societies' were generally based on 'clans' and 'lineages', which faded out with the development of the 'state'. The state was a monarchy, probably on the lines of Frazer's 'divine kingship' (see, e.g. Fortes and Evans-Pritchard, 1940, p. 18). Morgan was not stood on his head (the uncomfortable fate of so many social theorists). Rather he was laid on his side. His evolutionist model was made over into a timeless classification.

Yet the emphasis given to the 'lineage' in *African Political Systems* was symptomatic of a growing discomfort with the old 'clan' model in its pure form. The reason is evident from a review of contemporary discussions. A good example is the statement of the committee responsible for the fifth (1951) edition of the Royal Anthropological Institute's *Notes and Queries on Anthropology*. Perhaps because committees tend to compromise, the 'clan' was defined so vaguely that no sharp criterion of 'clanship' survived. A 'clan' was now 'a group of persons of both sexes, membership of which is determined by unilineal descent, actual or putative, with ipso facto obligations of an exclusive kind' (p. 89). Even the descent rule might be merely 'putative', and the ipso facto obligations, on inspection, turn out to be vague and indeterminate. 'Emphasis may be laid on the rule of exogamy ... descent from a common ancestor, or even in some cases, common habitation of a village or district' (p. 90), but a 'clan' need not be exogamous, totemic, or localized.

While retaining the concept, anthropologists increasingly relegated these vague 'clans' to the background of their descriptions and analyses. Like the creator figure in many African religions, one talked of the 'clan' with respect but it had little relevance to contemporary affairs; it had done its job in the distant past. Middleton and Tait explained in an influential essay that the term 'clan'

> is a long-standing one in anthropological literature and is generally used to refer to a unilineal descent group, especially when it is exogamous. *It consists of several lineages*, which may be segmented. It may be a mere category of dispersed people, not forming a corporate group and with only a vague notion of original common ancestry . . . *Its use is best restricted to unilineal descent groups . . . within which exact genealogical relationships are not traced . . . Exogamy and totemism are often given as defining attributes, but this is unnecessary* . . . (Middleton and Tait, 1958:4. My emphases)

This 'clan' was by now a very shadowy thing indeed. Exact genealogical relationships were not traced within it, and it was not necessarily exogamous or totemic. The one positive attribute it was allowed was that 'It consists of several lineages.'

The displacement of the 'clan' by the new 'lineages' in British anthropology was marked by the publication of *African Political Systems*. For the past forty years 'lineages' have been conventional appurtenances of Africanist monographs. In the United States there was a parallel development, motivated also by an uneasy feeling that the classical notion was unduly cumbersome. Murdock (1949), for example, suggested splitting the 'clan' or 'gens' into two: a totemic and exogamous descent group, which following Lowie he called the 'sib'; and a localized descent group, which he called the 'clan'.

Murdock's choice of terms added a fresh source of confusion to discussions between British and American scholars, but the trend was similar. If anything was to be salvaged from Morgan's model, to which all parties were apparently committed, then the old descent groups of the Morgan model had to be refurbished. They were split up into passive and active principles, the passive 'clans', having done a jolly good job through history, now giving way to the active 'lineages' or 'sibs'.

But these 'lineages' or 'sibs' were supposed to be endowed with the most important qualities which had once defined the 'clan' – unilineality, exogamy, localization, political identity, property rights, etc. (See, e.g., Fortes, 1953.) The classical model was salvaged by a verbal trick. Writing of 'lineages' rather than 'clans', Morgan's model of the gentile form of government was applied, lightly modernized, to the Nuer, Tallensi, Tiv, and various other African peoples.

The myth of the clan in Southern Africa

Morgan's original model was taken over with hardly any emendation by some theoretically inclined Southern Bantu ethnologists. Bryant, for example, wrote that:

> the fundamental unit in the Bantu political systems was the clan, i.e. the magnified family, in which all alike were descended from the same original ancestor, all were now ruled by that ancestor's direct living representative, and all (at least in those times), dwelt and moved together in one great block, but did not intermarry, mates being sought outside. (Bryant, 1929:15. Cf. Hoernlé, 1925)

This was the pristine state of affairs. By the nineteenth century the situation was clearly different. Bryant explained:

> The passing of Senzagankona marked the end and the beginning of two distinct periods in East-Nguni political history. On that day a long past of patriarchal rule was tolled to its grave and the tocsin sounded of a new era of autocracy to be inaugurated by his son . . . The primordial system of numberless clans and independent chieftains would, amidst much wailing and bloodshed, be gradually demolished, and upon and out of its ruins would be built up a grandiose nation ruled by an imperious despot. (Bryant, 1929:70-1)

The rise of the state ended the age of the clans, just as Morgan had said.

This orthodoxy survived the transition between the evolutionist amateurs of the early twentieth century and the functionalist professionals of the later period. Hilda Kuper (1947:11), for example, outlined a pure Morgan vision of Swazi history:

> (1) the period of migration of Bantu kinsmen organized into small patrilineal clans; (2) the contact of different clans and the growth of rival clan heads into petty chiefs with non-clansmen among their subjects; and (3) the dominance of one clan and the organization of subjects on a military non-kinship basis under the leadership of the head of the ruling clan.

Gluckman (1940:28; 1950:169) agreed with Bryant that essentially the same process was to be discerned in Zulu history. According to

Hammond-Tooke (1965:146–9), an original system of local clans was
also dislodged by the early state among the Cape Nguni, although 'It
is probably impossible at this point of time to reconstruct the process.'
As cautious a writer as Schapera (1956:30) could write that 'Among
Nguni and Tsonga . . . the clan was at one time a local group; many
tribes, indeed, seem at first to have consisted primarily of one clan . . .'

Despite this powerful body of opinion, there is next to no reason
to suppose that in Southern Africa a pristine age of clans really was
disrupted by the emergence of the early state. As Audrey Richards
pointed out with her characteristic good sense, the orthodoxy was
difficult to pin down. 'Kidd, whose whole thesis is a glorification of
the "clan system," never once explains exactly what he means by a
clan. Gibson, Casalis, and Kropf leave us in similar doubts . . .' (1932:
141). Indeed, 'it is difficult to decide whether the South African
clan was ever a strongly knit unit with important legal and economic
functions; and it is still harder to describe the part which it plays in
native society today' (p. 142).

When the Zulu expert Carl Faye (1923:102) consulted Radcliffe-
Brown in Cape Town about the use of the term 'clan' for the Zulu
isibongo, Radcliffe-Brown replied: 'The chief objection to the use of
the term "clan" is that it has been used so loosely in the past, for social
groups of very different kinds . . . I have not yet been able to settle
on a really satisfactory terminology for Bantu sociology . . .' In fact,
however, the problem was rather that if one defined the 'clan' in any
fairly rigorous and traditional way, then it was difficult actually to
find one.

There might be grounds for neglecting the political functions of the
'clan', on the grounds that these had been taken over by the 'states'.
Similarly, like Murdock, one could drop the demand that 'clans' be
localized. (Monica Wilson (1969:118), for example, wrote: 'A great
deal of confusion has arisen because one writer after another has used
clan both for the exogamous group claiming common descent, and for a
local group under a subordinate leader. In this book [*The Oxford
History of South Africa*] it is used in the first sense only.') Yet there was
no easy escape from the traditional requirements that the 'clan' should
be unilineal, exogamous and totemic, and each of these criteria was
troublesome.

The Sotho-Tswana had totems but were without exogamous groupings, while the Nguni, perhaps crudely 'exogamous', were usually not
totemic.[1] The Sotho-Tswana, indeed, were hopelessly refractory. One

recent writer claimed that 'clans and clan-like groupings exist in all Southern Bantu societies', but was immediately forced to concede that the Sotho-Tswana could only just be accommodated even on the most generous terms. 'Of such minor importance is clanship among Sotho-speakers that a number of authorities hesitate even to use the word "clan" in this connection, particularly as the group is not exogamous' (Preston-Whyte, 1974:201).

The 'clan exogamy' of the Nguni is also by no means obvious. In the first place, rules of exogamy did not exclude only marriages with lineal kin. In the second place, it was not true that even among Zulu- and Xhosa-speakers all marriages were banned between people who shared a common patronymic.[2] Bryant himself, committed though he was to the discovery of traces of an aboriginal gentile organization, was constrained to report that 'Since Shakan times, when the various clans became broken up and their members everywhere dispersed, these rules of "prohibited degrees" have not been so strictly adhered to . . .' (1949:484). On my reading of the evidence, no Nguni peoples had exogamous descent groups, unless one wishes to define in this way the category of immediate paternal kin.

This leaves only the last and the most fundamental criterion of 'clanship', that a 'clan' is a category of at least putatively lineal descendants of a common ancestor. Among writers on the Southern Bantu the assumption has been that this lineal recruitment was evidenced in the system of names and totems. Preston-Whyte (1974:201) has summed up the general view:

> Among the Nguni and Tsonga common clan membership is signalled
> by the possession of an eponymous clan name (Zulu and Swazi:
> *isibongo*; Cape Nguni: *isiduko*; Tsonga: *sibongo*) and among the
> Sotho by the name of a totemic species or object of praise (Lobedu:
> *motupo*; S. Sotho: *seboko*; Pedi: *moane* or *seano*; Tswana: *seboko*).
> Both clan and totem names are inherited partilineally but persons
> sharing them do not form, or even think of themselves as forming,
> a group of any kind.

This is by no means an extravagant claim, but on closer enquiry it too proves difficult to sustain. Among the Nguni there may be several surnames, used in different contexts, and acquired in various ways (e.g. Hughes, 1956:34–5), and a new *sibongo* might be adopted or be imposed by a ruler (e.g. Marwick, 1940:56–7). As Soga (1931:21) remarked for the Xhosa, 'the patronymic . . . is not a constant but a variable quantity.'

Similarly, the Sotho-Tswana and Venda have a variety of stories recording how individuals or even whole groups have changed their totems,
and some individuals and local communities may have several totems.[3]
Conversely, groups with no tradition of common origin may have the
same name or totem. There are no *sibongo* or totem groups, as Preston-
Whyte conceded; and it is not easy to pin down even *sibongo* or totemic
categories of people.

The 'lineage' alternative

The segmentary lineage model had rejuvenated the clan model in
African anthropology and a number of writers, perhaps dissatisfied with
'clans', tried to identify 'lineages' among the Southern Bantu. This was
not easy. Genealogies were very shallow, even in the male line, generally
extending to only one or two generations of deceased patrilineal
forebears.[4] There were no hierarchical arrangements of nesting lineage
segments. It was difficult to identify any particular 'lineage' activity
which might not more readily be attributed to the homestead or
neighbourhood or administrative ward. 'Lineages' therefore tended to
be invoked in a vague and general way, perhaps to indicate that the
fashionable modern authors had been duly studied.[5]

To cite one characteristic example, Hammond-Tooke (1962:58-60)
defined a 'lineage' among the Bhaca — 'an exogamous grouping of all
the people who trace their descent from a common grandfather or even
great-grandfather in the male line.' He could not, however, identify this
entity with any group the Bhaca conceived of or distinguished in action.
'There is no single vernacular word for the lineage but its members
conceptualize the group as *abantfu bomti*, "the people of the homestead," or *usapho*, which refers, however, more particularly to the
group of people residing in a homestead.' The Bhaca 'do not conceive
that the lineage ever splits and are at a loss to explain this inability to
trace the line further into the past.' It was little wonder that Hammond-
Tooke could not find any very specific functions for such a group
(cf. Hammond-Tooke, 1968).

Hughes (1956:36) found an ingenious way to display a command of
the vogue ideas while remaining faithful to his ethnographic materials.
He diagrammed a classic Nuer-type segmentary lineage system and then
explained that it did not exist among the Ndebele of Zimbabwe.

In retrospect I rather wish I had been as cut and dried (A. Kuper,
1970a). Among the Kgalagari the people sometimes talked as though

the descendants of each of the founding fathers formed a distinct category; and these categories were named after birds, animals, etc. While these broad categories were admittedly of little significance, I called the local village wards recruited from among them 'sub-clans'. I did not deploy 'lineages', and that is something for which I am grateful; yet all I had actually found was a mechanism by which local groups of agnates could define their identity and their relations to other groups in the village by projecting this back on to an origin myth of their people. By writing of 'sub-clans', I was giving a quite inappropriate image of what Kgalagari organization might once have been. The implication was that since 'sub-clans' still had political functions, 'clans' were the original political units. I shall later suggest a more realistic view of the situation, but my immediate point is that by searching out scraps of custom which we could label 'clans' or 'lineages' anthropologists were merely staving off the inevitable. The classical model had been patched and repatched, but was now beyond redemption. A fresh start was long overdue.

The ruling line

The obvious starting-point is not some mythical gentile organization which might once have flourished in Southern Africa but rather the familiar tribal polities which were described from the first moment of European contact and which in some places flourished well into the twentieth century.

Most of these political communities were divided into two categories, whom Schapera calls 'nobles' and 'commoners'. 'Nobles' were 'all people held to be of the same origin by descent as the chief. The rest are commoners . . .' (Schapera, 1956:56-7). This terminology has inappropriate overtones, suggesting a feudal system of some kind. Moreover there was often a shading off between the two categories rather than a fast boundary. Nevertheless, the terminology will be retained here for the larger states, such as the Ngwato or Swazi. But these distinctions were found even in a Kgalagari village; and my 'sub-clans' were really to be identified in relation to the founding or ruling lines of the various Kgalagari villages.

Members of the ruling line traced their genealogies back through males to the founder of the political community. Consequently the genealogies of ruling lines, exceptionally in Southern Africa, were often deep. They might even preserve the memory of earlier attachments to the ruling house of another tribe, from which they had seceded.

Internally the ruling lines were ordered more like European royal lines than classically conceived African lineages (as Fortes has remarked, 1970:282–3). What mattered was personal kinship relationship to the present ruler. Each time a new ruler acceded to power the internal relations of the ruling line were altered. Men who had been the most senior nobles were now pushed a step away from the source of power, perhaps being compelled to yield influence even to the younger sons of their brother or father's brother, the old ruler. The basic rule in the largest states and the smallest villages was that 'the more closely a man is related to the head of his group the higher his status within it' (Schapera, 1956:57).

Partly because so much was at stake for all members of the ruling line, the transition from one reign to another was by no means always easy and ordered.

> Owing to polygamy and the associated practice of ranking wives, disputes about the succession are almost inevitable. The brothers and other connections of each wife watch jealously over the interests of her sons, whose fortunes they usually do all that they can to promote, if only because they themselves expect to benefit in consequence . . . Even if the heir is definitely known and acknowledged, he is not always assured of the succession . . .
> Even if the heir does become chief, he may afterwards have trouble with his brothers or uncles . . . (Schapera, 1956:165–7)

Rebellion was frequent, as were preemptive strikes by the rulers. Gluckman (e.g. 1954) argued that these frequent Southern Bantu rebellions helped in some way to maintain tribal solidarity, but Schapera (1956:175–8) pointed out that on the contrary the normal result of rebellion was secession. Moreover, secession regularly occurred without rebellion.

> Among Bantu the creation of new tribes by fission is a constantly recurring feature of the political system. Disputes among members of the royal family often cause one of them to secede, and if accompanied by enough people he will usually start his own tribe. The great majority of existing tribes, in all divisions, are said to have originated in this manner; the reigning chiefs of different tribes in each division can consequently trace their descent back to a common agnatic ancestor . . . a seceding leader was often accompanied by

> some of his brothers and other close relatives, but . . . the bulk of his
> following was not necessarily related to him by ties of either blood
> or marriage. (Schapera, 1956:27)

The conflicts which led to secession were most likely to occur between
half-brothers by different mothers, belonging to different 'houses'.[6]

The process of internal differentiation was most clearly marked in
the system of appointments, often called 'placing'. This was the custom
by which a ruler placed his younger brothers or some of his sons in
positions of control over subordinate political divisions. The model was
the allocation of some estate property to each 'house' of a headman,
although ideally a ruler would carve new chiefdoms out along the
frontiers, or take followers over from weak foreign headmen. So long
as this was feasible there was no call to dispossess a member of the
ruling line. Monica Hunter (1936:380), for example, described the ideal
arrangements, with reference to the Mpondo:

> As far as possible the paramount appointed brothers and sons as
> district chiefs. He made no attempt to supplant a large and powerful
> district chief, or a less powerful chief who was a near relative of his
> own; but in smaller districts where the chief was not his own relative
> the paramount settled a wife, and the son of that wife on growing up
> became chief of the district . . . A number of the chiefs or large
> districts with which the paramount did not attempt to interfere were
> distant relatives of his own, their ancestors as sons or brothers of the
> paramount had been established as district chiefs . . .

A similar tradition existed throughout the region.[7]

Placing could no longer be carried out relatively painlessly, however,
when the boundaries of the community were fixed or even narrowed,
as they were with the imposition of colonial rule. Then the costs of the
system increased. As Hilda Kuper reported of the Swazi (1947:57-8):

> Formerly the king could find principalities for his relatives by
> expanding his terrain; now that all land is allocated and the
> boundaries of the country are fixed, he can only satisfy the claims
> of immediate kin at the expense of existing chiefs of royal or
> common descent.

Increasingly nobles began to preponderate in local headmanships
(Schapera, 1956:58-9), and new placings could be made only at the
expense of more distant noble relatives.

At the same time, the traditional option of fission was also increasingly difficult to achieve. Colonial rulers tried to maintain the integrity of the tribal governments, and there were fewer open areas to which a seceding leader could move. Since secession was no longer practical, subordinate office-holders tried to combat the increasing inroads on their privileges which followed from the development of the placing system.

The crisis in Lesotho

Lesotho, overcrowded and overcentralized, saw the worst internal crisis of the traditional polity. The Basotho state was formed in the mid-nineteenth century by a minor Sotho chief, Moshesh or Moshoeshoe. He successfully brought together various, largely Sotho, communities which had been devastated by the generation of unrest unleashed by Shaka's wars, prolonged by a wave of freebooting armies, and finally exploited by the Boer settlers of the Orange Free State.

Moshoeshoe's success was due in the first instance to his skilful diplomacy, in which he was assisted by the sophisticated missionaries of the Paris Evangelical Society. Internally, however, he employed classic Southern Bantu political techniques.

Initially Moshoeshoe and his relatives ruled directly over only a fraction of the communities which more or less fully accepted his overlordship. By the end of the nineteenth century, when Moshoeshoe's grandson Lerotholi became paramount chief, he was supported by all the sixteen principal chiefs of the country, 'of whom one was actually a son of Moshesh, ten grandsons, four nephews and one more distantly related' (Ashton, 1952:196). This achievement is readily explained. 'In their advance to supremacy, the Koena chiefs made use of two principal devices. One was intermarriage; the other was what has come to be known as the institution of "placing" . . .' (Hamnett, 1975:25). Hamnett underplays the importance of the marriage strategies, but gives an excellent account of the placing system and its logic (1975: ch. 2). The end result was that 'the political structure of Lesotho can be mapped fairly accurately on to the genealogical structure of the house of Moshoeshoe' (*ibid.*).

This was, of course, a success story from the point of view of the rulers, but difficulties soon became apparent, particularly at the lower reaches of the system. The trouble was that new appointments had increasingly to be made at the expense of previous appointments.

Political domains were continuously fragmented. By 1938 when the colonial government tried to rationalize the structure of political offices, they were forced to recognize over 1,300 lesser chiefs and headmen in a total population of under half a million; 'and there were probably about as many more headmen who considered they had a right to such recognition, some of them mere village heads . . .' (G. I. Jones, 1951:38-9).

Even with this fragmentation, sons of office-holders — whether major chiefs or minor headmen — were increasingly being set over their own father's brothers, who had in turn been 'placed' by their grandfathers. The logic of the system implied the continual degradation of all office-holders, aside from the Paramount, and with the partial exception of the great ward-chiefs.

The chiefs who were threatened by 'placings' argued their own claims in terms of a theory that Hamnett calls 'retrospective' but which might equally be termed 'descentist'. On this view:

> the dynastic relationships established by Moshoeshoe in his sons
> can be regarded as set up *once and for all*, in such a way that each
> father lives on, so to speak, in the person of his son. The four
> cardinal lines move forward in parallel lines from generation to
> generation, never losing their structural relationship to each other
> or their relative position within the hierarchy. (Hamnett, 1965:28)

The alternative view, the view of the office-holder placing his brothers and sons, is rather that 'each successive Paramount Chief, and *mutatis mutandis* each lesser chief too, becomes in his turn a "new Moshoeshoe," and can do again and on the same pattern what the father of the dynasty did before him' (p. 28). In practice, not unexpectedly, office-holders in a position to 'place' their sons did so. Only the most powerful ward chiefs were able to maintain the integrity of their domains. As a rule, what told was 'propinquity to the ruling house *of the day*' (p. 33).

The crisis in Lesotho was signalled by a dramatic escalation after 1940 in the number of so-called 'medicine murders', murders carried out in order to obtain human flesh used in making medicines which were believed to advance a person's political and judicial interests.

The anthropologist G. I. Jones was invited by the colonial administration to investigate. He found that most of the murders were being committed on the orders of minor chiefs and headmen. The cause was 'the unchecked development of certain parts of the Basuto political system, in particular the undue multiplication of minor chiefs and headmen, and the 'placing' system which gave them no real security of tenure' (1950:64). This insecurity was exacerbated by the attempt of the colonial administration, in 1938, to rationalize the number of traditional office-holders. At the same time there was a major national dispute over the succession, which had weakened the paramount chief. (This dispute was related to the most notorious of the medicine murders, for which two major chiefs had been brought to justice.)

The crisis in Lesotho was particularly dramatic, but the same factors were operating wherever the traditional political system continued to function under colonial overrule. With the circumscription of the tribal boundaries, which made secession impractical and allowed the 'placing' of junior sons only at the high cost of 'displacing' other nobles, huge strains were imposed on political office-holders.

The politics of marriage

Although, ironically enough, and in precise contradiction to Morgan, the nearest approach to descent groups in Southern Africa were the product of chieftainship, it is clear that these ruling lines were not like the 'lineages' of classical anthropology. Nor was secession equivalent to 'lineage fission'. Internally, each new reign precipitated restructuring of the status relations of the nobles, imposing new strains, initiating new breaks. 'Placing' threatened established leaders; secession movements menaced the ruler.

There was, however, another process which played an important part in the internal relationships of the royal line, and in the establishment of individual links with important commoners. This was the system of marriage alliance, a factor sometimes underrated in the literature.

Most Nguni groups did not favour (and might forbid) close-kin marriage in general, but the ruler himself was always permitted to marry within the ruling line. One consequence of such a marriage was to demote the woman's family. It might no longer be considered to belong to the ruling line. Among the Swazi, for example, they would lose the title Nkosi (H. Kuper, 1947:111). Soga (1931:104–5) related a probably mythical story about the great Xhosa chief Kreli, whose first wife was a royal:

> Such a marriage was contrary to Xhosa custom. The law against the marriage of blood relations was violated by it, therefore, as the

chief could do no wrong, a way out had to be found in order to legalise the marriage. The course adopted was the only one possible, and that was to reduce the Ama-Gwali clan's [sic] status by edict, to that of commoners . . .

The principal members of a clan [sic] descended from such a union usually follow the profession of diviners (witch-doctors), and in consequence become the religious heads of the tribe.

The Sotho-Tswana explicitly favoured marriage within the ruling line, a preference usually stated in the well-known words, *ngwana rrangwane*, *nyale*, *dikgomo di boele sakeng*, 'father's younger brother's daughter, marry me, that the cattle may return to the byre.' In an important series of papers, Schapera showed[8] that Tswana nobles had a particularly marked preference for FBD marriage. In a large sample, 51 per cent of marriages contracted by nobles were with relatives, including 11 per cent with first cousins or even closer kin. The comparable figures for commoners were lower, respectively 21 per cent and 6 per cent. (A higher proportion of men had married at least one close kinswoman, since polygynists tended to marry only one close kinswoman each (A. Kuper, 1975b).) Within the category of close-kin marriages the preference shown by nobles for FBD marriage was striking; and if the inner group of nobles — 'royals' — were considered, the preference was even more pronounced.

Table 1 Percentage of close-kin marriages with particular kin types (Tswana)

	FBD	BD	FZ	(All close agnates)	MBD	FZD	(Cross-cousins)	Others
Royals	51	11	5	(67)	16	11	(27)	6
Nobles	34	13	5	(52)	20	19	(39	9
Commoners	16	8	1	(25)	41	15	(56)	19

Sources: Schapera, 1957:152; 1963a:105. Cf. Ashton, 1952: Appendix III.

Schapera explained the preference for noble endogamy among the Tswana in terms of the political advantages offered by such marriages. The family of a wife and of a mother were expected to be reliable political allies. If they were themselves nobles, then their support was naturally even more useful. For their part the wife-givers could claim a place in the councils of their powerful affine. They tried to ensure that their sister's son succeeded to office, and if successful they would expect to exercise great political influence. Schapera suggested that these alliances within one royal family were especially valuable where royals were divided among different wards. This was the case among the Western Tswana. There each 'house' of a chief established a new ward, and Western Tswana royals showed a particularly marked tendency to endogamy (Schapera, 1963a).

These processes suggest the expectation of a status difference between Tswana wife-givers and wife-takers, wife-takers being politically more important figures. The mother's brothers were then less powerful nobles who in themselves posed no threat, and who supported the more powerful royal against his brothers. As Schapera summed it up (1963b:166-7):

> dynastic disputes are confined very largely to senior members of
> the royal line itself, i.e. to close agnates . . . On the contrary, a
> royal's non-agnatic relatives, especially his maternal kin, were usually
> among his leading partisans. A chief's wives were taken mostly from
> the families of his own local kin, or of other influential men in the
> tribe, or of the chiefs of other Tswana tribes; and the kinsmen of
> each wife watched jealously over her interests and did what they
> could to promote the fortunes of her sons. This, indeed, was one
> of the main factors leading to conflict between royal half-brothers.

Given the Tswana tendency to repeat alliances, an initial marriage with a father's brother's daughter might establish a tradition of marrying into that family. The wife-givers would now come to be defined as 'mother's brothers'. Matthews (1940:12) pointed to this tendency among the Tshidi-Rolong. Comaroff (1976, 1978) later showed that at least among Tshidi royals the redefinition of an agnatic relationship as a mother's brother–sister's son relationship was an issue of considerable political importance, since it implied that the 'mother's brothers' were now excluded from competition for office. He described the relationship of two important branches of the royal line to Chief Montshiwa (1849-96). Both had given wives to the chief's family, and one had come to be defined as 'mother's brothers', *bomalome*. The other family, however, 'resisted all attempts by Montshiwa and his sons to have them spoken of publicly as mother's brothers. In public contexts, the descendants of Mosela, themselves always regarded as the head of the opposition faction, constantly stressed that the marriages were FBD marriages, "as is Tshidi custom"' (Comaroff, 1976:101). (The third family, incidentally, had given wives to both these powerful rival factions, and was 'mother's brother' to both.)

Among both Sotho-Tswana and Nguni, then, marriages within the ruling line served further to redefine and rearrange status relationships and lines of conflict and support. Political marriages were also made with rulers of other communities, and with commoners at home; and the commoners themselves relied often on affinal and matrilateral connections with the ruling line at various levels of the political hierarchy. These issues will be dealt with more fully in the case-studies which follow. Marriage was a political matter in traditional Southern Bantu society. The present chapter has attempted to redefine the political context within which it should be analysed. The next four chapters deal with the political implications of marriage and bridewealth in representative Southern Bantu societies.

5   The Lovedu: marrying in[1]

Women as sisters and chiefs

Women rulers are comparatively common among the Sotho- and Venda-speaking peoples of the northeastern Transvaal.[2] The Lovedu, however, are exceptional in that the office of ruler has been regularly transmitted from each female ruler to a daughter born to the queen herself or to one of her wives. This is the most celebrated feature of the Lovedu political system, and it signals a remarkable transformation of the more general Sotho-Tswana structure.

The broad features of Sotho-Tswana political systems have already been sketched. There is typically an opposition between members by descent of the ruling line, and commoners. The royal line itself is always divided into factions, based initially on the various 'houses' of the chief but restructured at every succession, by personal ties of filiation and marriage. The ruler is characteristically at loggerheads with a faction of close paternal relatives, and each faction expects support from its maternal kin. Very commonly one of the royal families regularly provides the chief wife of the ruler. This tendency to royal endogamy is characterized initially by FBD marriage, redefined, as it is repeated, as MBD marriage. The relationship between the rulers and the main wife-givers is conceived of as one between sisters' sons and mothers' brothers.

Another general aspect of the political process is the 'placing' system. Just as a Sotho-Tswana father divides most of his wealth among his sons in his lifetime, his heir inheriting his position and any residue, so a Sotho-Tswana chief or headman 'places' his sons over the parts of his political domain, under his control (and, eventually, that of his heir), but over other subordinates including royals who had been 'placed' by one of his own ancestors.

Similar processes characterize the internal relations of the ruling groups at each level of the system, down to the smallest political sub-division of the tribe.

In the northeastern Transvaal women have a special position. They may hold office, in exceptional cases even transmitting office; and they may be expected to 'marry' women.

The role of women as uterine 'sisters' is also very highly developed. Everywhere amongst the Sotho-Tswana and Venda the eldest sister becomes the ritual head of a family, just as the eldest brother becomes the jural head. She has various duties, including the performance of rituals for her brothers' children, and the supervision of her brothers' inheritance. This role is particularly emphasized in the northeastern Transvaal. (See E. J. Krige, 1974:16–17.)

Every sister is also, ideally, paired with the brother who uses her bridewealth to marry a wife for himself. The linked sister then has particular ritual duties and rights over this 'house' of her brother. (See, e.g., E. J. Krige, 1964:177.) She has above all a claim to a daughter of her brother as a wife for her son: that is, as a daughter-in-law. From the point of view of her son, this would be a marriage with a MBD. Consequently a man's mother and linked sister are, as it were, partners in his marriage. This, Eileen Krige writes, is 'the most characteristic feature of Lovedu marriage'. It is even given recognition in the marriage ceremonies:

> After the wedding party of the bride and her companions has set
> out for the bridegroom's home, in the company of the groom and
> his companion, and *before* their arrival with the bride at her new
> home, she is taken to the home of the groom's cattle-linked sister
> to be introduced to her formally as a partner in the marriage; who
> will protect her and her children's rights even against her husband;
> to whom the bride can put all complaints and with whom she will
> find refuge. This is the house, also, to which the bride's *daughter*
> will one day go in marriage. All three, the husband/bridegroom, his
> cattle-linked sister and his mother play vital roles in the marriage.
> Very often a man's sister unofficially courts the girl on his behalf.
> (E. J. Krige, personal communication, 1980)

The Lovedu particularly emphasize this cattle-link between brothers and sisters, and the claim of a man to marry his MBD. This claim is very strong indeed. 'From the point of view of a man (or his mother) his marriage to his cattle-linked cross-cousin is preferential; from the point of view of a woman (or her house) such marriage is obligatory' (J. D. Krige, 1939:400).

MBD marriage (or its functional equivalents, marriage with a MMBD or MMBSD) is statistically common among the Lovedu. In two districts near the capital Eileen Krige found that about a third of all marriages are with a MBD, and (given the high rate of polygyny (E. J. Krige, 1975a:239)) about two-thirds of married men had contracted at least one MBD marriage (E. J. Krige, 1964:186).

If one wife is a cattle-linked MBD she must be the great wife and her son will be the heir. The houses which provide the main heirs, the pivots of the system, are therefore linked in an enduring series of marriage alliances, which yield a stable grid of social relations. The grid is not changeless, however. Political success and failure are reflected in changes in alliance relations.

Demographic accidents must also be coped with. What happens if a woman does not have a son or her brother has no daughter? (Cf. E. J. Krige, 1964:165-71; 1975a:243-6). If a man has no daughter to give his sister then sometimes the preferred marriage will simply be post-poned for a generation, his son's daughter being sent to marry her FFZS. For the husband this is marriage with a MBSD.

If a woman has daughters but no sons then she has various options. She may simply postpone the call for a daughter-in-law. She could pass her daughter's bridewealth on to her MB or MBS, but without requiring the immediate return of the wife. There would then be an extra 'house' owing wives to her heirs. Her daughter's son would marry a woman provided by his MMB or MMBS (thus marrying a MMBD or MMBSD). She might, alternatively, allow her husband or a FBS to use the cattle to marry another wife. In some cases, however, a woman may take a girl from her brother even though she has no son. She would then marry the girl to one of her own daughters. This is the essence of 'woman-woman marriage' among the Lovedu (cf. E. J. Krige, 1974). In the special case of a woman who herself holds an office inherited from her father in the absence of a male heir, woman marriage is a duty. In other cases women who earn cattle in one way or another (for example as doctors) may choose to acquire wives. E. J. Krige (1974:25) found, however, that outside the capital few women were married to women. At its highest, in one area only about 5 per cent of women had a female husband.

There are various ways of looking at these marriages, but where a woman office-holder marries a wife this is a form of levirate for a dead or unborn brother. The woman marries the girl 'born for' her dead or unborn brother, and the girl bears the heir to that dead or unborn brother. As J. D. Krige put it (1939:407): 'the marriage is really fictitious, the female descendant of the bride-receiving lineage

taking the place of her non-existent brother or of a male descendant
...' The woman office-holder continues in office until her death,
however, even if her wife has by then raised an adult male heir.

There are different structural consequences of woman-woman
marriage and MMBD or MMBSD marriage. In woman-woman marriage
the office-holding line is perpetuated by a legal fiction. In MMBD or
MMBSD marriage the line is dropped, its former wife-givers and wife-
takers being joined directly to each other.

(a) Woman-woman marriage

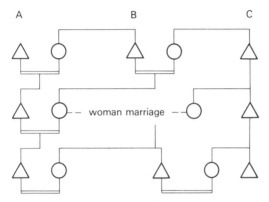

By a fiction line B survives.

(b) MMBD or MMBSD marriage

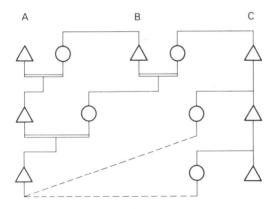

Line B drops out.

FIGURE 2 *Two Lovedu marriage types*

To recapitulate: the cattle-linked brother–sister bond is particularly emphasized in the cultures of the northeastern Transvaal. A woman brings bridewealth which is used to establish a 'house' for her brother. Ideally her brother marries a cattle-linked MBD. The new house bears her brother's heir, and returns a daughter to her, to marry her son. Statistically this ideal pattern is very common, and even demographic imbalances may be circumvented to enable the alliance pattern to be perpetuated.

A woman who has no son — and whose husband therefore has no heir — may marry the girl to her own daughter. Her brother's daughter's son will succeed to her husband's office just as he would have done if she had borne a son to marry the brother's daughter. If her husband has no office, then the bridewealth brought in by the daughters may simply be passed on to her brother or brother's son, a wife being returned in the following generation.

Cui bono? An office which in other Sotho-Tswana societies might have passed in the absence of a son to a man's brother or brother's son goes instead to a daughter. She is succeeded by her wife's son, who is ideally a MBDS. Presumably one beneficiary is the mother's brother, who will continue to claim influence and prestige as the father-in-law of the office-holder. In the case of the queen, mother's brothers may be councillors.

Others also stand to benefit, for during the tenure of an office by a woman her half brother or husband handles the public affairs:

> Just as a male ruler relies on his sister in ritual matters, so a woman ruler requires the help of a male relative for trying courtcases and other duties and activities that cannot be carried out by a woman. He acts in a rather menial capacity as her *modzeta* or assistant. (E. J. Krige, 1975b:59)

The abstract rules are perhaps not very illuminating in themselves. The political implications, however, are revealed by case materials. Before turning to the Lovedu succession itself, I consider the succession to the Khaha chieftaincy. The Khaha, a tribe closely associated with the Lovedu, share crucial features of Lovedu culture.

The Khaha succession

An excellent account of the Khaha succession has been provided by Jaques (1934), a colleague of Junod, specifically in order to illustrate the local complexities of female succession.[3] (Cf. van Warmelo, 1944.)

The first 'queen', Male, succeeded her father. She married her MBD Ngwanamaxoro, who bore the heir apparent, Sepeke. However, Male was briefly succeeded by her sister, Makhudu, who served as 'regent', and who was followed in turn by her son Mukwani, also as 'regent'.

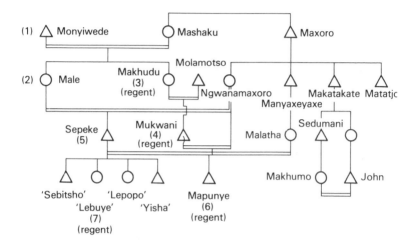

FIGURE 3 *The Khaha succession (after Jaques 1934. Van Warmelo, 1944, presents a slightly different version)*

Sepeke did at last succeed. He married, among other wives, two mother's brother's daughters, the senior of whom, Malatha, bore him four children including two sons. Yet he was succeeded not by one of his own children but by Mapunye. Mapunye's father was the former 'regent' Mukwani, and his mother was Ngwanamaxoro, widow of the old queen Male and mother of Sepeke. (On one interpretation Mukwani inherited the main wife of Male, his mother's sister. This would make Mapunye the leviratic child of Male by Ngwanamaxoro, and so the 'full brother' of Sepeke.)

Clearly the succession has oscillated not only between men and women but also — perhaps more crucially — between the son and grandchildren of Male and the son and grandchildren of Makhudu. The latter are qualified in Jaques's account as 'regents' but he notes the difficulty 'of distinguishing between chiefs who reign in their own right and those who are only regents', (1934:378). 'Regents' are, perhaps, chiefs from the lines of one's informant's rivals.

The final developments recorded by Jaques add poignancy to the story of fraternal competition. He considered the position of Sepeke's children to be so delicate that he gave them pseudonyms (as well as attempting to disguise the name of the tribe). 'Sebitsho', the heir apparent, died young and mysteriously, and after Mapunye's death the succession passed to Sepeke's second child, a woman named 'Lebuye'. But she 'preferred to abdicate in favour of "Yisha", her younger brother, and is presently only acting chief during the minority of the boy' (Jaques, 1934:381).

The final twist to the story is that the new heir, 'Yisha', is generally said to be the leviratic child of Mapunye, raised to Sepeke, his dead 'brother' and predecessor in office.

The accession of women, the ambiguous status of 'regents', the claims to genitorship, are all evidently aspects of competition between two royal families. But a third family is also represented in Jaques's genealogies, the family of Maxoro, who provided wives to the rulers, and who, through the marriages of Ngwanamaxoro, became wife-givers to both factions. This then is the family of mother's brothers, who may be expected to provide the main counsellors of the rulers, and whose role in political life may be just as significant, if apparently humbler.

The Lovedu succession[4]

The Khaha succession, for all its complexities, is comprehensible as a rough version of the Sotho-Tswana model. The real oddity is the succession of women. On one occasion the office was even transmitted from one woman to another, from Male to Makhudu, although Makhudu was defined as a 'regent' for her older sister's chief wife's son. Van Warmelo comments that the Khaha do 'not regard female chiefs with any special favour . . . it is more likely that females are only accepted when no males are available, but that perhaps the prestige of the queen Modjadji further north helped to overcome the common prejudice against female chiefs' (1944:24).

Among the Lovedu the complexities are greater, and three times in succession female rulers have been succeeded by their daughters. Professor Eileen Krige, who has with great generosity provided me with new materials and commented exhaustively on drafts of this chapter, has informed me that the last queen, Modjadji IV, died early in 1981, and that given the delicate political situation proper names should be avoided in the genealogy and the text that follows. I have naturally respected her wish.

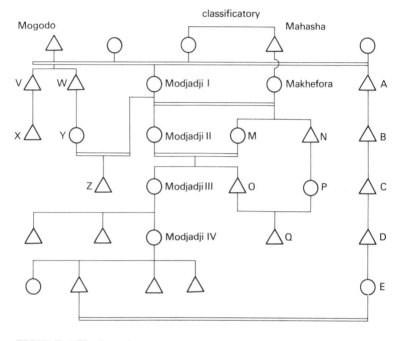

FIGURE 4 *The Lovedu succession*
          Sources: E. J. Krige (1975b) 70–1; and personal communi-
          cations from Professor Krige. An important misprint in the
          original has been corrected

There are various stories which account for the accession of the first queen. According to the version given in *The Realm of a Rain Queen*, the last king was Mogodo, who ruled the Lovedu in their old home in what is now Zimbabwe. The sons of his great house fought and despoiled their father, and were exiled. Mogodo had an incestuous relationship with a daughter of his second house, who succeeded him as Modjadji I, and who brought the Lovedu to the Transvaal. Modjadji I was in turn succeeded by her daughter, Modjadji II, who had been fathered incest-uously by Mogodo. By this version, then, the children of Mogodo's first house were exiled and died abroad, and he was succeeded by two daughters in succession, Modjadji I and Modjadji II (E. J. and J. D. Krige, 1943:8–10).

The main royal wife-givers were the Mahasha branch of the royal family. By one version of the story, Modjadji I was the daughter of a Mahasha woman. She herself married a MBD, a daughter of Mahasha. This woman's daughter in turn married Modjadji II and bore Modjadji III. (E. J. Krige, 1975b:70-2. There is a crucial misprint in the genealogy printed in this paper; fortunately Professor Krige has provided me with corrections.)

At this point it is necessary to consider the genitors of the queens. They attain a special prominence since all the queens except for Modjadji II bore their own successors. In theory one cannot know who the royal genitors were. 'The biological parentage of the Lovedu queens and of the children of *vatanoni* (wives) of the queen was always a closely-guarded secret. Anyone divulging the parentage of the queen or her children was liable to be put to death' (E. J. Krige, 1975b:70). None the less both E. J. Krige (1976) and Mönnig (1963) recorded detailed if slightly different traditions of paternal relationships.

But even if one can identify the genitor, what is his status? The formal rule is clear. 'The Lovedu genitor in woman-marriage holds no recognized position in the life of the family and should not be known as their father by his biological children.' And yet sometimes 'the genitor, by virtue of close relationship to the female husband and because of being resident in the same kraal, is able to play the part of father and gain some control over the children.' The queen's wives are more strictly watched, but ordinary women, fearing the claims of genitors, may even 'prefer not to appoint a genitor and leave the wife free to have children "in the bush" by lovers' (E. J. Krige, 1974:23).

Conflicting claims to paternal relationships in the royal family are politically significant. I have mentioned the tradition that Modjadji II was fathered incestuously by Mogodo, the father of her mother. According to another tradition, Modjadji II was fathered by a man from the junior house of Mogodo. This is the house of 'A', of whom the Lovedu say: '"A" is the termite heap from which comes out the queen ant' (E. J. Krige, 1974b, and personal communication, 1980). In the genealogy (Figure 4) this is the man 'A', founder of the line A, B, C, D. A also begot M, who married Modjadji II. Modjadji II was childless, though not barren. 'She had several abortions forced on her, because the fathers had not been acceptable as genitors of a royal child' (E. J. Krige, personal communication, 1980). This dramatically underlines the importance of the genitor (and, of course, the political constraints on the queen). However, the queen's wife and sister, M, did have a child. Modjadji II quarrelled with M and their common father A, and exiled them both. When they heard of the queen's death M and her children hurried back, M dying on the way (E. J. Krige, personal communication, 1980). Her daughter succeeded as Modjadji III.

It is important to underline the interpretation which the Lovedu give to the succession of Modjadji III. According to E. J. Krige (1975b: 72) 'the Lovedu always stress the fact that her mother, M, was a sister of the queen, not that M's mother, Makhefora, was a *motanoni* of the queen, nor that M herself was also a *motanoni* and her daughter an heir on that account.' Why do they present the complex situation in this way? Had Modjadji II been permitted to mother a child, the child would probably have succeeded her. Since she was not allowed to be a mother, who should succeed? Not a child she 'fathered' – i.e. the child of a *motanoni*, as one might expect if she were really an honorary man. Instead the succession passed to the child of a woman who substituted for her as a mother: her 'sister', M. Who then was the genitor of Modjadji III?

According to E. J. Krige (1975b), there are two lines of genitors. One line is that of the house of A (A, B, C, D in Figure 4). The other is the line of the excluded first house of Mogodo (V, W, X, Z). According to this version, A begot Modjadji II and also M, the mother of Modjadji III. Then the line of genitors shifted. X begot Modjadji III and also Z, who in turn begot Modjadji IV. The Kriges remark: 'in the fact that it was the line of Malegudu, great son of Mugodo, who provided the "husbands" of the last two queens, we may see perhaps an attempt to compensate the great son and retain his allegiance' (E. J. and J. D. Krige, 1943:171). But the prized, if secret, role of genitor was not allowed to rest with the line of Malegudu. D, a young man of A's line, was selected by the inner family council to beget the heir of Modjadji IV, but she had children by a commoner, described sometimes as a 'husband', sometimes as a 'paramour'. However, her son did marry the daughter of D.

Mönnig (1963:55–6) gives an account which is more favourable to the line of Malegudu, who, he insists, were really of the house of Mahasha's sister, and so by implication the true heirs of Mogodo. Mogodo is said to have fathered Modjadji II incestuously on Modjadji I. X then fathered Modjadji III, who succeeded therefore not only by virtue of her mother's position as Modjadji II's 'sister' or 'wife' but by virtue of her father's claim to the succession. X also begot Z by his

FBD, Y, who was a wife of Modjadji I. Z begot Modjadji IV by Modjadji III. The message is clear. The queens are the daughters and wives of the excluded line of Malegudu.

In her comments on a draft of this chapter Eileen Krige objected that I exaggerated the importance of factionalism in the royal families of the Khaha and the Lovedu. Evidently she felt that 'factions' were by definition highly institutionalized groups. However once it is accepted that factions do change (partly as a result of marriage and genetical links) there can be little room for argument.

One question which remains to be considered is why the genealogically correct heir was often passed over. The genealogy again and again shows excluded brothers, even older brothers, of the woman who in fact succeeded. One recurrent explanation is that the male heir died young, was physically or mentally incapable, or was exiled and killed after a quarrel. Another type of explanation is presented in the myths of the original kingly period, which preceded the age of the queens. These often tell stories of an elder son who is passed over in favour of a younger, on the grounds that the younger was mystically elected. 'Possession of the rain-charms which contain bodily remains taken from previous chiefs, purity of blood and divine ratification by the opening of the door to the "right" claimant at the time of the succession are sufficient to ensure that the successor has all the qualities necessary in the divine king' (E. J. Krige, 1975b:60).

Whatever the interpretation of particular successions, the problem remains that only among the Lovedu has the inevitable politicking yielded a line of (so far) four successive queens. To understand why this should have occurred the political situation must be examined more carefully.

The queen and her councillors

Comparing these accounts of the Khaha and Lovedu succession it is evident in both cases that at any time the royal family is split into two main factions, and that the succession of queens is a move in this game of intrafamilial politicking. The ambiguous 'regents' of the Khaha and the 'genitors' of the Lovedu are symptomatic of the competition for legitimacy, the ambiguities reflecting disputed claims. Among the Khaha the two main competing factions are both linked to one and the same wife-giving line. Among the Lovedu the competition swings between the lines of the other two houses of Mogodo, and is complicated by new splits between their descendants.

The queen herself has prestige and may at times exert influence, but there is a case for arguing that the line of queens is not politically dominant, and that more than male Sotho-Tswana chiefs they reign rather than rule. Like other women office-holders in the region, the queen is essentially a ritual rather than a political leader. Political power is in the hands of the royal councillors, the *vakololo*.

> The relation of the Queen to her *vakololo* or counsellors is of much the same pattern as that between uterine sister and brother in everyday life, the sister having ritual functions as priestess of the family, together with some control over her brother's household, while the brother is head of the family, responsible, if he is a headman, for holding court and dealing with political matters.
> (E. J. Krige, 1975b:67–8)

Alternatively (as will be seen in the case of some district heads), female 'rulers' placed by the queen may be assisted by their husbands.

Who then are these councillors who enjoy the substance of power? Studying the accounts given in the main sources (E. J. Krige and J. D. Krige, 1943:172–3; Mönnig, 1963:63; E. J. Krige, 1975b:62) it is quite clear that councillors compete and change, but that the leading councillors have usually been drawn from among the queen's closest relatives. Evidently competition is intense for a leading place in council, and the ideological claims of the contenders are based on kinship or claims as the queen's wife-givers (mother's brothers), or perhaps secretly as genitor 'husbands'. Eileen Krige summed up the selection of chief councillors over the last century in a personal communication to me:

> You will notice that these were all, over a period of nearly a century, either the M(other's) uterine B(rother), MBS, B or BS during the first 60 years (the reign of Modjadji III), and during the next 20 years (in the reign of the new queen Modjadji IV) a son and a grandson of her biological father, followed by her uterine B's pothumous son and her own son. All were very close relatives and members of the queen's own line of descent in the case of Modjadji III.

Perhaps this balance between queen and councillors helps to explain why queens have succeeded queens for four generations. With a weak chief, dependent to an exceptional degree on male councillors, the endogamous royal family shares power. The fissiparous tendencies of the Tswana are avoided. This may be in the joint interest of the powerful rivals within the royal family. As will be seen, they must present a united front against the district heads. More broadly, perhaps the weak central authority is best projected as above all a ritual focus, guaranteeing rain, symbolized by a 'divine' queen.

The royal wives and the district heads

The Lovedu court is only one power-centre in a highly pluralistic structure. The districts enjoy considerable autonomy and are articulated with the centre in various ways, most strikingly by a series of affinal relations involving the giving of wives to the queen and the 'placing' by the queen of some wives as district heads.

The queen is given many wives — by royals, district heads, other prominent men, and even by foreign rulers who wish her to make rain for them. The majority of these wives (*vatanoni*) are the daughters of district heads.

The giving of these women is regarded as a form of *hu lova*, an act which connotes 'showing allegiance, doing homage, paying tribute, honouring, but, above all, supplicating for rain. District heads *lova* in this way, it is said, in recognition of the land which the Queen has given them to rule' (E. J. and J. D. Krige, 1943:173-4). The queen may pay no brideprice, or offer a token payment when a woman is brought as a wife to replace her FZ.

The wives are expected to remain chaste, at least initially. Wives of good family who manage not to fall pregnant are specially rewarded, perhaps being given areas to rule. However, few *vatanoni* are chaste enough to remain on as wives of the queen.

Most wives fall pregnant and are sent home in disgrace. When her child is weaned the wife returns to the queen with 'pardon beer', and her father names another daughter to succeed her as a wife of the queen. The spoilt wife is then allocated as a wife to a political client of the queen. This process is known as *ho khobelwa*:

> to be allocated or divided out to someone, as in the case of the allocation of widows in the levirate. No bride-price is given to the Queen for such *motanoni*, since it is not ordinary marriage; but it is nevertheless regarded as full marriage and the children of the *motanoni* are all considered as the children of the man to whom she has been given. (E. J. Krige, 1975a:251)

The men to whom the wives are allocated are typically royals, district heads, or other prominent men in the tribe — precisely the men who send daughters to the queen. The men who receive *vatanoni* gain wives without brideprice as a gift of a patron (the queen); and they make the appropriate return of a daughter. (In some cases the queen will simply give a royal man cattle with which to acquire a wife.) So every man who receives a wife in this way enters into a new bride-giving relationship with the queen. The son of this wife will be his heir, and a daughter must be returned to the queen as a *motanoni*.

These marriages also create a link between the natal family of the wife and the family of her new husband. They are bound in a new marriage alliance, which should be perpetuated (E. J. and J. D. Krige, 1943:176–7).

Mönnig (1963:56) cites the example of Modjadji III's 43 wives. Twenty-nine were given her by district headmen, and 14 by royals. The queen retained 17 wives, and gave 12 to district headmen and 14 to royals, again dividing them between the main branches of the royal family. Eileen Krige (personal communication) reports that this is a gross underestimate. She has records of almost 100 *vatanoni* married to Modjadji III during the 65 years of her reign. Most of these came as follow-ups to a father's sister or a mother who had been a *motanoni* before.

Some wives — but only the daughters of royals — are 'placed' as district heads. *Vatanoni* placed as district heads are allocated husbands as well. The husbands normally administer the district and their sons succeed to the headmanship (E. J. and J. D. Krige, 1943:177). Districts may be broadly classified as those under one of the key royal groups and those under non-Lovedu headmen, the relative proportion being three to one. However, a considerable number in each category were originally 'placed' under a royal wife, passing only in the following generation to the eldest son of her husband.

It is not necessarily clear whether the district is allocated to a *motanoni* or to a man who is then also given a royal wife. It is a matter of nuances, as may be judged from E. J. Krige's comment (1975a:251) that sometimes 'when a man is made ruler of a district he is given a *motanoni* as well. If this *motanoni* is a member of the royal group and the man a commoner, the gift of a *motanoni* may actually detract from his position as she may be considered the real ruler.'

The formally subordinate status of the district head vis-à-vis the royals is also signalled by the system of 'mothers' who represent the district head at the court. A 'mother' is often a daughter whom the district head sent in marriage to the queen, or the son of such a wife (E. J. and J. D. Krige, 1943:187-8; Mönnig, 1963:64). Such 'mothers' are therefore royal sisters' sons or fathers' sisters' sons of those district heads they represent, integrating them upwards into the court.

The district head is also related to important sets of his subjects by marriage links. Like the queen in relation to district heads, a district head will stand to such people as wife-taker to wife-giver (e.g. E. J. and J. D. Krige, 1943:179), with the proviso again that wives (not sisters) may be reallocated down the hierarchy, so opening the way for a new upward stream of wives.

Endogamy and hypergamy

My analysis clearly suggests a stable pattern of hypergamy, such that wife-takers ('sisters' sons') are superior to wife-givers ('mothers' brothers').[5] This is a point which has been the centre of some controversy.

Leach argued in an important paper (1951; 1961:95-9) that wherever matrilateral cross-cousin marriage is found there will be a tendency for wife-givers generally to be of higher status than wife-takers, or vice versa. Among the Kachin, women married down, bridewealth passed up (and was associated with tribute). The Lovedu, he argued, had a 'Kachin system in reverse', wives and tribute beer moving up, bridewealth moving down.

E. J. Krige, however, retorted (1964:164) that there was no evidence for hypergamy. The royal group tended to be endogamous, relations between affines involved reciprocity, and, in general, Lovedu society was 'not a stratified society though the royal lineage enjoys great prestige'. In a later paper she returned to the attack (1975a:232-5, 241 n., 253-4). 'Obsessed with the Kachin association of a hierarchical class structure with asymmetrical cross-cousin marriage, Leach had read into his source material on the Lovedu what is not there' (p. 234). In fact 'there are no ranked local groups in Lovedu society'; questions of seniority, rank, power and wealth 'relate to the personal position of the individuals and bear no relation to any class structure in Lovedu society' (pp. 234-5).

Part of the disagreement seems to hinge upon different notions of what constitutes 'stratification'. Among the Lovedu economic differences are not great, and wealth in itself is not sought after. 'The true end of production . . . is almost immediate consumption, and prestige, insofar as it can be said to be associated with material goods, is gained rather by means of consumption of beer-drinks than by any saving for productive purposes' (E. J. Krige, 1941:3). Yet there are important differences in status and power. Moreover, these are bound up with the system of marriage alliance. For example we are told that 'many non-Lovedu lineages have, by virtue of marriage links through royal wives, a higher status and are more closely related to the Queen than sections of the Lovedu themselves' (E. J. Krige, 1964:156-7; cf., e.g., Mönnig, 1963:60). (As Eileen Krige emphasized in a personal communication, such links are personal rather than corporate in character. Indeed she would now avoid the term 'lineage' in writing on the Lovedu.) On my reading, there is a sufficient level of stratification to permit the application of Leach's model. He does not require the existence of a thorough-going feudalistic system of estates, as Krige seems to believe.

The evidence supports Leach's judgment that where asymmetrical marriages occur, women marry up. Unrelated women are given to the queen to solicit favours or to repay a debt or fine or as a form of tribute. 'Giving a daughter in marriage is a way in which a newcomer in any area might express indebtedness to a man, headman or other who has given him assistance and protection. Wives are also offered by commoners to the chief advisers of the queen in the hope of general recognition at the capital, advancement and improved social status' (E. J. Krige, personal communication). Mother's brothers are assistants and advisers; they are obliged to provide daughters for their sisters' sons, but the sisters' sons are not obliged to marry them. Sisters' sons represent district heads at court. Much case material in the literature can be interpreted in a way consistent with this interpretation, as Leach noted.

Moreover, even apparently contradictory customs seem in the end to support the view that hypergamy is expected. When the queen allocates wives to district headmen and others, the husbands do not pay bridewealth, and the wives are said not to be 'married off' but 'allocated', as with a man's widows, distributed by his sister. The husband is now bound to give his daughter to the queen as a wife, and she pays some bridewealth to him. Some of these allocated wives are of royal origin and are of higher status than their husbands: in such situations — obviously in recognition of the anomaly — the wife 'may be considered the real ruler' (E. J. Krige, 1975a:251).

This suggests one further possible element in the persistence of queens among the Lovedu. A queen, obviously, cannot marry up. If she then 'marries' a man, she would be marrying anomalously and would therefore 'be considered the real ruler'. This may be another way of seeing the relationship between the queens and the line of royal genitors.

Given a systematic status differentiation between wife-givers and wife-takers, the redistribution of wives by the queen may be used to adjust the relative status of individual royals and district heads. A man gives a daughter to the queen, and she places the daughter with a husband; the wife-giver and the ultimate husband are now linked as wife-giver and wife-taker, and, implicitly, inferior and superior. Since we lack a detailed account of which wives are allocated to whom, it is not easy to assess the importance of this element of the system, but the one extended example given by E. J. and J. D. Krige (1943:176-7) seems to confirm the potential. Eileen Krige, however, comments: 'There are social implications, mostly ephemeral, but relative status is not among these' (personal communication).

Bridewealth

Finally, the marriage system is shaped not only by political and status relations, but also by the bridewealth system, which among the Lovedu tends to perpetuate existing marriage alliances.

Bridewealth 'generally consists of some five to eight head of cattle, a number of goats and money (to the extent of at least £5)' (E. J. Krige, 1964:154). This was high relative to the tiny number of cattle in the reserve – some 3,000 head for a population of roughly 33,000 in the 1930s. Only the queen owned a substantial herd of cattle (J. D. Krige, 1939:394).

J. D. Krige calculated the importance of bridewealth exchanges in the economy (1939:396-7):

> *Munywalo* (bridewealth) accounts for over 95 per cent of all
> transfers of cattle; the only other considerable transfer of cattle
> occurs when judgment debts are paid, and 90 per cent of them have
> their origin in *munywalo*. In the total tribal economy of exchanges,
> purchases and sales, of whatever description, the cattle of *nywalo*-
> exchanges constitute about 20 per cent in value. No other single kind
> of transaction is comparable.

All but 400 of the total number of cattle in the society were required to seal the marriages contracted each year.

The consequence of this imbalance between the size of the brideprice and the number of cattle available to any individual was that a man could normally acquire a wife only with bridewealth brought in by the marriage of a sister, unless he could find a patron with cattle to lend him (against the return, eventually, of a daughter). The queen was the only substantial holder of unencumbered cattle, and so she alone could readily initiate new marriage relations. Ordinary people were effectively mortgaged to their sisters or their patrons, to whom they were obliged to return daughters.

The level of bridewealth relative to the number of cattle available clearly served to stabilize the flow of wives and so indirectly the series of patron-client relations which constituted the grid of the political system. The surplus cattle available only to the queen provided a measure of flexibility, permitting the initiation of new relationships from above.

Conclusion

I once described the Lovedu system as a women's lib version of the Sotho-Tswana model (A. Kuper, 1975b:139–43). There is something in that: women in the northeastern Transvaal enjoyed unusually high status and access to political and economic opportunity, and the sexual division of labour was less highly developed here than elsewhere. Yet it might be more accurate to say that the Lovedu arrangements were rather more the sort of thing that the women's movement derides as 'tokenism'. The female rulers had the glory, but the substance of power remained with their male councillors: half-brothers, husbands, or lovers.

Women held office as sisters, or in the case of ex-*vatanoni*, as wives. The peculiar development of the brother/sister relationship in this area, the women's ritual power almost overshadowing her brother's (or even her husband's), can be paralleled elsewhere among the Sotho-Tswana, but only as a possibility, intermittently and partially realized.[6] None the less these special developments should not be allowed to obscure the common features of all the Sotho-Tswana and indeed Venda systems. The male royals compete for power and intermarry; the more junior nobles and local leaders stand to them as wife-givers and mother's brothers. The Lovedu variant realizes one latent potentiality in this general scheme, but it belongs to the same family of systems.

Properly understood the Lovedu and their neighbours also provide an intriguing if remote echo of the Swazi balance between the king and the queen mother: but that is an issue for another chapter.

6   The Venda variant

Are the Venda an exception?

In his monograph on the Venda, Hugh Stayt (blinded in action during
the First World War but still a formidable ethnographer) drew attention
to three curious features of the kinship system which have continued
to excite the interest of commentators. First, Stayt suggested that a
woman was considered to be in some sense the 'wife' of her husband's
father, who had paid the bridewealth for her. This notion 'explained'
other features of the system, such as the terminological equation of the
wife's brother (and wife's brother's son) with the mother's brother
(Stayt, 1931:177ff).

Second, Stayt pointed out that the preference for mother's brother's
daughter marriage coexisted with an apparently contradictory preferential claim to the wife's brother's daughter. To add to the confusion, he
suggested a bizarre explanation for the claim to the WBD (p. 180):

> a man besides having the right to marry his wife's sisters is only
> prevented by their sex from being able to marry his wife's brothers.
> The claim over his wife's brother is then transferred to his wife's
> brother's daughter, whom he calls by the same term that would have
> been applied to his wife's brother if he had been a woman.

Third, Stayt suggested that the Venda have a system of double
unilineal descent. This would indeed have made the Venda unique in
southeast Africa. A subsequent ethnographer, Roumeguère-Eberhardt
(1963), adopted this view and explained some terminological identifi-
cations as the product of a combination of matrilineal and patrilineal
principles, plus the notion that a woman was really married to her
husband's father, plus a rule of matrilateral cross-cousin marriage; thus
boldly synthesizing a whole gamut of hypotheses.

The basic issues were later revived in a debate between de Heusch
and Adler. The starting-point was a paper in which de Heusch argued

that the neighbouring Lovedu and Tsonga represented two poles of a
radical transformation. The Lovedu had a classic elementary kinship
structure, based on a rule of preferential matrilateral cross-cousin
marriage. The Tsonga for their part had virtually completed the transformation to a complex structure where there are no preferential
marriages based on kinship. However, the transformation was not
complete. The kinship terminology was Omaha in type, but the Tsonga
permitted two secondary oblique unions, with the widow of the mother's
brother, and with the wife's brother's daughter. Moreover they were
characterized by a famous 'joking relationship' with the mother's
brother which marked the shock of the prohibition on marriage with
the mother's brother's daughter[1] (de Heusch, 1974).

Adler challenged this analysis by invoking the Venda. Like their
neighbours the Lovedu, the Venda had a rule of preferential MBD
marriage. However, according to Adler they exhibited precisely the
traits which among the Tsonga de Heusch had attributed to the abandonment of MBD marriage. Thus they had an Omaha kinship terminology,
they permitted marriage with the WBD, and men joked with their
mother's brothers. In a rejoinder de Heusch challenged parts of Adler's
argument, but by implication accepted the ethnographic statements he
made about the Venda. De Heusch suggested that the Venda might
represent a stage intermediate between the Lovedu and the Tsonga
(Adler, 1976; de Heusch, 1976).

At this point half a century of debate comes full circle. Even before
Stayt published his monograph, Junod had distinguished two types of
kinship system in Southern Africa. In one a man had a special right to
marry his matrilateral cross-cousin. In the other a man had a prior
claim to marry his wife's brother's daughter. These two systems would
seem logically to be mutually exclusive, since a man's WBD is his son's
MBD. However, the Venda appeared to combine the two preferences,
although Junod reported that marriage with the WBD was very un-
common. The anomalous situation, he suggested, was a consequence
of diffusion. The Venda system 'contains elements of another origin',
which he took to be Kalanga (Junod, 1927, I:302–3).

Shortly afterwards Eiselen argued that marriage with a MBD or a
WBD, or indeed the sororate, represented 'various ways of fulfilling the
obligations attending the exchange of one's daughter and sister respectively for valuable property' (Eiselen, 1928c:428). Although from one
point of view functionally equivalent, MBD marriage still represented
an evolutionary advance on a rule of WBD marriage, and the two

evolutionary stages were to be found in Southern Africa. The Venda and the Swazi, however, represented transitional systems in which the two possibilities briefly coexisted.

Broadly speaking, Junod, Eiselen and de Heusch present substantially the same hypothesis, though their arguments are couched respectively in terms of a diffusionist, evolutionist and structuralist transformation. In all their models the Venda represent an anomaly, combining the very features which serve to contrast the polar types.

Facts and clarifications

Before assessing the place of the Venda in broader perspective it is essential to be clear about the central features of their kinship system. Given the detailed and reliable ethnographies published by Stayt and by Van Warmelo and Phophi,[2] as well as other, lesser, but often helpful reports, one might assume that at least the facts of the matter were beyond dispute. Yet although controversy has indeed concerned explanations rather than basic facts, it is necessary to re-examine some crucial ethnographic assumptions. I list them as a series of questions, and deal with them in order. (a) Does a man 'marry' his son's wife? (b) Has a man a marriage claim on his WBD? (c) Do the Venda have a system of double descent? (d) Does the uterine nephew make aggressive claims upon and/or 'joke' with his mother's brother? (e) Is the kinship terminology particularly remarkable, and/or is it an Omaha terminology?

(a) Does a man 'marry' his son's wife?

This would certainly qualify the Venda to be Africa's Murngin or Miwok. It is apparent, however, that we are dealing with a legal fiction.

A man must provide bridewealth to procure one wife for the eldest son of each of his own wives. The woman married with bridewealth provided by a man's father, his *dzekiso* wife, becomes his great wife, and the heir is chosen from her 'house'. Stayt reported that a *dzekiso* wife calls her fiancé's father 'husband', and her fiancé 'child'. He calls her *mmane* (= mother's younger sister or mother's junior co-wife). This odd arrangement persists only until the final marriage rite is performed, after which the girl takes up residence with her husband. Stayt commented (1931:149):

> Although it is quite understood that the girl is to become the bride of the son, it is the father who pays the lobola (brideprice) and is

consequently recognized by the parents as being her legal husband, and he is responsible to them for her well-being.

Van Warmelo's picture is similar. He adds that all the girls of the bride's party are *mmane* to the groom until the marriage ceremonies have been completed, but notes that a man may continue in some circumstances to refer to his wife as *mmane* until his father is dead: '. . . even though he knows that the girl will be his wife, he treats her as if she were the wife of his father' (*Venda Law*, I:197). It was formerly the custom in some families for the father (or elder brother, if he provided the bridewealth) to sleep with the new bride for a few nights before handing her over to her husband, since, as the Venda put it, 'a child cannot open a cattle kraal' (*ibid.*: 209).

Both Stayt and Van Warmelo agree that the terminological identification of a wife as mother's co-wife is temporary, and that it is subsidiary to a more conventional notion that a woman really is married to her husband. The identification is a way of expressing the relationship between the girl and her parents, on the one hand, and the person who provided bridewealth for her on the other. Van Warmelo pointed out that where a man provides bridewealth for a younger brother, the wife will for a time address the older brother as 'husband', and be termed 'older brother's wife' by her real husband. Similarly, where a woman provides her son with the bridewealth he needs to acquire a wife, the wife termed *tshiozwi* ('female owned') is called 'mother-in-law' by her co-wives. Her children, however, trace their kinship connections through their 'real' fathers, as do children of a *dzekiso* wife, or a wife provided by an older brother (*Venda Law*, II: 367–71, 397).

Stayt and also Roumeguère-Eberhardt have attempted to explain certain features of the terminology as consequences of the notion that a woman is married to her husband's father. Thus, for example, my wife's brother is 'really' my father's wife's brother, and hence my mother's brother. This is far-fetched, unnecessary, and raises more problems than it appears to resolve, as I shall attempt to demonstrate later.

(b) Does a man have a marital claim to his wife's brother's daughter?

A man's WBD is normally his son's MBD. It is apparent, therefore, that a right to the WBD runs counter to a right to the MBD; at least, if these rights are unequivocal.

The Venda have a strong preference for MBD marriage, including under this head marriage with a MBSD 'and in fact all those girls of his maternal uncle's family (*lushaka*) whose fathers his mother calls "brother" or "brother's son"' (*Venda Law*, I: 29). Mother's sister's daughters are unmarriageable, but aristocrats (as amongst other Southern Bantu peoples) also favour marriage with patrilateral cross- and parallel cousins, and even half-sisters. Such marriages are permitted to commoners, but rarely occur, and there are ideological objections to them (*Venda Law*, I: 1–20; Stayt, 1931: 176; Lestrade, 1930).

In addition, men have a claim upon certain female relatives of their wives. According to Stayt (1931:179):

> A Venda man has the prior right to his wife's younger sisters and must be consulted before a sister is given to any other man. If he consents to 'untie' his sister-in-law she may marry elsewhere. He may only marry his wife's brother's daughter when there are no sisters-in-law available.

Such claims are not recognized by the courts (*Venda Law*, II: 373–7). It seems reasonable to conclude, with Junod, that WBD marriage, while permissible, is infrequent, and that 'the Vendas definitely belong to the category of tribes where it is the son who marries his cousin and not the father his niece' (1927, I: 307).

Adler is therefore clearly overstating the case when he writes that among the Venda, 'a man has (as among the Thonga and the Lovedu [sic]) a secondary marriage claim (*un droit matrimonial secondaire*) to his wife's brother's daughter, whom he calls "my little wife"' (Adler, 1976:23). De Heusch, equally, is not justified in arguing that contrary to the Lovedu the Venda place great ideological weight upon this oblique marriage with a WBD (de Heusch, 1976:41). Adler in fact goes further, committing himself to the view of Roumeguère-Eberhardt (1963:41) that ideally a Venda man's great wife is his MBD who in some sense is then also seen as his father's wife. Thus a man marries his MBD and simultaneously his father marries his WBD!

Several authors have attempted to explain other elements of the kinship system, and particularly aspects of the kinship terminology, by invoking this claim on the WBD. It is apparent, however, that the claim is not emphasized ideologically, is rarely exercised, is not legally enforced, and should be understood as no more than a possible fall-back position should a man's wife have no sisters. It is unlikely that such a marginal aspect of the system could *cause* other features. The apparent incompatibility of 'claims' on the WBD and the MBD also becomes less problematic when the restricted nature of the claim to the WBD is appreciated.[3]

(c) A system of double descent?

Stayt's judgment that the Venda have a system of 'double descent' refers above all to a system of spirit organization. The system's 'importance is essentially linked with the ancestor cult' (Stayt, 1931:185, 245, 260). A black bull is associated with male paternal ancestors, a black she-goat with female maternal ancestors, and the two sets of spirits are invoked in different contexts and by different congregations. There seems, however, to be no basis for talk of 'matrilineages', and although a patrilineal principle orders residence, succession and inheritance there are no patrilineages either. Neither Stayt nor Van Warmelo suggest a relationship between this cultic organization and rules of marriage, group organization, or kinship terminology.

(d) Does a man joke with his mother's brother?

This is important, because in de Heusch's theory a joking relationship with the mother's brother signals the abandonment of a marriage claim on the MBD (de Heusch, 1974). On the basis of a casual aside dropped by Roumeguère-Eberhardt (a footnote to a Venda rite; 1963:32), Adler (1976:24) suggests that a Venda uterine nephew can joke with, and snatch goods from, his mother's brother. De Heusch (1976:43) accepts this. However, the weight of the evidence is quite unequivocal. Stayt (1931:176) wrote:

> Generally when children are old enough to leave their mother they go to the home of their maternal uncle and live with him for a few years. They always treat him with respect and deference, and must give him any of their personal possessions, as clothes and implements, that he may demand. Even when grown-up the children are bound to help him with his work whenever he demands their services.

Junod's evidence is particularly interesting here, as the author of the classic account of the avunculate among the Tsonga. Junod (1927, I:306) concluded that a man's relations with his sister's children 'are kindly, but by no means so easy as amongst the Thonga. He can punish them, if he sees fit to do so'.

The joking relationship (as among the Lovedu) is with cross-cousins.

(e) Is the kinship terminology peculiar (or only the explanations of it)?

The presumed existence of a 'double-descent' system, the fiction of marriage with a son's wife, the supposed right to marry a wife's brother's daughter, and the preference for matrilateral cross-cousin marriage have all been invoked at various times to account for features of the kinship terminology. Although the terminology has been so elaborately explained, in part, it is remarkable but, alas, true that nobody has hitherto attempted to analyse it as a whole. Attention has been directed to specific equations, and in particular to the way in which certain affines on the wife's side are merged terminologically with consanguineal kin. A rapid review of these theories will illustrate the ways in which the dubious ethnographic assumptions already discussed have been put to work.

The issue which has exercised commentators is quite simple. The Venda classify certain affines as consanguines. Thus WF, WM, and MBW are *makhulu* ('grandparent'), and WB, WBS, and WBSS are *malume* ('mother's brother').

Junod felt that this would all make sense if only mother's brother and wife's father were identified with each other (as are MBW and WM in the terminology). He argued that the terms *malume* and *makhulu* were in fact 'almost the same', but this argument depended upon a dangerous and unjustified analogy with the Tsonga terminology, a classic Omaha system, which Junod in any case did not clearly describe, and which he failed to understand (see A. Kuper, 1976:112–13; Lounsbury, 1964:374). If these two terms could be merged by the anthropologist, then, in Junod's view (1927, I:306), they stood in opposition to *muduhulu* ('child's child' and '(man speaking) sister's child') as wife-givers to wife-takers. Neither Stayt nor Van Warmelo understood these terms in this sense, however, and both must be given greater weight in Venda matters than Junod. Stayt (1931:176) glosses the relationship between father-in-law and son-in-law as one between *makhulu* and *mukwasha*, the latter being a purely affinal term 'applied to a man who brings cattle into the family'.

Van Warmelo's comments are scanty. WM and MBW are both classified as *makhulu* since, in the event of matrilateral cross-cousin marriage, they are one and the same person. He suggests that for similar reasons '*Malume* for wife's brother (i.e. wife's guardian) and maternal uncle also becomes clear' (1931:109). What is not clear at all on this reasoning is why WF is classified not as *malume* but as *makhulu*.

Stayt also concentrated upon special facets of the problem, attempting, for example, to explain the fact that WB and WBS are classified as *malume*. He explains this identification by postulating various marriages, including 'marriages' with a son's wife. The argument is illustrated by Figure 5.

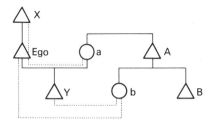

FIGURE 5 *Hypothetical son's wife marriage (Venda)*
The dotted lines represent marriages postulated in the
argument

Ego's wife's brother A is 'really' his mother's brother, because
Ego's wife a is 'really' the wife of his father, X. Ego's son, Y, follows
the rules and marries his MBD, b. However, b 'really' becomes the wife
of her husband's father, Ego. Her brother B, though by conventional
reckoning Ego's WBS, is thus 'really' his WB (Stayt, 1931:177–8).

Stayt's argument breaks off at this point. However, there is no
apparent reason for the classification of B now as Ego's mother's brother
— unless we are asked to assume that poor b ends up as the 'real' wife
of Ego's father! Moreover, Stayt makes no attempt to account for the
fact, which he records, that WBSS is also classified as *malume*.

Roumeguère-Eberhardt was also particularly concerned with the
combination of affines and consanguines in the categories *makhulu,
malume* and *muduhulu*. Rather in the manner of Junod, she argued that
makhulu/muduhulu are opposed as wife-givers/wife-takers, but she
went further, arguing that *makhulu* meant specifically 'grande vieille
mère' (Roumeguère-Eberhardt, 1963:48). The *makhulu* are then related
to the *malume* as wife-givers and their husbands, and women in the
bride's female line are the true wife-givers, representing the 'matrilineal'
or 'feminine' principle. These hypotheses are directly contradicted by
the facts, for *makhulu* means any grandparent, and WF is termed
makhulu. The term *makhulu* is also applied to FFB, FFZ, FMB, MFZ,
etc., and among affines it is applied not only to both the parents of the
wife but also to MBW, WBW, WMB, WFB and WFZ.

This appeal to a Venda system of double descent by no means
exhausts Roumeguère-Eberhardt's fund of explanatory principles.
Like Stayt, she derives terminological consequences from the supposed
marriage of a woman to her husband's father, and she further invokes
the rule of matrilateral cross-cousin marriage. On her argument, these
two rules partly coincide, since in the ideal case of a *dzekiso* marriage

with a MBD, a man marries his MBD while his wife 'really' marries her husband's father. However, according to her, they represent two principles, 'masculine' and 'feminine', which pull in slightly different directions, so that, 'La terminologie de parenté repose ainsi sur l'enchevêtrement et la complémentarité de ces deux coutumes' (1963:48).

Figure 6 illustrates a slightly simplified example of the reasoning Roumeguère-Eberhardt (*ibid*.: 48) bases on these principles.

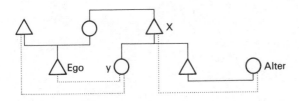

FIGURE 6 *More hypothetical marriages (Venda)*
The dotted lines represent marriages postulated in the argument

Why, she asks, does Alter call Ego, her HZH, *muduhulu*, which she glosses as 'child's child'? First of all, Alter is 'really' married to X, her husband's father. X's daughter, y, although apparently married to Ego (her FZS) is 'really' married to Ego's father, and is thus, in a manner of speaking, Ego's mother. If y is Ego's mother, then clearly X is Ego's mother's father (rather than mother's brother). Therefore X calls Ego 'child's child'. Alter, as X's wife, will follow suit.

Unfortunately for the argument, Ego will stubbornly call X *malume* and not *makhulu*. The reasoning in any case reveals grave methodological errors. First of all, even more strongly than Stayt, Roumeguère-Eberhardt has to postulate a series of potential marriage links in order to explain the terms used by real affines for each other. By Occam's Razor, the purist will object, this is a trifle elaborate. Second, even if one swallows the elaborate hypothesis, it will not serve to account for other elements of the terminology. Roumeguère-Eberhardt does proceed to explain the classification of HFZH as 'child's child', in an argument of Byzantine complexity, but could she account in these terms for the classification under the same rubric of CDH, HZC, HZDH, and so on (see Table 2b)? Third, the attempt to link terminology and marriage patterns is made without reference to the purely affinal categories used by the Venda. If her argument were to be sustained she would have to explain why the purely affinal categories *mukwasha* and *mazwale*, which, following

Table 2a Venda and Lovedu kinship terms: Consanguineal

Venda term	Primary designation	Further extensions recorded by:			Lovedu term	Extensions
		Van Warmelo	Stayt	Junod		
khaladzi	(m.s.) Z; (w.s.) B	(m.s.) FBD MZD (w.s.) FBS MZS			*kgaitsadi* (m.s.Z, w.s.B)	identical
khotsi	F				*papa* (F)	
khotsi muhulu	FoB	MoZH HoB (w.s.) oZH	WoZH		*ramoholo* (FoB)	MoZH
khotsi munene	FyB	MyZH HyB (w.s.) yZH	WyZH		*rrangwane* (FyB)	MyZH
makhadzi	FZ				*rrakgadi* (FZ)	
makhulu	PP	WP WPP MBW WBW WBS WMB WMBW WFBW	FFB FFBW FFZ FMB FMBW FMZ FMZH MFB MFBW MFZ MFZH MMB MMBW MMZ MMZH SWP WFB WFZ WMZ		*koko* (PP)	MBW WP WBW
makhulukulu	PPP					
malume	MB	WB WBS	WBSS		*malume* (MB)	WF
mmane	MyZ	FyBW (m.s.) oBW FyW	FyZW[1]	FBSW	*mmane* (MyZ)	FyW FyBW oBW
mme	M				*mma* (M)	

mme muhulu	MoZ				*mmamoholo* (MoZ)	FoW FoBW WoZ
muduhulu	CC	FoBW FoW WoZ (m.s.) ZC HZH HZC HZDH CDH (m.s.) ZDH	FBDC MZDC BSC ZSC WZSC	DH FZH FZDH (m.s.) ZH (m.s.) FBDH	*modoholo* (CC)	(m.s.) ZC DH (m.s.) BDH
mukomanana	(m.s.) oB/ (w.s.) oZ	(m.s.) FoBS MoZS (w.s.) FoBD MoZD HoW HoBW			*moholo* (oB, oZ)	FoBC MoZC WoZH HoW
murathu	(m.s.) yB/ (w.s.) yZ	as for *mukomanana*, with 'y' replacing 'o' (w.s.) yZH			*moratho* (yB, yZ)	as above, 'y' for 'o'
muzwala	FZC/MBC				*motswala* (FZC/MBC)	
muzwala-zwalane	FZCC/MBCC					
mwana	C	(m.s.) BC FBSC MZSC WZC WBDH[2] (w.s.) BC ZC FBDC MZDC HBC	WBDC MZSC		*ngwanaka* (C)	BC (w.s.) ZC HyB
tshiduhulwana	CCC					

Table 2b Venda and Lovedu kinship terms: Affinal categories

Venda term	Primary designation	Further extensions according to:			Lovedu term	Referents
		Van Warmelo	Stayt	Junod		
mazwale	HP/SW	HFB HMB HFZ HMZ CSW HPF and 'W of any mwana'	BSW WZSW DSW SSW		ratswale mmatswale ngwetsi	HF HoB HM HoBW SW (m.s.) yBW BSW HyBW
muhadzinga	HW (co-wife)					
mukwasha	DH	(m.s.) ZH FZH FBDH BDH (w.s.) ZDH HBDH, and 'H of any mwana'		MBDH FZDH	tsetsi	BDH (w.s.) yZH HZH
mulamu	WB					
munna	H		HB HF[3]		monna	H
musadzi	W	WyZ	BW SW[3] WBD WyZ WBD WBSD[4]		mosadi	W
musadzana	'little wife'					
muvhuye[5]	HZ (w.s.) BW				mohadibo	(w.s.) BW HoW HZ

Sources: Van Warmelo, 1931:108–18; Stayt, 1931:172–84; Junod, 1927:496–503. Van Warmelo's diagrams occasionally give infor-mation not summarized in his list of kin terms, and similarly Stayt's text provides a few terms in addition to those listed in his summary. The source used for the Lovedu is Mönnig, 1961.

[1] A Venda woman may marry in her own right.

[2] This term is given by Roumeguère-Eberhardt (1963:40).

[3] Temporary designation. See text.

[4] Stayt gives WBDD in his list, but WBSD in the text, which is in my view correct.

[5] Some use a Sotho form, *muhalivho*.

Stayt, she identifies as wife-givers and wife-takers, order affines in a way which differs from the classification of affines as *makhulu* and *muduhulu*, i.e. in consanguineal categories. (Compare Tables 2a and 2b.)

Adler drew a particularly radical conclusion from the classification of WB, WBS and WBSS as *malume*, 'mother's brother'. *If a man marries his MBD* then WB = MBS, WBS = MBSS and WBSS = MBSSS. Therefore, Adler argues, 'on aboutit à une terminologie incontestablement omaha'; indeed, he claims, 'curieusement, plus omaha que celle des Thonga' (Adler, 1976: 23). There is, however, a difficulty with this argument. The Venda classify cross-cousins as *muzwala*, and do not 'skew' them, as in Omaha systems. Adler notes this 'incohérence' but dismisses it as an illusion. A man has a 'droit matrimonial secondaire' over his WBD, and in any case is the real husband of his son's wife. Thus MBD is really father's wife − thus mother, and her brother, the MBS, is thus really mother's brother. The patrilateral cross-cousin is ignored, though the identification of FZC and MBC must surely scupper the argument. The argument's impossibility is, however, neatly demonstrated by accepting Adler's challenge and considering what happens over three generations.

On Adler's argument, no longer novel to us, Ego 'really' marries his WBD, y, who may also be the wife of his son. However, by the same argument, Ego's wife, x, is 'really' married to his father. In consequence y is his 'real' MBD, and we are still left to explain why her brothers should be called *malume*!

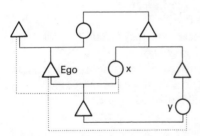

FIGURE 7 *Yet more hypothetical marriages (Venda)*
The dotted lines represent marriages postulated in the
argument

Adler also suggests that an Omaha principle is to be discerned in the Venda rule that if two unrelated men marry a pair of sisters, then their children cannot marry each other. This is, however, simply another way of saying that one cannot marry mother's sisters' children, a rule which applies among many peoples who favour matrilateral cross-cousin marriage.

To sum up, all these authors have concentrated on a limited range of terminological equations, in the main those by which certain kin of a wife are classified with 'mother's brother' and 'grandparent'. All are vulnerable to the same basic criticisms:

a. They do not attempt to account for the system as a whole, or to explain particular features in relation to the system as a whole; and they ignore kin-types which might contradict their arguments.
b. Their 'explanations', even of these restricted features of the terminological system, all require them to postulate 'marriages' which, though fictitious or exceptional, are supposed to *cause* the features they are trying to explain.

The whole theoretical effort may be summed up as the 'explanation' of three kin categories (*makhulu*, *malume* and *muduhulu*) as the products − at least in part − of three marriage prescriptions, with the MBD, SW and WBD, two of which have, to say the least, a dubious ethnographic status.

The terminological puzzles become manageable immediately one treats the kinship terminology as a whole, and places it in comparative perspective. Table 2 sets out the Venda and Lovedu terminologies. It is obvious that they are very similar. The Lovedu even share the famous Venda equation MBW = WBW = WP = PP. Viewed holistically the two terminologies are fairly commonplace examples of the 'Iroquois' class of kinship terminologies. Their unusual feature is the classification of certain affinal types, which so many commentators seized upon. Precisely how unusual a feature this is must remain in question, since work on affinal classifications is still fairly undeveloped. However there is nothing 'Omaha' about it, nor can it be related to a notion that a man's wife is 'really' his father's wife, since the Lovedu do not share this idea. Viewing the classification in the first place as a linguistic phenomenon, it can be accounted for by a reduction rule which treats inmarrying women as 'mothers' and outmarrying women as 'daughters'.[4] Formally the basic rule may be stated as follows:

> *Let a man's wife as a linking relative be regarded as structurally equivalent to his mother, and conversely, let any linking female*

relative's husband be regarded as structurally equivalent to her son.

♂W . . . → ♂M . . . ; . . . ♀H → . . . ♀S

Sociologically speaking, this reduction rule need imply no more than the asymmetrical transmission of women in marriage, which is a consequence of the MBD marriage preference shared by the Lovedu and Venda.

The father's sister

Some of the most remarkable features of Venda culture turn out on closer examination to be artifacts of the ethnographers, while others can be shown to be unexceptional and unproblematic. Properly understood, the similarities between the social structure of the Venda and Lovedu are evident. Nor is this a surprising discovery. Both tribes were formed by off shoots of the Karanga who imposed themselves as ruling sections upon the same stratum of northern Sotho communities. The Venda retain a Karanga grammatical structure, but Sotho is the main source of their vocabulary,[5] while the Lovedu language is completely Sotho in form. J. D. Krige long ago stressed the 'intimate and age-long relationships between Venda and Lovedu' (1937:325), and indeed according to some Venda sources the Lovedu are of Venda origin (Van Warmelo, 1974:78).

Yet despite the basic identity of the two systems, and although the Venda system is not structurally anomalous, there is a little-remarked but significant difference between the Venda and the Lovedu which is directly relevant to the structural model which I am developing in this book. One expression of this difference is the contrast between the central position of the 'father's sister', the *makhadzi*, among the Venda, and the role of the 'sister' among the Lovedu.

The significance of the father's sister is particularly apparent in the case of the official *makhadzi* of a chief. A new chief is appointed together with an official 'brother', who is normally the oldest son of the second house of his father, and an official 'sister', who is normally the oldest daughter of the third house. During his reign the sister has some importance, but essentially as a shadow *makhadzi*. She comes into her own when her brother dies. She and the official 'brother', the *khotsimunene*, should witness her brother's death and continue the government during the interregnum. The *makhadzi* announces the death officially to the inner council of the chiefdom, and in the case of a disputed succession her voice is decisive. The *makhadzi* must marry a royal or a son of a neighbouring chief, but even after her marriage she generally remains in the chief's capital. She may lodge with one of his wives, like a Lovedu 'sister'. The *makhadzi* receives many of the formal honours of chieftainship, including a share of all taxes, and she can intervene in major political decisions and grant appeals against the judgment of the chief (Stayt, 1931:195-7, 205-9).

In the case of commoners too the father's sister plays a crucial role. She certifies the succession to her brother, and if he has no son in his chief house she will oversee the appointment of a substitute. She names the children of her brother, and when they are shown to the moon, in the typical Southern Bantu rite of aggregation for young babies, the moon is called *makhadzi*. She is also the 'mouth', the intermediary, between her brother's children and their paternal ancestors (Stayt, 1931:88, 90, 168, 249-50).

The Venda chief's sister is generally termed *khadzi*, 'sister', but she may also be termed *makhadzi*, in which case the father's sister is distinguished as *makhadzi vhamusande* (Stayt, 1931: 198). Moreover a chief's wife is sometimes also termed *makhadzi*. Stayt suggested that this usage 'is readily explained by the fact that the chief's great wife is often also his sister, and so called by the people *makhadzi*; possibly it used to be a marriage injunction for the chief's sister to be his great wife' (Stayt, 1931:208). This is far-fetched, since the Venda chiefs never had a particular preference for half-sister marriage, simply tending like most Sotho-Tswana royals to marry patrilateral kin. Another possibility is that chief's wives provided by the father's sister would be called *makhadzi*. This is on the analogy of the Venda custom discussed earlier, whereby a wife is associated with the person who provided bridewealth for her. A wife provided by a man's mother, it will be recalled, is termed 'mother-in-law' by her co-wives (see p. 80). The circumstances in which a father's sister would provide a wife for the chief have been described by Stayt. 'If the wife designated to bear the heir is barren, or if she dies before bearing an heir, she is replaced by one of her sisters, or the *makhadzi* will provide the chief with a second royal wife' (Stayt, 1931:208).

Another, related, difference between the Venda and the Lovedu concerns the provision of bridewealth. Among the Lovedu a man takes the cattle paid for his sister and uses them to acquire a wife for himself. Among the Venda a woman's bridewealth passes first to her father, mother and mother's brother. The father is responsible only for providing the great wife of his oldest son. This son is then supposed to provide bridewealth for the next son, and so down the line, except that the marriage of the youngest son may be financed by his mother. The 'sister's' contribution to her brother's marriage is recognized, but it is indirect, operating via her father or older brother.[6]

To phrase the matter more generally, the tie between a man and his cattle-linked sister is equivalent among the Lovedu to that between a man and his father. According to the Kriges: 'The weight of the social structure, in all complicated cases, balances unevenly between the cattle-descent and cattle-linked houses' (E. J. and J. D. Krige, 1943: 180-1). Among the Venda the 'cattle-descent' relations with the father and with older brothers are more significant, perhaps in part because more cattle are passed from father to son in bridewealth payments and in inheritance. This basic difference feeds through into the operation of the bridewealth system, where the Lovedu 'sister' has such a direct role; and so into the contrast between the position of the Lovedu 'sister' and the Venda 'father's sister'. Fundamentally, however, the two systems are very similar to each other, and they do not differ markedly from the Pedi or from Sotho-Tswana systems more generally.

7   The Swazi: marrying up

Politics and the formal analysis of marriage rules

Many Southern Bantu political communities bound together populations of diverse origin. One of these groupings generally enjoyed a privileged political status. I have mentioned the position achieved by Moshoeshoe's Kwena among the Southern Sotho, and discussed the political situation of the central Lovedu group in relation to the various districts. Among the Swazi the Dlamini enjoyed a similar pre-eminence. As was the case among other dominant groups, the marriage choices of the Dlamini ordered the internal relations of the most powerful families, and shaped the relations of these families to influential men belonging to other groups.

Hilda Kuper pointed out the importance of Dlamini-Tembe alliances at an early stage of Swazi history and continued (1947:17):

> Diplomatic marriages continued to be made for national purposes. Wives were selected for Mswati from many subject groups, and marriage ties were created, not only with powerful chiefs, but with insignificant commoners. His harem was the largest in the land . . . His kinsmen also, because of their high status and the wealth that went with it, possessed many women. The Dlamini clan multiplied more than all others and the bond of Dlamini blood ramified throughout the nation.

These marriages yielded, in the first place, useful alliances. 'Female relatives of the king are politico-economic assets to be judiciously invested. The more important princesses are given as wives to foreign rulers and non-Dlamini chiefs.' 'A wise king recognises the value of *bunini* (kinship). It extends throughout the nation, linking him by blood and marriage with chief and commoner, wealthy and poor' (H. Kuper, 1947:58, 60. Cf. H. Kuper, 1978:344–5.)

Secondly, the accumulation of wives at the top of the hierarchy is both cause and effect of the aristocrats' wealth in cattle. 'Cattle, the main goods in circulation, are exchanged primarily through marriage,' and aristocrats, on the whole, give less for their wives than they receive for their daughters. 'Cattle come to aristocrats rather than go from them on the marriage market' (H. Kuper, 1947:152). Similarly, wives come disproportionately to aristocrats, partly as a consequence of their privileged position in the cattle-bridewealth system.

Disproportionate accumulation of wives seems to bring a gain also in agricultural productivity, for it has been demonstrated that in Swaziland the larger the homestead (i.e. the greater the number of women workers) the more efficient the production of maize, and the greater the likelihood of a surplus (Daniel, 1964:226–33). (The wives of the king, however, 'are not primarily workers', and he receives tribute service from the general public (H. Kuper, 1947:84–5).)

Observations of this sort, and the obvious conclusions drawn from them, are of course fairly routine in Africanist anthropology. Unfortunately, these arguments seldom take account of the formal system of marriage exchanges. A recent contribution to the discussion of Swazi marriage and politics begins, for example, by stating an unexceptionable aim: 'a consideration of the formal rules of marriage and the extent to which they promote and maintain differences of rank and wealth in Swazi society.' Yet the author almost immediately adds: 'Marriage to the paternal and maternal grandmother clan is not considered, because its significance lies more in ritual and the ancestor cult, rather than in the distribution of wealth and political control' (Derman, 1977: 119, 122). But the formal marriage rules are not discrete 'ritual' phenomena. On the contrary, they signal the mechanism by which the Swazi aristocracy actually operates in the field of marriage relations. Nor should the rules be ignored on the questionable grounds sometimes given, that they are not typically Nguni, and may be of Sotho origin.[1] If the formal marriage rules are neglected, the particularity of the Swazi system is lost. The rules are intrinsic to the system, and represent neither a marginal ritual flourish nor an unintegrated borrowing.

Descent categories, rank, and marriage rules

One reason for the failure to appreciate the significance of the formal rules was perhaps the persistence of Morgan's inappropriate model. Swazi ethnographers conventionally described marriage rules in 'clan' terms. Later 'lineages' were introduced. Both usages caused needless perplexity.

Hilda Kuper wrote: 'There is no specific word for a lineage: the closest approximation is the word *lusendvo*, which was originally applied to the entire clan but is now restricted to the effective family council which coincides roughly with a lineage' (1950:87). In other words, *lusendvo* means 'effective family council'. Any attempt to drag in 'clans' and 'lineages' under the pretext that *lusendvo* used to mean something of the sort must be viewed with scepticism.

Objectively there seems no need to posit the existence of 'clans' or 'lineages' among the Swazi. 'Clans' (i.e. categories of people with one surname) were scattered throughout the area, without organization or common identity. Hilda Kuper suggested that 'The clan structure was broken by the rise of military age classes owing allegiance to the head of the Dlamini clan' (1947:115-16). Whatever substance such historical speculations might have, there were evidently no 'clans' to be found in recent generations. Not surprisingly, therefore: 'Segmentation of the Swazi clans has not given rise to any distinctive interlinked lineage structure, that is, to a structure in which the links are remembered' (H. Kuper, 1950:87).

Similar objections apply to a 'clan' model of the system of ranking. Not even 'the Dlamini' form a single ranked category. 'The more remote Dlamini of all lineages are described as "just of the *sibongo*" and merge, for practical purposes, with the masses' (H. Kuper, 1947:111-12).

I regard it as unhelpful to talk of marriage rules, or ranking, in 'clan' terms. The real structural units, which act, rise and fall in status and enter into alliances are not clans but homestead groups, or more specifically local headmen and their dependants. This corresponds to the unit which is actually termed *lusendvo*. My analysis will assume that these local family heads are the nodal figures in the social network to which the marriage rules refer.

Marriage prohibitions and preferences

The basic prohibition is upon marriage between a man and a woman with the same *sibongo*, or patronymic, which passes from a father to his children.

The literature is less clear about first cross-cousin marriage. Engelbrecht (1930:1) claimed that all first-cousin marriages were forbidden, and Marwick (1940:52) reported a prohibition on MBD marriage. According to H. Kuper (1947:96; 1950:103-4) either cross-cousin may be married, but marriage with a first cross-cousin is discouraged.[2]

There is, however, agreement that a MBD should properly be married to replace a man's mother in his homestead. A Dlamini informant put it in this way:

> I should marry the child of my *malume* (MB) when my father is dead. When he is still living it is not allowed because she is your father's *umlamu* (WZ) and he may marry her. She is your *umzala* (cross-cousin) and is called your mother. You should marry her, it is the law: you pay cattle, you *lobola* her with the full number of ten cattle.
>
> Her child does not become heir in your hut. She is put in your mother's hut even if your mother is still living. If your mother dies, although you have more wives, she remains in this household of your mother's. (Ziervogel, 1957:73)

Whether one's mother is alive or not, then, the MBD is 'mother'. ('She will not be taken out of the great hut because she is said to be my mother' (Ziervogel, 1957:75).) There is a special duty to marry her if your mother is dead; though she may not be married if your father is still alive. According to Hilda Kuper, even in this situation there is a certain ambivalence, however, and first cousins may be avoided (1950: 104). Finally, a wife who is a MBD cannot be the great wife, and her son cannot succeed.

The positive preference is that a man marry a *gogo*, a 'grandmother'. This may be a *gogo lotala babe*, a 'grandmother who bore my father', or a *gogo lotala make*, 'a grandmother who bore my mother'. Of the two a paternal 'grandmother' is especially preferred.

Obviously a genealogical grandmother is not being indicated. The preferred woman would be of her husband's own generation, or be younger than him, but she would come from the family of his mother's mother or the family of his father's mother. Ethnographers have commonly expressed the preference as if it were for a woman from the 'clan' of a grandmother. I shall rather use a genealogical specification, identifying the closest genealogical relative who would fit the descriptions available. I therefore interpret marriage with a *gogo lotala babe* to mean in the first instance marriage with a FMBSD. A *gogo lotala make* would, similarly, mean a MMBSD.[3] If the ideal marriage with a FMBSD is made, she would become the great wife and her eldest son would succeed her husband.

Figure 8 presents a model of FMBSD marriage over three generations. The resultant alliance structure is unusual, since it is based upon an alternating mechanism. Each line must have two heir-producing lines of wife-givers, who provide the heir's mother in alternate generations.

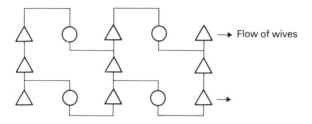

FIGURE 8 *FMBSD marriage (Swazi)*

Hilda Kuper's diagrammatic representations of the marriage system show Ego's line and the 'clans' of mother, father's mother and mother's mother (1947:95; 1950:106). This identification of three lines of wife-givers coincides with the Swazi specification of the three forms of kin-marriage. Accordingly I have developed a model which incorporates three lines of wife-givers and, mirroring them, three lines of wife-takers, in addition to the line of Ego. As the model shows, the third line of wife-givers, the line of the *gogo lotala make*, is the line of wife-givers to Ego's wife-givers.

There are further indications in the literature which help in the development of the model. The Swazi recognize the possibility of reversing the direction of the exchanges, but deprecate it. Hilda Kuper notes (1950:106) that the Swazi feel men of wife-giving lines should have no claim on women of lines that give wives to Ego, 'though if they should intermarry many families rejoice that the "cattle have returned home". Other Swazi disapprove of such ties, saying it is too like "buying from each other"'. Father's sister's daughter marriage is also frowned upon (H. Kuper, 1950:106).

Hilda Kuper reports (1947:95) the intriguing fact that 'a woman is not encouraged to marry a man with the clan name of her grandparents'. If this rule is rewritten to specify the genealogically closest kinswomen whom a man would then not be encouraged to marry, one finds that the disfavoured marriages would be with a FBD, FFBSD, FZD, FFBDD, FFZSD and FFZDD. The first two women, the FBD and FFBSD bear the same *sibongo* and are ruled out by the basic exogamy principle. FZD and FFBDD are daughters of men who took wives from Ego's

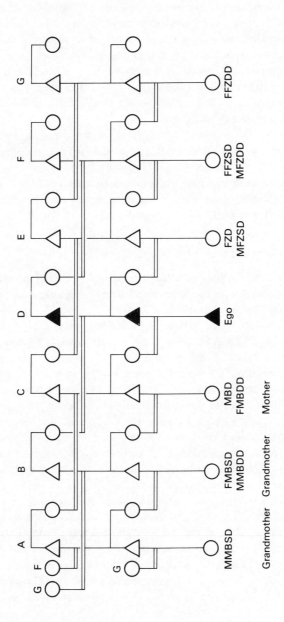

FIGURE 9 *The Swazi model*

close agnates in the previous one or two generations. FFZSD and FFZDD are similarly from lines of wife-takers, or wife-takers of wife-takers. This rule therefore underscores the undesirability of reversing the direction of exchanges, even in alternate generations.

I suggest that the most economical way of representing the system, while taking into account all the constraints presented by the Swazi, is to maintain a uni-directional flow of wives, which implies that Ego's wife-givers must themselves take wives from other lines. The seven-line model in Figure 9 thus makes certain simplifying assumptions, but takes into account all available material.

To sum up, the proposed model generates a unilateral transmission of wives, as in an elementary system of matrilateral cross-cousin marriage, but each local line has two primary lines of wife-givers. These supply his line with wives in alternate generations. This is a system of unilateral marriage alliance but with an oscillating action, so that the system repeats itself only every second generation.

The developmental cycle of the domestic group

The oscillation of alliance relationships is not an isolated peculiarity of the Swazi social process. It is matched by a specific developmental cycle of the domestic group.

The common Nguni pattern is to divide a polygynous homestead into right-hand and left-hand sections. The senior section is expected to succeed to the headmanship, while the other will split off, forming a separate local grouping when the headman dies, or when the eldest son in the 'house' reaches maturity. The Swazi, in contrast, stress the unity and continuity of the homestead unit, and the great house is not generally clearly identified during the lifetime of the headman. The leading woman in the homestead is the 'mother', representing the dead headman. Subordinate homesteads, including any homestead set up apart by the new headman, are bachelors' barracks (*lilawu*) in relation to the main homestead of the 'mother'.

Like some other Nguni aristocrats, Swazi headmen tended to marry their great wives late. The first-married wife would not normally bear the successor, and often the house of the heir was identified only after the headman's death. These factors further complicated the developmental cycle of the homestead group. For one thing in consequence of these principles 'the heir . . . is frequently a minor . . . Guardianship is consequently recognized as part of the machinery of succession' (H.

Kuper, 1947:101). Except in the case of the king himself, the guardian would normally be the eldest son of the first-married wife, who was customarily debarred from the succession.

Another consequence is that the mother of the heir would often be a young woman when her husband died. Until her son grew up and formally succeeded, the homestead 'mother' would still be her late husband's 'mother', her son's 'grandmother'. Ideally her son would eventually marry a 'grandmother', and she would bear his heir. The 'grandmother'-wife would, as the Swazi say, 'wake the hut of granny' and also 'wake the hut of father' (H. Kuper, 1950:105). The developmental cycle of the domestic group therefore incorporated in its own action the mechanism of oscillation which characterized the system of alliance.

Marrying up and choosing the heir

Swazi marriage choices were guided not only by kinship-based preferences but also by a bias in favour of hypogamy. Marriages with women of superior rank were highly valued. '"Marrying up" is a well-known practice among the Swazi. Though a person without rank or substance cannot aspire to the daughter of a prince or chief, a wealthy commoner is sometimes accepted as a son-in-law' (H. Kuper, 1947:113). These marriages would imply adjustments in the bridewealth price. A princess marrying down might command twice the average rate, and 'it is generally accepted that the more important a woman the higher her *lobola* value' (H. Kuper, 1947:98). Even in recent times if a marriage was initiated by the groom's party the bridewealth was inflated, while if initiated by the bride's party it was below what might otherwise have been expected (Derman, 1977:123).

Not every marriage was hypogamous, and indeed hypergamy occurred too, being marked – as Derman's observation indicates – by a reduction in the brideprice. At the top of the system a king or chief would normally pay no brideprice at all. Yet in general men tried to 'marry up'. Marriage into the family of a man with power marked a rise in status and was expected to deliver concrete benefits. Thus Swazi would argue that 'So-and-so should have rights over a large arable area since his wife is the sister of the chief, or because his father was chief deputy to the previous chief; while the relatively small arable holding of another family is easily explained in terms of their being new arrivals in the area, with no close connections with any of the mighty' (Hughes, 1961:265).

Where a man had married several women, over many years, the selection of the great wife, and so of his heir, had important consequences. The choice would naturally take account of any kinship ties to each wife's family and of their political status. The kinship preference did not, however, necessarily work against the desire to marry up. Since the ideal kinship marriage pattern implied a unilateral transmission of wives, it could accommodate a systematic status difference between (superior) wife-givers and (inferior) wife-takers.

The considerations involved were clearly enunciated by a Swazi aristocrat, who identified 'four ways of enabling a wife to succeed to her husband's estate if he has many wives' — i.e. four tests which determined which wife should be great wife and 'mother' of the heir.

(a) The *Endziswa* wife:
The wife called *umfati wekwendziswa* is also called the wife of the *sikhoti*: she is the one whose father causes her to *gana*, saying: 'My child, Buhlaluse, I want you to go, my child, in order that we may take you over there to the Mdzabuko's so that you may find me some calves' . . . On the death of her husband she is the person to succeed when there are co-wives; she has a higher status than the co-wives, those who are not *endziswa*-ed.
(b) *Gogo lotala babe*:
The one who has a higher status than the *sikhoti* wife is the wife from the clan of your father's mother; she is above all. By calling her 'grandmother' the grandmother herself is not meant; any girl who is born of the clan of the mother of your father is indicated. By saying she is your grandmother the old woman who bore your father is referred to because of her clan name.
(c) *Gogo lotala make*:
The third one is the wife from the clan of the grandmother who bore your mother. When there is no one from the clan of father's mother she is likely to succeed. If they bring her with a gall-bladder she will say that she was indeed *gana*-ed. Having been brought they treat her like a *sikhoti* wife. She succeeds like an *endziswa* wife; after all she had *gana*-ed.
(d) A wife of higher birth:
The following is done by ordinary citizens: If a girl of an important family comes along, whether she be of the royal clan or the daughter of a district chief, she is indeed the successor. Even if she found an *endziswa* wife or wives from the grandmother's clan, she is still the most important; she succeeds to the kraal.

(Glossary: *endziswa* = to be made to marry; *umfati wekwendziswa* = a married woman who was caused to marry; *sikhoti* = a woman given in marriage by her father, and not courted in the usual way; *gana* = to become betrothed; *gogo lotala babe* = grandmother who bore my father; *gogo lotala make* = grandmother who bore my mother. (Glosses from Ziervogel, 1957.))

Summary statements of the rules may be found in various ethnographies, and without significant variation. (See, e.g., H. Kuper, 1947:90-6.)

To sum up, in specifying marriage preferences the Swazi identify certain kinswomen as favoured spouses; value marriages with women of higher status; and prefer marriages arranged by the parents of the couple, particularly those initiated by the parents of the bride.

These preferences presumably constrain marriage choices, but we lack the statistical material to be sure. They certainly constrain the selection of the heir-producing house in polygynous families. This is crucial to the structure of social relations, since the rich and powerful are polygynists, and the ties traced through homestead 'mothers' are of particular importance.

The queen mother

The first two wives of a young king are said to be provided by the nation. 'They are chosen from special clans, the Matsebula and Motsa, and are known as his 'right-hand queen' and 'left-hand queen' respectively' (H. Kuper, 1947:80). Neither will bear an heir to the kingship.

The king may also marry a close relative, a 'sister'. The Swazi indeed insist upon the significance of this royal privilege. '"We are one with the Tembe; their king, like ours, marries his sisters"' (H. Kuper, 1947: 12). Luc de Heusch has suggested that these rumours of royal incest must be related to a broad substratum of Bantu myths of royal incest, and in general he is certainly correct. (See de Heusch, 1982.) Yet such a marriage might have significant political consequences. Hilda Kuper described the effect as a form of 'clan fission'. 'Dlamini clan fission was periodically induced by the King ostensibly to enable the King to marry women who are otherwise forbidden by the law of exogamy' (H. Kuper, 1947:111). What happened was that the family of the wife would *lose status*. They might even have to abandon the title Nkosi ('chief'), which marked membership of the aristocracy.

The process contrasts with the common Sotho-Tswana pattern in which women marry up and a 'mother's brother' group of royals is defined as the regular source of heir-producing wives. There too the wife-givers lose status in the royal group, being defined as a separate section, but their women are always the ruler's great wives. This is not the case with the Nkosi Dlamini wife. 'Under no circumstances whatsoever could this girl be considered a candidate for the position of the King's main wife and the future queen mother' (H. Kuper, 1947:111).

Neither of the ritual wives can be the great wife. If the king marries a close kinswoman who bears the same patronymic, she is also barred from the position of queen mother. Who then bears the heir to the throne? To recapitulate:

> The Swazi, unlike some other Southern Bantu, do not automatically accept the first wife as the great or main wife. It is usually only after the death of the husband that a council chooses the heir by determining which of the wives of the deceased holds highest rank. In certain cases, one wife is married when the man is well on in years according to a ritual that leaves no doubt as to her superior status in his harem. Prominent men, chiefs, and especially the king, are expected to contract a marriage of this kind, in order, no doubt, that the identity of the heir may be unquestionable. At the same time, he will be too young to challenge his father's power during the patriarch's lifetime. Even in these cases, however, the child is never publicly announced as successor, and open discussion is discouraged. The fiction of equality is studiously maintained until after the father's death, when the actual appointment is made. (H. Kuper, 1947:88-9)

Even apparent clues to the succession might be provided only after the event. For example, the king did not formerly *lobolo* his wives, and Sobhuza is said to be the first king to pay *lobolo* (H. Kuper, 1947:112, 153). (This was true of even lesser chiefs. 'When a chief takes the girl of a commoner to wife and gives cattle, the natives are not disposed to consider this as *lobolo*, because he could have withheld it' (Engelbrecht, 1930:14).) Bridewealth for the queen mother, however, should be provided by the leading men of the country. Yet 'if the queen mother is chosen after her husband's death, these cattle are given retrospectively' (H. Kuper, 1947:111).

Queen mothers seem once to have come from the families of leading chiefs who had been incorporated (or were being incorporated) into the kingdom, but there has been at least one commoner queen mother. Hilda Kuper also noted 'a tendency to repeat marriages with a clan that has provided an outstanding queen mother. Thus LaNgolotsheni, Sobhuza II's mother, was selected because she belonged to the Ndwandwe clan, the clan of the famous LaZidze' (H. Kuper, 1947:112). This case is suggestive, but it must be set in the context of the succession of a series of recent queen mothers and kings.

Fairly detailed stories are available only for the past five generations (but see Matsebula, 1972:4–6). Ngwane, the hero-founder of the Swazi, was succeeded by Ndvungunye, who was succeeded by Sobhuza I. 'Ndvungunye's principal wife had been Lobija, who had no child. So when Ndvungunye died Sobhuza was adopted by Lobija . . .' (Matsebula, 1972:8). However, Sobhuza soon established his real mother, Somnjalose Simelane, as queen mother, and according to Hilda Kuper she 'restrained her son and won for the mother of the Dlamini ruler a special place in ritual and in government' (H. Kuper, 1947:12–13). If Ngwane may be considered the founder king, his grandson's 'mother' was the founder queen mother.

Sobhuza I led his people to the modern Swaziland. 'It was Sobhuza's policy to avoid conflict with superior forces; by marriage alliance he sought the goodwill of powerful kings and demonstrated his own peaceful intentions' (H. Kuper, 1947:14). A notable marriage was with a daughter of a powerful and often antagonistic neighbour, Zidze, chief of the Zulu Ndwandwe. Her son Mswati succeeded Sobhuza I.

The new queen mother has left a great reputation for wisdom. She and her son were joint innovators. 'Mswati, encouraged by his mother, organized all subjects into age groups' (H. Kuper, 1947:15). This innovation contributed to Mswati's notable military success. During his reign hitherto independent chiefdoms were brought under Dlamini control.

When Mswati died there was a disputed succession. Hilda Kuper gives the following account:

> Mswati's mother and one of his half-brothers, Ndwandwe, were
> acting regents for the young heir, Ludvonga. Suddenly Ludvonga
> died. The council held that the Prince Regent had murdered him in
> order to obtain power for himself, and so the Prince Regent was
> clubbed to death. Thereupon, older sons of Mswati wrangled and
> intrigued, coveting the kingship, and the army was divided behind
> rival claimants. Finally, influenced mainly by the Queen Regent,
> the nation . . . agreed to accept the quiet, motherless Mbandzeni
> as king. (H. Kuper, 1947:20) (Cf. Matsebula, 1972:24–9.)

What happened in theory was that Mbandzeni, whose own mother was dead, was 'put in the stomach' of Sisile Khumalo, who had been chosen as queen mother, but whose own son Ludvonga had now died. A complication immediately arose, for Mbandzeni took to wife a woman who had been betrothed to Ludvonga. This raised the possibility that his child by this woman might be regarded as a leviratic son of Ludvonga, and so as the rightful heir to the throne. In any case when the new wife had a son the child died mysteriously, and the queen mother fled. Another widow of Mswati, who had looked after Mbandzeni as a child and was of the same 'clan' as his real mother, was appointed queen mother (H. Kuper, 1978:21–2).

When Mbandzeni died the inner council was divided between two possible queen mothers. One was of the same family as Sobhuza I's mother, the famous founder-figure of the office of queen mother. However, a commoner was chosen, and her son Bhunu became king in 1890. Bhunu died in 1899, at the climax of the great national *ncwala* ritual, leaving behind him three sons by three different wives. 'Though the numbers were relatively few, the choice was difficult. The princes deliberated and argued, referring to precedent and manipulating complicated principles of succession, starting from the rules that a king is king by the blood of kings, and a king is king by his mother' (H. Kuper, 1978:31).

The first wife, laNkambule, was of the same family as Mbandzeni's mother. The second, laNdwandwe, was of the same family as Mswati's mother. The third, laSimelane, was of the family of Sobhuza I's mother – the family which had also very nearly provided the heir to Mbandzeni. Eventually the Ndwandwe wife was selected, and so Sobhuza II succeeded as king (*ibid.*).

Clearly there is a tendency to repetition in selecting queen mothers. Candidates tend to come from a few families, although they do not hold a monopoly, as is indicated by the succession of the commoner Gwamile and her son Bhunu. Moreover, no two successive queen mothers have come from one family. The tendency to oscillation is evident, though given the stakes and the competition the oscillation is not unexpectedly less smooth than would be the case if the alliance model were mechanically applied.

One major rivalry is clearly between the Ndwandwe and the Simelane. The Simelane provided the great wife of Ngwane, who was in semi-mythical terms the founder of the office of queen mother. Mbandzeni had a Simelane wife who was very nearly selected as queen mother, and Bhunu also had a Simelane wife who was nearly chosen as queen mother. Sobhuza I married an Ndwandwe great wife, and his great-grandson Bhunu also married a Ndwandwe, who came to office with her son Sobhuza II.

The internal competition is evidenced by the stalemates: the confused succession to Mswati eventually yielded the 'motherless' Mbandzeni, and the selection of a commoner woman as queen mother on his death. Another significant pointer to internal conflict is the shift in queen mothers on at least two occasions — from Sobhuza I's adoptive mother to his 'real' mother, and similarly from Mbandzeni's adoptive mother to a co-wife and relative of his 'real' mother, who had brought him up.

The forces engaged in the competition are the 'houses' of the leading contenders, and their mother's relatives. These affines are necessarily interested since 'the queen mother's close relatives also influence national affairs . . . The close maternal relatives of the king, more especially his *bomalume* (maternal uncles), usually receive, if they do not already hold, posts in the central government . . .' (H. Kuper, 1947: 59). One appreciates why the Swazi emphasize the selection of the queen mother rather than the nomination of a king.

Leaving to one side the problem of fixing the succession, the very fact that the queen mother is so significant a figure demands comment. A satisfactory discussion of this role would demand a far-ranging study of Swazi politics and ritual,[4] but I confine myself here to the marriage system. In most Nguni systems the leading woman in the homestead is the great wife. Here the great wife is selected only after her husband's death, and so the mother's central position in the homestead is unchallenged. Among the Sotho-Tswana — and particularly in the northeastern Transvaal — the sister has a prominent position in her brother's home, and the position given the 'mother' and queen mother among the Swazi recalls the roles of the 'sister' and queen among the Lovedu. Luc de Heusch (1982) has identified ritual transformations between the roles of the Lovedu queen and the Swazi queen mother, but there is also a structural transformation at the level of the systems of alliance. This is the shift from a system of MBD marriage, in which the sister is the lynch-pin, to the FMBSD structure, in which a homestead 'mother' is replaced by her grandson's wife.

8   The Tsonga: marrying out

Junod's ethnography

In 1895 Henri Junod, a missionary with the Swiss Romande Mission in Mozambique, received a visit from the distinguished statesman Lord Bryce. Lord Bryce had been struck by the poverty of the information available on the tribal peoples of Southern Africa, and he remarked to Junod: 'How thankful should we be, we men of the nineteenth century, if a Roman had taken the trouble fully to investigate the habits of our Celtic forefathers!' This observation, Junod reported, was a revelation to him:

> Up to that date I had already collected some Ronga tales and studied some curious customs of the tribe. But the science which I was pursuing as a favourite pastime was Entomology. Delagoa Bay is a splendid place for beetles and butterflies ... Since that time Ethnography has more or less supplanted Entomology. I started on the systematic and thorough investigation which Lord Bryce recommended to me, and I very soon found out that, after all, Man is infinitely more interesting than the insect![1]

The consequences of this encounter were of the greatest importance to African anthropology, Junod compiling over a long period what is still one of the finest reports of any traditional African way of life. For present purposes his ethnography represents the best account of a Southern Bantu kinship system which lacks positive kinship marriage preferences. On some crucial points, moreover, additional material of great importance was published by Junod's colleagues, the Rev. A. A. Jaques, André Clerc and E. Dora Earthy.

The bridewealth system

At the turn of the century, when Junod lived amongst them, the Tsonga occupied small settlements, each typically housing a patrilocal extended family which seldom reached even three generations in genealogical depth. There were no patrilineal groupings beyond the small fissiparous local family settlement.

For most purposes inheritance and succession passed down a line of brothers before being transmitted to the next generation. This is exceptional in Southern Africa. Furthermore, the house-property system was not as highly developed as in the southern tribes, but the house remained the unit of marital exchange. A man traditionally had a prior claim to his house-sister's *lobolo* and he could enter into *lobolo* contracts without interference from the head of his homestead.[2]

The *lobolo* payment was by far the largest and most important of the prestations and counter-prestations which accompanied the establishment of a marriage. It was also a major problem to assemble. Cattle were the ideal bridewealth medium, but southern Mozambique is an unhealthy area for livestock, and they were scarce. Citing Portuguese sources, Harris (1959:57) reported that 'even before the final pacification of the Thonga area in 1895 the English pound had already become the most prevalent form of brideprice'.

The possibility of substituting cash and perhaps sometimes other articles did not, however, make matters much easier for the prospective groom, since the cash price constantly inflated. Junod reported in 1912 that a commoner's daughter could command £20, and in the 1927 edition of his monograph noted that the price had risen to almost £30. In 1938, Clerc talked in terms of £30 to £40, which he said was equivalent to 10–12 head of cattle. In the next decade a source in the Transvaal reported bridewealth rates of between 9 and 13 head of cattle, conventionally valued at £5 a head, and so yielding a cash equivalent of £45 to £65.[3]

The high and rising price served to prevent easy access to the bridewealth circuit. As migrant labourers began to go to Johannesburg, some young men earned their own bridewealth, although this must have been a difficult feat even well into the twentieth century. In the inter-war years Tsonga migrant labourers in South Africa earned only £3–£4 a month, and comparative data suggests that they could have saved only £3–£7 from an average tour of migrant labour.[4]

Reports from the 1930s and 1940s reflect a new development, which probably foreshadowed the breakdown of a closed bridewealth circuit. This was the payment of bridewealth by instalments. Junod wrote that the transfer of the bride to her husband's home was delayed until bridewealth had been paid in full (1927 I:107). Clerc, however, reported in 1938 that in the south of Junod's area, 'It is rare that the whole *lobolo* is paid cash down, it is enough to make a deposit of £1–£10 for the marriage. The rest of the debt will be paid little by little.' This arrangement 'gives a chance to the young bachelor as against the old and wealthy polygamist.'[5]

Traditionally, however, the bridewealth circuit was virtually closed. This ideal was evidently maintained even as the system began to break down. Clerc (1938:96), for example, reported that a wife who had been married with the *lobolo* received for a sister was superior in rank to a woman married with savings from migrant labour, or with *lobolo* borrowed from someone else, although normally the first married wife was the great wife.

Not only was entry into the bridewealth circuit largely restricted to those who received bridewealth, but there was also an explicit rule against leakage from the circuit. *Lobolo di fanela ku buyisa nsati*, the bridewealth payment must bring a wife. It was not to be divided but should be conferred entirely upon 'the oldest bachelor who is most closely related to the bride' (Clerc, 1948:100). The bride's full brother alone enjoyed the unencumbered use of the *lobolo* as of right, and such a right passed to her half-brother or patrilateral parallel cousin only in the absence of a brother in her own 'house'. Such a close kinsman might use the *lobolo* over the head of a full brother if the latter were too young to marry, or if a bridewealth debt was outstanding. If he were to do so, he immediately became indebted to the full brother, owing him a payment. Debts incurred in this fashion were strongly enforced, and inherited. They might be covered by pledging the *lobolo* of the debtor's daughter.

The situation was made more complex by a rule that *lobolo* might be reclaimed in certain circumstances: for example, if a man's wife voluntarily left him, or if he expelled her as a witch or adulteress, or because she was childless. Since the *lobolo* payments were relatively so high, and the accumulations of capital seem to have been largely restricted to these sums, circulating on the closed track of marriage exchanges, the demand for the return of *lobolo* could set off a chain reaction of divorces. As a rule, when a woman married, her brother used her *lobolo* to acquire a wife for himself. Should she now be divorced he might be obliged to divorce his own wife in order to recover the *lobolo* to pay back his former brother-in-law. The alternative was to provide a substitute wife, commonly his daughter, sometimes an unmarried younger sister, and, in exceptional circumstances, his own wife, his brother-in-law's wife's brother's wife. Jaques reported (1929: 334) that he knew of some cases in which such marriages with a WBW had been necessitated, but these were 'very rare, as, even if all other possibilities have been exhausted, the *mukongwana* may redeem herself by giving a daughter or a niece, whom a man is obliged to accept in compensation, even if the girl offered is yet a child'.

The closed bridewealth system therefore implied the existence of a shadow circuit of debts. This was the source of much contention and litigation. Indeed, 'ninety per cent of the civil cases are in connection with *lobolo*' (Junod, 1927, I:439).

Junod described a typical case, though with a tragic end. A woman named Gidhlana ran away twice from her husband Khandela, and the second time refused to return to him although her parents did their best to persuade her, and although her uncle thrashed her with a stick. At home a young man named Gudu, from a neighbouring village, proposed to her, and she accepted him. Gudu subsequently left for Johannesburg, but Gidhlana was abducted on his behalf by his elder brother. After some negotiation the traditional settlement was made, and her parents reconciled themselves to Gidhlana's marriage to Gudu.

At this point Khandela confronted his former wife's parents, demanding the return of the *lobolo* cattle he had paid for her. This put Gidhlana's parents in a quandary.

> They had just used the *lobolo* of Gidhlana to buy a wife for Mubene, her brother. The money had already been given to the Moyane clan from which a girl had been chosen by Mubene. They consequently went to the Moyanes and asked them to return the money. But the Moyanes said: 'Your money has already gone further. We have used it to buy a girl of Madjieta for our son. We will go and fetch it'. So two projected marriages were prevented; they would have been annulled, had they been already concluded! In this way Khandela found his money!

When Gudu eventually returned from Johannesburg and took Gidhlana as his wife, her parents expected at last to recoup all their losses. 'Hoping that he had earned some money, [they] went to him and said: "You have spoilt our flock . . . Now pay."' But Gudu did not have the money, and his elder brother persuaded Gidhlana's parents to accept instead the promise of the bridewealth which would one day accrue for Gudu's young sister, Shaputa.

Later Gudu and his family moved, and Gidhlana contracted leprosy and eventually died. When Shaputa married, Gudu's family refused to pass on the bridewealth they received for her, arguing that the debt owed for Gidhlana was cancelled since 'no claim is accepted for a leper, for one drowned in the river, or for anyone who dies from small-pox or from the assagay.' Junod reported that litigation was continuing (1927, I:506–9).

In another case a man was driven to suicide by the behaviour of his ward, a brother's daughter, who five times deserted different husbands, leaving behind her when she finally escaped to the city a nightmarish tangle of *lobolo* claims (Junod, 1927, I:280n.).

In Junod's view (by no means the conventional and naive missionary response of the day): 'These complicated relations due to the *lobola* poison the whole of native life . . . the *lobola* question fills the African village with hatred and bitterness. The *milandju*, the debts!' (1927, I: 282. Cf. Clerc, 1938:104). He quoted the moving plea of a Tsonga evangelist, who invoked the image of the slave-trade, still a living memory in the region:

> These *lobolo* debts are ropes which start from the neck of one and go to the neck of the other. Though your father dies, this rope still ties you, you are kept tied to your father's bones by this accursed rope! Others will get drawn into its coils and the strands become entangled round you! Cut it and be free! (Junod, 1927, I:531)

To see only the debts, and the consequences of personal indebtness, is, however to perceive the system only from one, very special, point of view. Structurally the binding and enduring nature of the debts signal the existence of a durable series of marriage relations, integrally con-nected with each other and burned into the consciousness of the actors in the form of a record of debit and credit. As Lévi-Strauss remarked (1969:467), referring particularly to Junod's ethnography:

> once *lobolo* is received it immediately commences a new cycle . . . Scarcely is it received than it is re-invested for a wife for the brother or cousin of the young bride. As a thread runs through a piece of fabric, *lobolo* creates an unlimited series of connections between members of the same group, and between different groups.

This is the proposition of the Tsonga evangelist, although expressed in another idiom, and formulated from a different perspective.

The avoidance of the wife's brother's wife

The system of kinship relations among the Tsonga has two remarkable features: the joking relationship with the mother's brother, which has become a classic focus of anthropological debate; and the avoidance relationship with the wife's brother's wife. Both can be explained in terms of the *lobolo* system.

The two main categories of affines are termed *mukonwana* and *namu*. An informant told Junod, '*Bakonwana* are those persons who produce wives for you; *tinamu* are those persons who produce children for you, because they are your presumptive wives. Even if you do not marry them, their children will call you father.' This is a crude gloss, but adequate for present purposes. *Bakonwana* are respected, and 'it was in the relation with two women of the wife's family that the respect of *bukonwana* is pushed to the greatest extent: the wife's mother and the wife of the brother-in-law. In these cases there is not only respect but *avoidance*.' The wife's brother's wife (WBW) is termed the 'Great *Mukonwana*', and in relation to this woman 'the avoidance is pushed further than with the mother-in-law' (Junod, 1927, I:237, 238, 241).

The WBW is closely identified with the wife's mother, the other main avoidance relative in the category of *bakonwana*. She seems in fact to take the place of the wife's mother. Among some Tsonga groups, 'My mother-in-law brings our *mukongwana* . . . to our kraal, "to show her where we live". She says to my wife, "This is your mother. I am getting old and shall not be able to come and see you often. But she will come and know that she is here at home"' (Jaques, 1929:333). Similarly, when a man first marries he stays in the hut of his wife's mother when visiting her family. After his wife's brother has married a woman with the *lobolo* which he paid, he lodges with the wife's brother's wife (Junod, 1927, I:241–2).

Junod characteristically explained the avoidance rules in terms of potential marriages. Among the Tsonga a man can claim a wife's younger sister or a brother's daughter as a secondary wife; a claim which he enjoys through his wife (Junod, 1927, I:261–2). The WBW is therefore a potential mother-in-law, and so associated with the actual mother of a man's wife, and consequently avoided. However, with his scrupulous regard for what his informants told him, Junod admitted that:

in the case of the wife of the brother-in-law, there is still another element: 'The oxen!' This woman has been acquired by the oxen paid by the man to obtain his wife, and this explains the uneasiness which characterizes their relation.

This second reason is perhaps more readily recognized by the Thongas than the first; they sometimes tell you that it is the only reason. (Junod, 1927, I:242)

The importance of the bridewealth factor is underlined by the fact that (according to Jaques, 1929:332) the WBW, Junod's 'Great *Mukonwana*', is more commonly termed *nyatihomu*, 'of the cattle'.

Because she is acquired with the *lobolo* paid for his own wife, a man's WBW is in a sense 'his' wife. He paid for her, if indirectly. Moreover, she is the ultimate guarantor of his marriage. If his marriage fails, his wife's brother will be obliged to return the *lobolo*. If he cannot, and if he can find no substitute wife among his sisters or daughters, then in the last resort he must send his own wife as a replacement.

Lévi-Strauss suggests that the WBW is equivalent to a sister: 'Everything takes place as if, instead of being at the end of the process, she were at its origin, or as if I had exchanged the "great *mukonwana*" for my wife' (1969:469. Cf. F. Hanson, and F. Miller, 1977). But why should she then be avoided? Lévi-Strauss, thinking purely in terms of the exchange of a sister for a wife, elided the bridewealth transaction. It is because the great *mukonwana* was bought with bridewealth cattle which I paid, while being in fact married to my wife's brother, that my relationship with her is 'uneasy', structurally ambiguous, and so contained by a rule of avoidance.

One might even explain the avoidance relationship with the wife's mother in similar terms. Viewed diachronically, a man's outlay in acquiring a wife is recovered when he receives bridewealth for her daughter. In a sense the man who marries the daughter *lobola*'s the mother. This may seem far-fetched, but after all a man who cannot raise the bridewealth payment for his wife may pledge the bridewealth to be received for a (perhaps unborn) daughter. If the mother is indeed ultimately paid for by the bridewealth received from her daughter's husband, then their relationship is clearly ambiguous, and so expressed in avoidance behaviour. Taking the argument one step further, the payment received for the daughter retrospectively finances the *lobolo* payment made for the mother, but it also immediately finances the payment for the brother's wife. Consequently the brother's wife is identified with the mother, and replaces her as the great *mukonwana* of her daughter's husband.

The mother's brother and the mother's brother's wife

The classic anthropological problem raised by the Tsonga ethnography concerns the 'joking relationship' with the mother's brother. The category of 'mother's brothers' is merged in some Tsonga group with 'grandfathers', but 'the *kokwane* or *malume*, with whom I am the most familiar, is the one who has acquired his wife with the *lobolo* of my mother' (Jaques, 1929:344).

The 'joking' has two main expressions:

1 A man 'jokingly' treats his mother's brother's wives as his own wives. They engage in sexy banter, and he demands that his uncles' wives provide him with food.

> Sometimes the *malume* himself points to one of his wives and says to the *ntukulu*: 'This is your wife. Let her feast you well!' The woman much enjoys the situation . . . She makes a feast for the *ntukulu* and calls him *nkata*, husband. It will sometimes go so far that the nephew will say to the uncle: 'Please make haste and die that I may have your wife!' 'Do you intend to kill me with a gun?' says the *malume* . . . But all this talking is a mere joke. (Junod, 1927, I:233)

The mother's brother must patiently endure the 'joking' of his nephew, but commentators have too often neglected the fact that the mother's brother's wives 'joke' with the boy on their own account.

> I may one day go to pay a visit to my *kokwana*. I have washed well and anointed myself with oil; I have put on my best skins and stuck some beautiful feathers in my hair, which is nicely combed. As I approach his kraal, my *kokwane*'s wives see me and say to each other, 'Here is our *ntukulu* coming, let us play a joke on him.' They catch hold of me. As they are four or five women and girls, they overpower me, carry me by the legs and arms and throw me on the ash-heap. One of them says: 'Bring some water.' Water is brought, and they mix it with earth and smear my face and my whole body with mud. Or they smear me with women's ochre. They ruffle my hair, take away the nice feathers and stick in ridiculous little fowl's feathers. They sprinkle my head with ashes. They have torn away the belt of skins around my loins and laugh at me. I likewise try to defend myself by tearing their dresses, but they hold me fast. Then my uncle, my *kokwane* arrives. He will clap his hands to greet me, and will say: 'O, my *ntukulu*! Do not be angry. You know that these

foolish women are your *bakokwana*, and that it is only a joke.'
He will order his wives to kill a fowl or a goat in my honour. They
will then wash me with clean water, anoint me with oil, comb my
hair, and adjust my skins. We shall then eat together and be merry.'
(Jaques, 1929:344)

Rather than talking of 'joking' with the mother's brother, one might
more accurately say that the Tsonga man has a reciprocal joking relationship with his mother's brother's wives, of which his mother's
brother is the long-suffering observer. A key element in the 'joke' is the
real possibility that the nephew may claim a widow of his mother's
brother as a wife.

2 Secondly, and at least partly quite distinct from this 'joking', the
mother's brother and sister's son stand in a special ritual relationship
to each other; and here the relationship is not solely between the cattle-
linked mother's brother and his sister's son. The relationship exists (at
least in some Tsonga groups) also between men and their grandchildren
and their father's sister's children; all of whom are classified together
by the 'Omaha'-type kinship terminology. Basically the *kokwane* or
malume sacrifices for the *ntukulu*, and the *ntukulu* must attend sacrifices
performed by the *kokwane*. Towards the end of the ceremony the
batukulu snatch part of the sacrifice and run off with it, pursued by
other participants. The Tsonga say that the *batukulu* represent the
ancestors. The sacrificing relationship is also said to rule out marriage
with sister's daughters.[6]

I am particularly interested in the 'joking relationship' with the mother's
brother's wife. Junod himself explained it as a throwback to an original
system of 'mother-right', an exercise in conjectural history which led
Radcliffe-Brown to propose an alternative psychological theory which
has, ironically, only an historical interest today.[7]

More recently Luc de Heusch has attempted to explain the Tsonga
avunculate in terms of alliance theory. The Tsonga system exists in
close proximity to the Lovedu and Venda, who have elementary
kinship systems based on preferential matrilateral cross-cousin marriage.
According to de Heusch, the Tsonga system must be analysed as a step
— a long step — on the path from such a system to a truly complex
kinship structure in which such repetitive kinship marriages are prohibited. As a general rule 'those kinship systems, in which the aggressive
privilege of the uterine nephew is found, occur at the point where the
elementary structures (which call for one or the other form of marriage

with the cross-cousin) hinge with the complex structures which do not permit this primary union' (de Heusch, 1974:615).

The Tsonga system retains echoes of the proscribed marriage with the MBD: a man may marry a distant matrilateral relative, and there are two secondary and oblique marriage claims, to the widow of the mother's brother, and to the wife's brother's daughter as a subordinate wife. 'However, these two oblique marriages are not symmetrical and reverse replicas of one another. In demanding the daughter of his wife's brother, ego's father renews an alliance; in claiming with virulence the widow of his maternal uncle, whom he pretends to wish dead, ego destroys this same alliance by a regression to incest' (pp. 614–15). This indeed is the underlying message of the nephew's aggressive claims. He is acting out the structuralists' version of incest — making 'a derisory attempt at least partially to annul the exchange made in the preceding generation, taking back that which had been given' (p. 613). The joking claims of the sister's son to his uncle's wives are therefore a symptom of the wrenching transformation which the Tsonga system is undergoing, a harking back to the formula of matrilateral cross-cousin marriage. In short, 'the aggressive claim of the nephew is only another indication of the closing of an elementary structure, that which establishes the marriage with the matrilateral cross cousin' (p. 615).

De Heusch's alliance theory has something in common with Junod's explanation of the Tsonga avunculate. Junod took the view that the avunculate represented a throwback to a primordial state of matriarchy. The residual inheritance rights of the sister's son, for example, were to be understood as 'a most vivid representation of a right which no longer exists, having in fact become obsolete, but which asserts itself in virtue of the survival of an old custom' (Junod, 1927, I:270–1). De Heusch similarly evokes agencies from the tribal past. 'It is exactly as though the spectre of marriage with the daughter of the maternal uncle (that would transform the ambiguous relationship of the uncle and of the nephew into one of alliance, thus putting an end to its confused character) prowled around on the periphery of the Thonga system' (1974:614). I find these explanations unsatisfactory, preferring not to use historical speculations in this way. While rejecting Radcliffe-Brown's own alternative explanation of the Tsonga avunculate, I sympathize with his view that as far as possible the springs of social action should be sought in contemporary institutions.

An alternative line of argument is suggested by the Tsonga themselves. This relates the nephew's claims to the *lobolo* system. A woman demands a return from her brother because she brought in the bride-wealth which he used to marry a wife. This gives her the right to claim a brother's daughter as a co-wife. Among the Lenge she may even seize a brother's daughter and keep her as a servant, releasing her only if she bears a daughter to replace herself. But it is when her brother dies that she asserts her claim most dramatically. Among the Lenge the sister may 'pounce down on her brother's *muti* . . . and take possession of some of his belongings − including his wife and child − while the widow meekly begs her deceased husband's sister to allow her to remain in the kraal' (Earthy, 1933:14−18). Among the Ronga she will demand one of her brother's widows for her son, saying: 'Has this widow not been bought with the money which I secured for the family by my marriage?' If there is trouble the *ntukulu* may carry off the widow, saying 'Good-bye! I go with my wife!' His uncle's family is virtually helpless.

> They had better consent to it at once, because it not infrequently happens that the *ntukulu*, if repulsed that day, will go to the family of the woman and claim the money (*lobola*) paid for her by her late husband, saying: 'That *lobola* comes from my mother. If you do not give us our wife, if you allow her to stay with another man, then give us back the money.' (Junod, 1927, I:210)

My conclusion is that the joking claim to the mother's brother's wives, and the real claim to the mother's brother's widow, are both rooted in the *lobolo* debt a man owes his sisters. This was the view of Junod himself before he was converted to the matriarchy theory. The argument has a certain comparative force too, as may be seen even from the cases de Heusch himself cited in his essay, namely the Tetela of Zaire and the Dan and Dogon of West Africa. In these societies, de Heusch pointed out:

> the nephew makes reference to his mother, relies upon her to put forward a claim . . . The Tetela used in front of me almost the same words as those that Marie puts into the mouth of the Dan: 'My uncle has given my mother to other men, and he has consumed the marriage wealth, that which he has is therefore mine.' (De Heusch, 1974:610)

This argument suggests a link between the joking relationship with the mother's brother's wife and the avoidance relationship with the wife's brother's wife − and there must surely be a connection, since a man's wife's brother's wife is his son's mother's brother's wife.

A man avoids his WBW because although (a) she is his 'wife', being bought with his *lobolo* cattle, she is (b) in fact his wife's brother's wife, and as such (c) the ultimate guarantor of his marriage. He will marry her if his alliance relationship with his wife's brother totally collapses. These delicate possibilities are contained by the avoidance relationship.

A man jokes with his mother's brother's wives because (a) they were bought with *lobolo* cattle earned by his mother, who may therefore claim them for him, but (b) they are married to his mother's brother and will revert to him only if his uncle dies. Moreover, his marriage to them would (c) resolve his father's claim without dissolving his father's alliance relationship. These deductions from the logic of the *lobolo* system are not of direct practical importance — the claim on the uncle's widow is seldom exercised and is not significant. They are, however, of considerable ceremonial importance in that they express and contain the structural implications of the *lobolo* system, resolving the ultimate contradictions of *lobolo* as a principle of organization. The issue is one which was clearly understood by a missionary observer. 'In the Ronga tribe, the same *lobolo* can be used to bring about several marriages. Here is a contradiction in the two attributes of the *lobolo*: it is the only given sign that a marriage has been arranged, and, at the same time, it is used to conclude several marriages' (Clerc, 1938:79).

Marriage regulations

The *lobolo* system is invoked to define the boundaries within which marriage should occur, for if marriages are made beyond the political and moral community then bridewealth claims cannot be depended upon. As one of Junod's informants explained, marriages outside the community are risky because:

> 1) If the marriage were unsuccessful, the parents-in-law against whom the claim would be brought might run away with wife and oxen, and we should lose our herd. 2) If our oxen multiplied in the other clan, we might be tempted to go and make war on our parents-in-law in order to appropriate the cattle. So blood would be shed on account of our oxen! (Junod, 1927, I:260)

First-cousin marriage is prohibited, second-cousin marriage is permitted only after a ritual has ended the relationship, but at least in some areas third cousins are marriageable, 'they belong to families which were relatives yesterday'. According to Junod, this rule was more strictly enforced with respect to father's kin, and matrilateral second cousins were marriageable. Clerc reported that 'A man may take a wife in the *muti* (homestead) where the paternal or the maternal grand-mothers of his mother were born.'[8]

The reason that patrilateral kin marriages were particularly prob-lematic, according to Junod, was to be found in the workings of the bridewealth system.

> Should a woman who is a relative on my father's side become my wife and should our union be put an end to by quarrels, I should go to her father to claim the *lobolo*. If her father happens to possess no oxen to return to me, he will have to go to his relatives to get them . . . He may have to come to my own father, who is his brother and belongs to the same family, a consequence which would be indeed absurd, because then I should myself pay the debt due to me. (Junod, 1927, I:256)

A further series of prohibitions flow from the passage of *lobolo*. Because marriage payments link several marriages in one series the possibility of counterposing debts must be avoided. Clerc explained that these rules flowed from *bukongwan*, which he glossed as 'relation-ship of oxen'.

> The *bukongwan* prevents matrimony between the sisters, nieces, etc., of a man and all the people who have taken, or might have taken, possession of the *lobolo* paid by that man. (A man can take possession of a *lobolo* by reason of his relationship to a wife or by reason of old debts of *lobolo*.) The *bukongwan* also prevents a marriage taking place between a man and all the women who might have been married by transmission of the *lobolo* paid by that man at the time of his marriage. (His own wife being an exception.) (Clerc, 1938:80)

In other words, bride-givers and their bride-givers cannot become bride-takers.

These prohibitions tend to suggest simply the scattering of marriage choices which has traditionally been assumed to characterize 'Omaha' systems, of which the Tsonga are an example. However, there is a new trend to see more long-term repetitive alliance patterns even in Omaha systems;[9] and this directs attention to the admittedly thin and scattered indications in the Tsonga ethnography that there are positive kin-marriage preferences.

Two rules have already been stated. Women of the homestead of either maternal great-grandmother are marriageable. In other words, matrilateral second cousins can be married. Patrilateral third cousins are also marriageable. A third rule is reported by Jaques, in a frustratingly vague passage. Discussing the category of 'great-grandchildren', *switukulunguhe*, he comments: 'It often happens that my other sons marry girls among my *switukulunguhe*, i.e., their grand nieces. This is done "in order not to lose the kinship with these children"' (Jaques, 1929:341). Presumably this means that men 'often' marry the grandchildren of their siblings. Finally, a modern source dealing with the Hlanganu, like the Ronga one of the southern Tsonga groups, reports the existence of a preferential marriage with a woman of the line into which a man's mother's brother married, while marriage with a woman of the line into which the father married is prohibited (Kotzé, 1978:25). The existence of such a rule would give new content to the claims a man makes to the wives of his mother's brother.

These are meagre hints. Any bricks built with these straws must be suspect. Nevertheless it is tempting to see what would happen if the Lovedu-Swazi series is stretched one step. Among the Lovedu a man repeats his father's marriage and marries a MBD. Among the Swazi he repeats his father's father's marriage, and marries a FMBSD. Among the Tsonga he may repeat his father's father's father's marriage, marrying a patrilateral third cross-cousin, a FFMBSSD. If he does so, and given a seven-line model of the Swazi type, he can be shown also to repeat the marriage of his mother's brother (see figure 10).

One may even perhaps incorporate Jaques's tantalizing clue, by referring to the Omaha rules of kin classification. It will be seen that according to the model a FFZDD would be marriageable. By the appropriate Omaha reduction rules she would be classified together with the 'grand nieces' whom Jaques singled out as preferred spouses. A parallel clue is provided by Jaques's observation that the FZD is called 'wife', although she is unmarriageable, and that ribald sexual joking is permitted with her. Terminologically the FFZDD and ZDD are identified with the FZD.[10]

A scatter of alliances?

Tsonga chiefs, like ruling families throughout the Southern Bantu area, tend to marry endogamously and to form repetitive marriage alliances with other powerful families.[11] Despite hints that elements of repetitive alliance may be present in the general marriage system, commoners

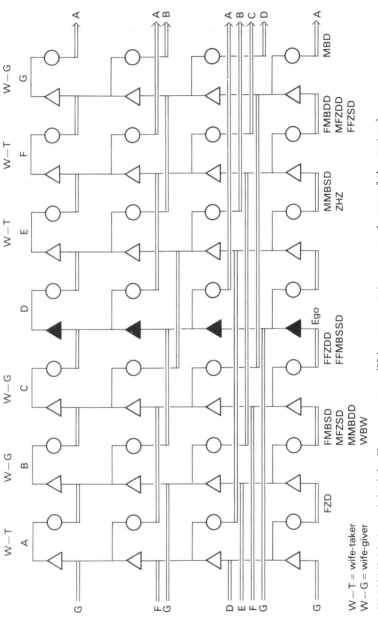

FIGURE 10 *A model of the Tsonga system.* (H is necessary to assume closure of the system)

W – T = wife-taker
W – G = wife-giver

apparently scatter their marriage links, a characteristic feature of 'Omaha' systems. The consequences have been well described by Webster, with special reference to the closely-related Chopi:

> kin terms and exogamy rules combine to provide a system which has the effect of spreading ties horizontally . . . Alliances are impermanent and do not follow recognisable patterns . . . This has the effect of producing a largely egalitarian society . . . Insofar as marriage alliances are ephemeral, the lack of continuity from generation to generation ensures that no one group monopolises power and status . . . (Webster, 1977:202)

Webster further suggested that this broadcasting of marriage alliances fostered individualism, 'big-man' political strategies, and ultimately a pluralistic and unstable power structure. Presumably such a state of affairs would in turn encourage people to keep changing their marriage alliances.

The analysis is plausible, and supporting evidence can be found in the marriage preliminaries. There is hard bargaining over bridewealth, and it is quite common for young men to short-circuit the stately marriage negotiations and to stage a 'marriage by capture', which dramatizes the social distance between the parties, but also brings out an essential feature of these marriages, the expectation that they will join people distant from each other yet equal in status.

Putting the hypothesis slightly differently, the Tsonga commoners seem to be operating a marriage strategy which spreads alliances laterally rather than integrating families hierarchically into chains of patrons and clients, as happens for example among the Sotho-Tswana, Venda and Swazi. This may be a function of the relative ethnic homogeneity of the non-Shangaan Tsonga chiefdoms, and the (perhaps consequent) lack of strong central control. Yet if the Tsonga represent a relatively democratic Southern Bantu system, they are also the people amongst whom market operations are most developed, and where the speculative potential of the *lobolo* systems has evolved most fully. Tsonga men may be relatively free of direct political control, but they are chained by debts, which inhibit their marriage choices and link marriages in series which produce their own characteristic structural consequences. The relationships with the MBW and the WBW signal the complex and profound implications of the Tsonga *lobolo* system.

Part three

Transformations

9   Wedding ceremonies

Brides for bridewealth

Willoughby (1923:110) wrote that 'a careful study of the usages of many tribes convinces one that the public reception of the bride-price and handing over of the bride would validate the marriage, even if all other ceremonies were omitted.' Legal commentators have tended to add that the consent of all parties, including the bride, must be given (e.g. Whitfield, 1948:85), but that is unlikely traditionally to have been essential. In any case the ceremonial as well as the legal emphasis is upon the transfer of the bride to her new home, and the transfer of the bridewealth cattle to her father's cattle-byre.

This central exchange, ceremonially spotlighted, is, as it were, bracketed by more private rituals and transactions. These include the betrothal, the fixing of the bridewealth price, the making of offerings to the bride's father's ancestors, etc. Then after the public excitement of the wedding come the observances which mark the bride's more or less gradual and complete incorporation into her new home.

The Sotho-Tswana and Nguni vary, however, in the emphasis given to these two ceremonies which mark every marriage. The Sotho-Tswana emphasize the bridewealth payment. Among the Nguni the public emphasis is upon the transfer of the bride. This contrast between the Sotho-Tswana and the Nguni is carried through to the details of the ceremonies. As an initial crude approximation, one might say that among the Nguni the initiative lies with the bride and her party, and the main ceremonial acts are staged at the groom's home. A woman may choose her husband and present herself at his home. While her father is setting the bridewealth price, she may visit her fiancé at his home for sexual relations. Then the transfer of the bride to her new home is elaborately celebrated, while the delivery of bridewealth to her father, which often happens later, is by comparison a muted affair.

Among the Sotho-Tswana and the Venda, in contrast, a man or his father chooses a bride. The man woos the girl at her home and once they are engaged he may visit her there for sexual relations. The bride-wealth is paid at the bride's father's home with considerable ceremony, while the subsequent transfer of the bride to her new home is given little ritual emphasis.

The contrast carries over to the period after the wedding. The new Nguni bride enters into an humiliating novitiate, marked by *hlonipha* avoidance behaviour, before eventually achieving the status of a wife in the new homestead. The Sotho-Tswana wife normally enters her new state with little ceremony and without enduring a period of extreme subordination.

I shall briefly describe the main features of these two types of wedding, and will then attempt to explain the contrast offered by the main Southern Bantu traditions.

The Nguni wedding: Kohler's account

Various sources present detailed descriptions of Nguni wedding cer-emonies.[1] None is 'typical', of course, but Kohler's (1933) texts and commentary provide a convenient and reliable basis. They deal with the Khuze and Bhaca of southern Natal, so incidentally serving as a bridge between the reports dealing with the Zulu and those dealing with the Cape Nguni.

Young men court girls, but 'A girl is said to choose (*qoma*) a sweet-heart, while the lad is said to 'cause to choose' (*qomisa*) the girl in question' (Kohler, 1933:32).[2] Thereafter, although strictly the girl should wait until formally betrothed, 'it is customary for girls to steal off after dark when everybody is asleep and to spend the night at the kraals of their young men, returning early in the morning before their absence can be noticed' (p. 35). They are expected to confine them-selves to *hlobonga,* external sexual intercourse, and defloration is punished with a fine.

Having chosen her lover, the girl takes the next step, making the betrothal visit. She *gana*'s her man, and he is said to *ganisa* her: to cause her to *gana*. She presents herself at her future husband's home at night, with girl companions. They are taken into a hut and a goat is killed for them. Until this is done they cannot touch any food. At the same time a messenger is sent to the girl's father to tell him that his daughter has gone to *gana* at such-and-such a village.

Next morning the girls bathe in the river. On their return the future bride is presented with special blankets and ornaments. She covers herself in the blankets and begins observing the rules of avoidance and decorum called *hlonipha*. The girls who accompanied her now collect firewood for the people of the homestead, and then leave, the bride remaining behind for a while with only one companion.

The next months are spent arranging for the wedding. During the period of negotiations the young woman visits her future husband's home frequently and she and her fiancé engage in external sexual intercourse. The visits are meant also to spur her husband's family on to completing their payments.

The amount to be paid in *lobolo* is set by the girl's father. He negotiates with an intermediary appointed by the boy's father, and the cattle are handed over in instalments, again by intermediaries.

The successive payments of cattle are every time acknowledged by the despatch of presents of beer and firewood from the bride's kraal. Such a present is called *umbondo* and represents a public and formal acknowledgement of receipt. The women and especially the young girls of the bride's village take these presents to the home of the bridegroom, their arrival being celebrated by the consumption of this beer and meat. (pp. 63–4)[3]

(In Zululand this beer is often called *ingquibamasondo* — wiping out of the cattle track (E. J. Krige, 1936.133n.).)

The low-key serial payment of the bridewealth cattle completed, preparations are set in train for the main event of the wedding, the formal delivery of the bride. First the bride's party prepare beer, and then they set off, arriving at the groom's homestead at dusk. They are welcomed with the slaughter of a goat, before which they cannot be persuaded to enter the homestead, and then they are given meat to eat.

The following morning the groom's father slaughters an ox for the bridal party, and the young people of both families go to the river to bathe and then dress up in their wedding clothes. After feasting on roast meat and drinking beer the dances begin, each party dancing as a group.

The high point of the ceremony occurs in the afternoon, beginning with the speeches, particularly the speech of the groom's father.

Thereupon the father of the bridegroom greets the bridal *umtimba* in a great speech, expressing his joy at their arrival and inviting them to the wedding dance in his cattle kraal (*isibaya*). This enclosure is surrounded by a living fence of agaves, under which his fathers and grandfathers rest in their graves. The spirits of the ancestors have

seen with grief how the *lobolo* cattle left their kraal, and to-day
they must be reconciled to this loss by the sight of the handsome
intombi now arrived in their stead. Her fruitfulness will increase
the wealth of this *isibaya*, maintain the ancestors' position of honour
and add to the strength and prestige of the sib. Her full and well-
built body is worthy of the seed of his ancestors. And he praises
them by reciting their *izibongo*. The fertility of this woman makes
closer the contact between the spirit world and the life in his kraal.
For her wedding dance therefore the bride must enter the *isibaya*,
in which she may never again set foot as long as she remains capable
of reproduction, for the cattle kraal is sacred to the ancestral spirits;
it is their resting place, where he himself will also one day sit in his
grave under the agaves ... (p. 79)

The bride's father may respond, praising his daughter and confiding
her to the care of her new family.

Then comes the bridal dance in the cattle-byre. The groom and his
father and relatives are waiting at the upper end of the byre, while the
bride and her party enter at the lower end, dancing up to them. The
bridegroom seats himself on a mat they spread out, and then the bride
and two girl companions dance before him. She carries a spear and
dances violently, stabbing with it; and finally breaks it.

The celebrations now proceed, the only important observances
remaining being the presentation of various gifts to her new relatives
by the bride, and the semi-public defloration of the bride, which occurs
on the second or third night.

During the afternoon before the consummation of the marriage the
bride's companions receive the special *mekeza* goat from the groom and
then sing, again and again, a special song — 'He has eaten the cattle,
the poor (bride), orphan of my father, we have taken (the cattle) back,
she is now an orphan' (p. 85). That night the bride is deflowered and
shouts — '*Maye webabo!* I have been spoilt!' 'Before the people have
gone to bed the shouting of the bride is heard. The next day she is
much troubled because she is now a woman ...' (p. 86).

The new wife must observe the most stringent avoidances, associated
with the names of her in-laws, the cattle paths and fronts of the huts,
and certain foods, particularly sour milk, meat, fowl and roasted maize.
After a month or so some restrictions are lifted, but the prohibition on
sour milk persists until after her first child is born.

Other rites

Kohler's description is in outline applicable to the general run of Nguni weddings, but some other rites are often described in addition. Kohler is unusual in the lack of emphasis he gives to the slaughter of an ox for the bride by the husband's family, on the day of the main wedding dance. Most other descriptions emphasize this event and the associated customs. Fuze's (1979:36–7) description (of the Zulu rite) may stand for many:

> the bridesmaids slaughter the *umbhubuzo* beast (*bhubuza* means to steal or capture) in honour of the bride. They do the selecting themselves . . . if the person who stabs it (who is always a man of the husband's family) does so without killing it outright, it is a serious fault, and the spear with which he stabbed becomes the bride's, to be redeemed with a forfeit . . . The beast is slaughtered as the bridesmaids chant, 'May it rise! Yes, may it rise!'

It must then be carefully skinned, and the bride should puncture the stomach herself. She is smeared with the gall. Other authors stress that the gall-bladder of the ox is tied to her wrist, and add that the husband's father must cover the wounds of the ox with white beads.

Other descriptions also often stress that the bride pretends to run away during the wedding; or even that men from her village mount a ceremonial rescue attempt. Among the Zulu she may, on the morning after she has slept with her husband, creep with her bridesmaids to the cattle-byre and pretend to escape with the cattle (e.g. Braatvedt, 1927: 562). The bride may also be 'abducted' at the start, rather than presenting herself at her future husband's home. Such an 'abduction' (*thwala*) is particularly common among the Cape Nguni (see, e.g., Van Tromp, 1948:64–75). It is often planned by the girl's father because '"her parents do not like to hear their daughter cry". When a girl leaves her home to be married she is obliged by custom to weep and make a fuss about going' (Hunter, 1936:188).

The Cape Nguni stress another ceremonial event which is rarely reported for other Nguni. This is the ritual unveiling of the bride and her bridesmaids on the main wedding day. The bride and her bridesmaids are brought into the cattle-byre, where they must kneel on a mat and uncover their bodies for the inspection and comments of the men. They then withdraw, the bride leaving a present, traditionally a spear, under the mat for the ancestors. The unveiling is then repeated in one of the huts for the benefit of the women of the homestead.

Sotho-Tswana weddings: Hoffmann's account

A good description of Sotho-Tswana wedding ceremonies[4] to set
beside that provided by Kohler for the Nguni, is given by Hoffmann
(1913) in texts collected among the Northern Sotho.

Hoffmann's informants begin with marriage to a mother's brother's
daughter, the preferred form. After his initiation a young man is
given a spear by his mother's brother. This represents a promise that
he will be allowed to marry the uncle's (perhaps still unborn) daughter.
In due course he delivers the bridewealth for her, and the mother's
brother slaughters an ox for him and hangs its stomach fat in strips around
his neck and the necks of his intermediaries and of the bridesmaids.

Where an unrelated girl is being courted, the man's father opens
negotiations through male intermediaries. If the approach is acceptable
the girl's family sends a woman intermediary with a present of snuff-
tobacco. This indicates that the engagement is agreed, and that cattle
must now be paid for bridewealth.

The cattle are delivered by a party from the groom's home, and
after extra demands are made by the bride's family, they are accepted.
One is then slaughtered, and the groom's party is feasted and given
beer. Although Hoffmann's informants do not repeat this, the groom
or his representatives are festooned with the innards of the ox killed
by the bride's father.

There follows a period during which the suitor and a male friend
periodically visit the fiancée's home, staying overnight and being
entertained by the girls of the homestead. The man is impatient to
take his promised wife home, but the girl's parents are evasive. A
woman intermediary is sent and is told that more cattle must be paid,
a cow for the mother and an ox for the father of the bride (cf. Jacottet,
1896:115). Then yet another ox may be demanded from the young
man. He may also be asked to build a house for the girl's parents,
finally demanding her from its rooftop. Eventually — after perhaps a
year of visits by the man to his fiancée and the repeated demands of her
parents — they agree that he can take his bride home.

The girl now displays reluctance. She must be enticed from her hut
with gifts, and so to the entrance of her father's homestead, and,
gradually, to the home of her new husband — constantly resisting,
constantly being lured on by gifts.

At the home of the groom the bridesmaids who accompany the
bride collect firewood and are given meat to eat. The people of the

homestead celebrate and dance: but after two or three days the girls go home again, taking the bride with them. Eventually she returns, without a fuss, bringing a present of beer; but she returns to her parents again when she first menstruates at her new home and when she finds herself pregnant with her first child.

When she leaves his home the bride's father makes a long speech, stressed by many sources (though not by Hoffmann's informants), and corresponding to the speech made by the father of the Nguni groom when the bride is presented at his home. The Sotho father begins by warning his daughter against all the accusations which will be levelled at her — that she is lazy, adulterous, even a witch. Then:

> Look after your husband, he has *lobola*'d you with cattle; spread mats for him; get up early in the morning and draw water; you must boil it so that it washes your husband; you must cook porridge for your husband, you must make light beer on seeing your husband hungry . . . You must look after your mother-in-law, and pour for her light beer; and pour for your father-in-law light beer . . .
> (Ziervogel, 1954:91 — a Pai (Eastern Sotho) text)

The ceremonies compared

Some reports of Southern Bantu marriage ceremonies diverge from the type-cases I have presented on various points. There is often not enough evidence to be sure whether these variations are significant or whether they can be written off (for present purposes) as the product of Christian influence, observer bias, or other extraneous factors. Some variants are clearly significant, and will be discussed, but in general I judge the descriptions of Kohler and Hoffmann (with the additions already noted) to be reasonably representative. The Venda (e.g. Stayt, 1931:142-52) correspond closely to the Sotho-Tswana form, but the Tsonga (e.g. Junod, 1927, I:101-25) appear to have developed an intermediate ceremonial structure.

Comparing these two ceremonial types the first point to stress is that they both refer constantly to the cosmological ideas discussed in an earlier chapter. The roles of ancestors, cattle, men, women, beer hardly need comment. The identification in many contexts of the bride's party as female and of the groom's party as male is evident. A more detailed consideration of the rites would reveal the rich symbolic references to these cosmological ideas encoded in the use of colours, times of day, spatial relations, etc.[5]

I wish, however, to concentrate on the way in which the two sets of ceremonies diverge, for this brings me to the social relations being ritualized. The divergences are striking and systematic: it is not too much to say that the Nguni and Sotho-Tswana marriage ceremonials represent systematic transformations of each other. Not only do the Nguni emphasize the delivery of the bride and de-emphasize the delivery of the bridewealth, while the Sotho-Tswana ritualize the delivery of the bridewealth cattle rather than the arrival of the bride at her new home. The transformations apply even to the detailed stages of the ceremonies. The following table makes some of the more evident contrasts:

	NGUNI	SOTHO-TSWANA
Preliminaries	Girl chooses lover.[6]	Man chooses girl.
	Girl visits man for love-making.	Man visits girl for love-making.
	The girl's party presses for the completion of the bridewealth payment.	The man's party presses for the transfer of the the bride.
Main ceremony	*Delivery of the bride.*	*Delivery of the bridewealth.*
	At the groom's home.	At the bride's home.
	Groom's father kills ox; bride covered with its bile and wears its gall-bladder.	Bride's father kills an ox; groom (or representative) is covered with bile and wears its gall-bladder.
	Groom's father makes main speech.	Bride's father makes the main speech.
Aftermath	New bride isolated from her parents and avoids her in-laws (*hlonipha*).[7]	Bride's integration is eased by regular visits home and by reasonably easy relations with her in-laws.

The obvious question to pose is, what do these ceremonial contrasts 'say' about the formal relationships between the parties of bride and groom?

Status difference

Examining the Southern Bantu data, one might guess that the Nguni, who ceremonially give the initiative to the bride and her party, expect the bride to be marrying down, while the Sotho-Tswana, who ceremonially give the initiative to the groom and his father, expect the bride to be marrying up. Alternatively (following Bloch's (1978) suggestion) one might suspect that the ritual inverts the real status relationships.

In fact the situation is more complicated. Among the Nguni alone various contrasting status relations are expected and ritualized. Among the Zulu, for example, the expectation is that the parties will be equal; or, as one informant put it: 'Both think that they are superior, and each therefore is very strict about their due respect from the other' (E. J. Krige, 1936:153n). The Zulu term for one's child's parents-in-law is *umlingane wami*, my equal. Krige stresses that in the wedding ceremonies among the Zulu 'the most noticeable fact is the rivalry between the two parties, which culminates in the wedding dances ... Each group tries to show the other its superiority, and the bride and bridegroom each have the support of their whole kraal' (1936:138). She cites a vivid description of the *uMcwayo* competition during singing –

> The performers sit on the ground, their bodies thrown into all sorts of positions, the arms moved about in different ways, all being done with the object of seeing who can perspire most. A kind of rivalry is started between the visitors and the visited. I have on such occasions seen the perspiration actually running in two streams from the doorway. The one party having done their level best, the floor is swept clear of perspiration and the other party have their innings.
> (E. J. Krige, 1936:131)

The parties also insult each other in the often obscene *qhubushela* songs, and genuine fights may break out. Only with the marriage feast is there 'an end to the antagonism and henceforth there is only interchange of presents between the two groups, and efforts at friendliness' (E. J. Krige, 1936:122).

Among the Swazi, in contrast, the expectation is that a woman will marry an equal or an inferior, and the marriage ceremonies stress the superiority of the bride and her family.[8] At every stage they must be courted by the groom and his family, whom they treat with elaborate disdain. They insult their hosts, who cannot retaliate but rather placate them with gifts.

The Cape Nguni are different again. Among the Xhosa, and possibly more generally in the Cape, 'There seems to be a general rule that a woman should marry a man of her own status or one of higher status;

but a man may, without shame to himself or his family, marry a woman of lower status than himself' (Van Tromp, 1948:31). Their wedding ceremonies imply the inferior standing of the bride. On arrival the bridal party is abused and even ritually attacked, and it cannot retaliate in kind. (The bride's parents never accompany her to her wedding.) The bride's party gives presents to the groom's, even, for example, in order to be allowed to enter the cattle-byre for the main part of the ceremony.

To sum up, then, the expectations of relative status of the parties to the marriage vary among the Nguni, and these expectations are expressed in the ceremonial, but within the framework of the general Nguni assumption that the initiative is normally taken by the bride or her father, and that the central drama is that of her transfer to the groom's home.

Among the Sotho-Tswana there are indications that a similar range of possibilities is to be found. Ashton, for example, reports that among the Southern Sotho a woman is expected to marry an equal or an inferior (1952:15), but the wedding ceremonies do not obviously reflect this. There is at least some stress on competition and equality. For example, after the bridewealth has been agreed and accepted the bride's father slaughters an ox, which is cut up competitively. 'The girl's people skin the left side of the beast and the boy's the right; all work fast, for it is said that the side to finish first will dominate their future relations' (Ashton, 1952:68). That night the young people flirt but the older people meet in another hut, facing each other and engaging in ceremonial banter. 'Later a special pot of beer is brought in and this brings the raillery to an end. The beer is placed exactly between the two groups and meticulously shared out, an unusual feature being that each group has its own server' (p. 69).

One might argue that here at least, as Bloch suggests, the status difference is formally denied in the ritual; but if the Southern Sotho are the only Sotho-Tswana group for whom a tendency towards hypergamy has been reported, they are also the only Sotho-Tswana group amongst whom the brideprice is set by the wife's family. (See Poulter, 1976:91.) Elsewhere among the Sotho-Tswana there is, if anything, a slight tendency to expect the bride to marry up (as in father's younger brother's daughter marriage, a favoured marriage type), and the brideprice is always set by the groom's party.

It should be noted that there are often differences, relevant to this problem, between the ceremonies of aristocrats and commoners. However, there is in my view insufficient material to establish the precise nature of these variations.

The conclusion seems to be that while expectations of status differences between the families of bride and groom may be expressed in the ceremonials, these differences cross-cut the Sotho-Tswana/Nguni opposition, and so cannot account for the systematic contrasts which have been identified between the Nguni and the Sotho-Tswana and Venda marriage ceremonies.

The boundaries of affinity

The other obvious variable to consider is the presence or absence of a preferential marriage rule. Broadly, the Sotho-Tswana prefer first-cousin marriage, particularly (at least for commoners) mother's brother's daughter marriage; while the Nguni ban cousin marriage. There are exceptions. The Southern Transvaal Ndebele retain their Nguni language but favour matrilateral cross-cousin marriage. Their marriage ceremonies are 'Sotho-Tswana' in form, suggesting either that there is indeed a correlation between the type of marriage rule and the wedding ceremony (at least in this culture area), or else that the Southern Transvaal Ndebele are simply more acculturated to Sotho custom than has sometimes been believed to be the case (cf. Van Warmelo, 1974:67).

The Swazi case is more complex. The Swazi prefer a form of second cross-cousin marriage which they interpret as 'grandmother' marriage, since it repeats the alliance of a man's grandfather. This is reflected in the wedding ceremony. When the bridewealth cattle are delivered, the groom's party announce, 'We *lobola* a grandparent' (H. Kuper, 1945: 153). An old woman from the groom's homestead:

> suddenly bent double, wriggled like a snake, beat her head and lay still. The *umtsimba* stopped their mournful *mekeza*, clapped their hands, and sang: 'Grandmother dies. Who will cook for us?'
> Whereupon the bride placed a string of beads on the old woman's head and a new blanket round her shoulders. The girls shouted: 'Wake, granny!' The old woman stood up energetically and admired her presents. (H. Kuper, 1945:152. Cf. Ziervogel, 1944:52)

Apart from these direct evocations of the preferential marriage rule, however, there is nothing in the Swazi marriage ceremonies to suggest that the bride is less of a stranger than among other Nguni.

Such exceptions to one side, are there grounds for thinking that the preferential marriages rules of the Nguni and the Sotho-Tswana are integrally related to their respective wedding ceremonial forms? The alternative possibility is that they are linked by historical accident only, representing two more or less independent elements of a particular cultural tradition, like a characteristic form of pottery and a taboo on eating fish. The transformations I identified between the Nguni and Sotho-Tswana ceremonial forms may be significant merely as ethnic markers.

One obvious connection between the marriage rules and the ceremonial forms is that the Nguni wife is expected to be a stranger, while the Sotho-Tswana wife is expected to be a relative (cf. Preston-Whyte, 1974:204-5). This is reflected in Nguni marriage ceremonies. To take some obvious examples, the bride is sometimes forcibly 'abducted', she may be treated as a captive, though often an honoured captive, she is sometimes ceremonially 'rescued', she may try to flee, etc. Afterwards she endures a long period of liminality, marked by *hlonipha* observances, before being integrated into her new home.

The Sotho-Tswana also stress the reluctance of the girl to leave her parental home, but the break is not so marked or final, and the social distance she must travel not so great.

Another factor is less immediately obvious. I have suggested that one of the key differences between the Nguni and the Sotho-Tswana marriage rules is that they imply a different evolution of affinal relations in time. The Sotho-Tswana marriage ideally implies future marriages with the same family. Indeed, these may be sealed in the previous generation. The Nguni marriage, in contrast, normally excludes automatically any future intermarriage in the next generation, and certainly does not imply such future marriages (the Swazi and Southern Transvaal Ndebele apart).

This contrast suggests that there is also an integral link with the central drama emphasized by each cultural tradition in wedding ceremonies. The Nguni ritualize the initiation of the marriage, the transfer of the bride; the Sotho-Tswana emphasize the completion of the marriage, the payment of the brideprice, the marriage having been initiated when the participants were children. The two ceremonies appear to contrast more strongly than they do, perhaps, because the real transformation is between two stages through which they all pass: one marking the transfer of the bride, the other marking the handing over of the brideprice. These balance each other and are distinguished by ritual inversions of each other. The Sotho-Tswana and Nguni differ so much in their wedding ceremonies, therefore, because they stress different moments of the process, so concentrating their ceremonial on one or other of the two transfers which make up every Southern Bantu wedding.

This may clarify also the Nguni tendency to stress the initiative of the bride and her father, and the Sotho-Tswana tendency to give the formal initiative to the groom and his party. These initiatives are appropriate to the two parts of the wedding. In the transfer of the bride she and her father have the initiative. This is the dominant theme among the Nguni, but among the Sotho-Tswana the muted ceremony of bride transfer still occurs very much at the moment chosen by the bride's father, who tantalizes the groom by dangling the promise of delivery before him for months. In the transfer of the bridewealth cattle the groom's party has the initiative. This is the dominant theme of Sotho-Tswana marriage ceremonies,[9] but again among the Nguni the delivery of the cattle is done on the initiative of the groom's party, the bride's party being passive and supplicant.

Valuable confirmation of the argument is provided by linguistic data. I asked the linguist Dr Erhard Voeltz what to make of the Nguni usage whereby a woman is said to choose her husband, while he is chosen or causes her to choose. He replied:

The two words [Sotho and Zulu] that we choose to equate with the English 'marry' . . . represent different stages in a process, that of becoming married, rather than the single act. Thus, the Zulu:- *gana* marry, choose a husband, constitutes the earlier step. Cf. the Sotho cognate: – *kana*, to choose a boy or girl in a game. Now, the Sotho: – *nyala* pay brideprice, marry, is to be compared, properly speaking, with the Zulu: – *lobola* 'pay brideprice'.

The difference between the two has only secondarily something to do with who chooses, etc., but rather [with] at what point one considers the 'marriage' to have taken place.

10   The system on the ground: the homestead layout

Circular plans

Some years ago one of the very few structuralist anthropologists to contribute to Southern African studies complained that 'Aucune étude n'a encore été consacrée à l'organisation spatiale et aux relations qu'elle implique chez les Bantu du Sud-Est' (Roumeguère-Eberhardt, 1963:77). This was not strictly accurate. For example, Holleman (1940) had provided an important analysis of the Zulu homestead, borrowing something of the methods and concerns of the Leiden school's studies in Indonesia; and one cannot ignore Walton's (1956) wide-ranging if unsystematic treatment of the Southern African village. Yet the topic has been largely neglected[1] despite the highly-ordered nature of the Southern Bantu homestead and the legal and symbolic significance of the traditional homestead plan.

I shall begin with the arrangement of women's quarters around the cattle-byre in Nguni societies, a matter which caused serious problems for the compilers of Codes of Native Law a century ago (see, for example, Kerr, 1961:42-6).

The arrangement of the huts shown in Figure 11 is superficially similar, but the differences in detail are suggestive. There are four basic variations. First, the entrance to the cattle-byre may be placed facing or opposite the wives (though an additional private entry may be provided at the top of the cattle-byre of an important man, among Zulu and Swazi). Second, the placement of the second and third senior women varies, both absolutely and in relation to the relative distinction between 'right' and 'left' sides of the homestead. Third, the absolute positioning of 'right' and 'left' is not fixed. And fourth (though this cannot be read from the diagram) there is variation as to the description of the senior woman, A, who occupies the *indlunkulu* or 'great hut'. She may be a 'mother' or a 'great wife', or first a 'mother' and then a 'great wife'. It should be stressed that there is no obvious linking of the variables: thus Bomvana and Zulu reverse each other's orientation of the cattle-byre and of right and left sections, but have the same organization of second and third senior wives; the Mpondo share the Bomvana orientation of the byre, but reverse their denomination of right and left and of the second and third senior wives; the Swazi share the form of layout of the Mpondo, except that they reverse the orientation of the byre; and so on.

Despite this apparently wilful amount of play (perhaps not without significance in the marking of ethnic identity) an underlying regularity is evident in the spatial organization of the homestead. The circular or semicircular plan is ordered (to follow Lévi-Strauss's (1956) usage) both diametrically and concentrically. This yields in the first instance two basic spatial oppositions: between 'right' and 'left', and between the centre and the sides. The right/left opposition orders wives by seniority; the centre/sides opposition contrasts kinsfolk and wives.

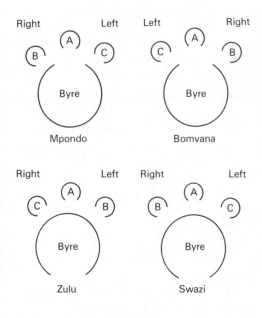

The letters A, B, C indicate the order of
seniority of the women

FIGURE 11 *Arrangement of women's quarters around the cattle-byre (Nguni)*

The centre/sides dichotomy is particularly stressed by the Swazi, and the significance of this opposition overrides that between right and left. This is associated with the fact that the Swazi do not designate a 'great wife' (the mother of the heir) while the headman lives, and insist that the great hut be occupied by the headman's 'mother'. Thus:

> In charge of the great hut is the most important woman of the household — the mother of the headman, or if she is dead, a substitute 'mother'. Wives are not as rigidly organized into two or three major units as among the typical Nguni, their placement depending largely on the whim of the headman. (H. Kuper, 1952: 16–17)

Yet the right/left opposition does not completely disappear. Marwick (1940:28-9) described a right/left arrangement of wives (reflected in Figure 13), and Hughes devoted a special appendix to the problem, concluding that while:

> in the ceremonially significant royal Homesteads a clear distinction is drawn between the 'right' and 'left' hand sides . . . most Swazi are completely unconcerned as to which are the 'right' and 'left' hand sides of their own Homesteads . . . The evidence of informants is contradictory . . . (Hughes, 1972:338-9)

Among the other Nguni groups, on the contrary, the right/left opposition is dominant, and sometimes the separate existence of a central 'great house' is elided. However, the centre/sides dichotomy normally remains as a secondary theme. Thus Holleman drew attention to the tendency of the Zulu initially to identify the great hut with the mother. (Cf. Mayr, 1906:458.) When she dies the great wife moves into the *indlunkulu*, but its association with a kinsman of another generation is maintained through the institution of the *uyise wabantu* ('Father of the kraal-people'), described as:

> a peculiar figure in the kraal . . . the first son of the fifth wife of the head, who lives as a second inhabitant of the main hut with the *inkosikazi enkulu* ('mother'). It is said of him that he stands *emadlozini*, by the ancestor spirits, that he is the keeper of the old hearth-stones, the guardian of the old kraal.
> While the older brothers are potential heads of new homesteads, he continues with the old, to which he is bound fast . . . (Holleman, 1940:36)

The Bomvana and Xhosa tend to stress a simple dichotomy between the 'great house' and 'right-hand house', and even where a 'left-hand house' is instituted 'in character it ranks as an additional support of the great house' (Soga, 1931:54). However, important chiefs may turn back, though less forcefully, to the idea of a house which represents the historical and kinship-based continuity of the homestead, and set up a 'House of the Grandfathers', a *Xiba* house.

> If a chief found that he had already nominated the various houses and ranked them, but was desirous of magnifying the honour of a wife, he would put this wife in his, the chief's, own mother's kraal. The son of this wife now ranks as a younger brother of the chief, his father. (Cook, 1931:16; cf. Soga, 1931:50, 54)

Thus, as Holleman stressed for the Zulu:

> The Nguni homestead should not be divided only into two halves, the *uhlangothi* and the *isibay' esikhulu* (i.e. right and left), but for greater accuracy must be divided also into the old and permanent (*indlunkulu*) and the young, which is destined to split off (the two sections and their huts). (1940:36–7)

The relative stress laid on these two principles varies, and their coexistence seems intrinsically fragile. Ideologically, the Swazi stress is on the continuity of the homestead, and this is reflected in a preferential marriage rule, with FMBSD (father's mother's brother's son's daughter), each headman's heir-producing marriage therefore ideally repeating that of his father's father (see Chapter 7 above). Among the Bomvana and Xhosa, in contrast, homestead fission is a built-in expectation, continuity underplayed. Soga speaks of the right-hand house among the Xhosa being 'almost co-equal in rank' with the great house, enjoying 'a semi-independent character and constitution, the object of whose existence is to spread out the tribe on a two current basis . . .' (1931:56). The Zulu seem to lie between the two extremes, though at different stages of the development cycle of the homestead the relative weighting of the two principles changes.

Swazi models

These dimensions of the homestead structure only provide a preliminary orientation, however. In order to elaborate the analysis it is necessary briefly to concentrate upon one particular system, and I have selected the Swazi because the ethnography is particularly rich. Hilda Kuper,

Marwick and Ziervogel all provide descriptions of the Swazi homestead in the 1930s and 1940s, particularly the large aristocratic homestead, and they permit us an inside view of some fundamental Swazi conceptions. Their descriptions are of the Swazi homestead a generation ago, when 'the average number of occupants per homestead was 7.2 for commoners and 22.5 for aristocrats' (H. Kuper, 1952:16).

The sketches of Nguni homesteads in Figure 11 represented only the homes of the women and their orientation about the cattle-byre. This simplified view of reality reflects the descriptions given by some informants, but Hilda Kuper was echoing the terms of another common indigenous model when she wrote that 'In each homestead or local division there are three key structures: the *sibaya* (cattle-byre), *indlunkulu* (great hut), and *lilawu* (bachelors' quarters)' (1947:38). The wives are absent in this model, the headman represented as a bachelor. This needs some comment. In contrast to other Nguni, the Swazi headman is not associated with the hut of a particular wife, and ethnographers working before the last war commented that as an innovation some married men were only just beginning to establish private married quarters for themselves. Marwick (1940:21–2) records a headman building such a hut for himself and making it *rectangular*, i.e. symbolically modern in form. The Swazi emphasize that the headman occupies the *lilawu* himself if he is unmarried, and that if he remarries and establishes a homestead apart from his mother this is also merely a *lilawu* in relation to the main homestead with his mother's *indlunkulu* (H. Kuper, 1947:39). Translating the texts of a Swazi noble, Ziervogel (1957:14) produced a diagram of the Swazi homestead representing precisely the elements picked out by Hilda Kuper. (See Figure 12.) In this model, then, the emphasis is entirely upon the elements of continuity in the homestead, and thus upon the headman/mother relationship; the wives are excluded. One might almost say that in this model the development cycle of the domestic group is frozen at an early stage.

The exclusion of affines in this model is more thorough than may seem apparent at first glance. Both the *indlunkulu* and the cattle-byre are associated among the Swazi with the ancestors and the kin of the headman, and with the exclusion of affines. Thus:

> The 'great hut', often decorated with skulls of cattle sacrificed to the headman's ancestors, is used as the family shrine: in the rear, the headman offers libations of beer and meat . . . The shrine is

specifically dedicated to the headman's senior paternal relatives . . .
While daughters-in-law must avoid the 'great hut' out of respect,
their children may even sleep in it . . . (H. Kuper, 1963:19–20)

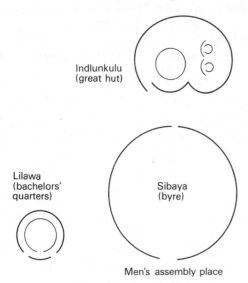

FIGURE 12 *Ziervogel's sketch of the Swazi homestead (after Ziervogel, 1957, 14)*

Similarly, wives are excluded from the cattle-byre. Moreover, just as
married sisters of the headman are symbolically represented by cattle
in the byre which were received as brideprice for them, so wives are
associated with cattle which have left the byre as brideprice. Dead
headmen are buried in the byre, and their spirits are invoked there by
day as they are in the *indlunkulu* by night. Cattle are sacrificed to them.

A consideration of this model directs attention to the relationship,
neglected so far, between the *indlunkulu* (the great hut) and the cattle-
byre. To understand this, a third dimension must be charted, again
diametric, but crossing the right/left line at right-angles. This is an
opposition between 'up' and 'down', or west and east. Among all the
Nguni, the cattle-byre is built to the east of the *indlunkulu*, or if the
homestead is built on sloping ground, as is preferred, it is built below.
(Cf. Shaw and van Warmelo, 1972:25 et *passim*.) Thus the great hut
and the cattle-byre are opposed as west to east or as 'up' to 'down'.
The *lilawu* stands to these structures as 'side' to 'centre', and Marwick

(1940:28) places the bachelors' quarters 'always at the tip of the crescent which forms the *kunene* (right) side of the village', which is where it appears in Ziervogel's sketch and other diagrams. Indeed, all the other dwelling huts are opposed to the *indlunkulu* along two dimensions, as 'down' or east to 'up' or west, and as 'sides' to 'centre'; while the bachelors' hut is again opposed to the wives' huts as 'down' or east to 'up' or west, and perhaps as 'right' to 'left'. (See Figure 13.)

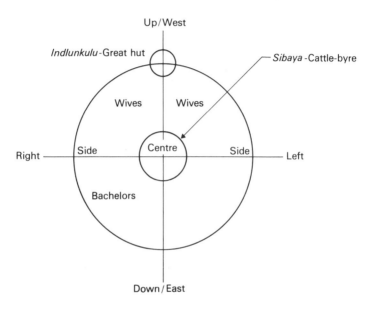

FIGURE 13 *The symbolic dimensions of the Swazi homestead*

The Nguni hut

Like the homestead, the hut (beehive or rondavel) is circular in plan, and the layout of hut and homestead have much in common, although the hut has its special features too. Within the circular hut, the Nguni stress a right/left division, 'right' being very generally associated with men, 'left' with women. The right/left orientation is, seen as it were from above, the reverse of the right/left orientation of the homestead. That this principle is systematically applied may be judged from the example of Bomvana. It will be remembered that the Bomvana homestead reverses the right/left orientation of the Swazi, Zulu and Mpondo.

The Bomvana hut again reverses the orientation of the Bomvana homestead (or, at least, the left side of the hut as one enters is the male, the
right the female — we do not know how they are designated by the
Bomvana) (see Figure 15).

Other already familiar dimensions are also invoked. The rear of the
hut is a raised sacred area, associated with the ancestors. At the centre
is a raised hearth, with three hearthstones, one of which points to the
back, is sacred, associated with the ancestors, and never moved. Visitors
stay near the entry, and dogs sleep there. (See, for example, Hunter,
1936:38; Marwick, 1940:32; and Berglund, 1975:102-4.) There is thus
a central line drawn through the hut, with the most sacred position on
it the rear (and thus probably western-most) spot.

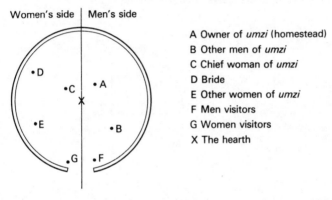

FIGURE 14 *A group of people in a Mpondo hut (Hunter, 1936:38)*

That the right/left opposition is subject to modification through the
superimposition of a centre/sides dichotomy is nicely illustrated in
Monica Hunter's sketch of the positions assumed by a group of people
in a Mpondo hut (Figure 14). The husband and his chief wife sit on the
male and female sides respectively, but both are also closest to the centre
and (with the exception of the bride) nearest to the rear of the hut.

Although these principles are very general, there is again room for
variation. The right/left opposition may encode relative seniority rather
than gender. Thus Jenkinson (1882:38n) noted that if a headman sits
in a hut with his sons he will sit on the right, the sons on the left; but
that if he leaves the hut, the senior son will move to sit on the right.
Hunter pointed out that in contrast to the Mpondo, the Xhosa divide

the hut into a back half, in which the men sit, and a front half, in which the women sit (1936:38). The Bomvana vary the Mpondo pattern in a different way. The right-hand side, as one enters a hut, is the female section, the left-hand side the male section. There is also an inner/outer division, such that the inner part of each section is peculiarly the domain of the husband and wife respectively (Figure 15a). But if a new-fangled door is installed, which is so hinged that it swings inwards into the man's section, then the wife's place is no longer the inner part of the woman's section, but rather the outer part of the man's section. The husband keeps his place, and the traditionally female half of the hut is set aside for the children and male visitors (Cook, 1931:159–61). Here, therefore, the inner/outer opposition comes to override the right/left opposition, 'inner' being redefined by the inward-opening door which provides an inner half, itself divided into front and rear.

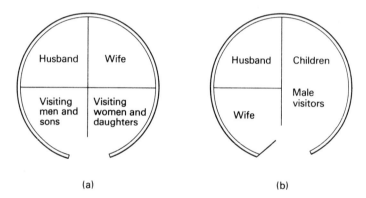

(a)   (b)

FIGURE 15 *The effect of a door opening inwards on the organization of a Bomvana hut*

The Nguni and the Sotho-Tswana models

Despite superficial (but interesting and suggestive) variations, the Nguni homesteads all share a fundamentally similar spatial idiom, which gives meaning to, and governs, their physical arrangement. Indeed, the variations themselves help reveal the ordered nature of the underlying structure, a point to which I shall return.

All the Nguni homesteads may be represented by two underlying plans, one concentric and one diametric. In the concentric representation, the centre is opposed to the side or the periphery, and the inner is contrasted with the outer. In the diametric representations, there is a longitudinal opposition between 'right' and 'left', and a latitudinal opposition between west (or 'up') and east (or 'down'). Variations between the systems occur in two ways. First, different dimensions may be given greater or lesser prominence, and second, the social relationships associated with particular spatial dimensions may vary from system to system, or even in different contexts within one system. For example, although the right/left opposition recurs constantly, it may in some contexts or systems be overriden by another opposition: by the centre/side opposition in the Swazi homestead, or the inner/ outer opposition in the strange case of the Bomvana hut with the modern door. Moreover, one cannot know in advance whether the right/left opposition will be used to symbolize an opposition between male and female or between senior and junior; nor even which term of the social opposition will be identified as 'right' or 'left', or which half of a circle will be defined as 'right' or 'left'.

Although the spatial concepts of the Nguni have not systematically been examined before, the conclusion that a common 'Nguni' system exists is not surprising. The broad identity of the Nguni cultures is generally recognized. It is perhaps more interesting to discover the same underlying structures among the Sotho-Tswana, particularly in view of the conventional though not wholly reliable opposition between the stereotypically isolated Nguni homesteads and the agglomerated Sotho-Tswana villages. Of course, there were traditionally isolated Southern Sotho homesteads, and this is a settlement pattern found among even Tswana chieftaincies at times of weak central leadership, when the town dissolves (cf. A. Kuper, 1975a:144–6). There were also agglomerated settlements in some Nguni chieftaincies and states, with settlements in Swaziland of up to 3,000 in the nineteenth century (H. Jones, 1968: 12). Even in the Cape the modern one-family homestead is perhaps a new development. Hunter (1932:681) for example remarks that 'Within the memory of living men in Pondoland, it was usual for twenty or more married men, related in the male line, to live together in one *umzi*'. I would be inclined to argue that agglomeration and dispersal of settlements has more to do with political conditions than with cultural differences within the Southern Bantu cluster, but it must none the less be admitted that while the spatial arrangements of the now relatively simple southeastern homesteads yield fairly easily to analysis, the superficial complexity of the generally more agglomerated northern and western settlements seem to pose problems of a different order. In the event, by applying the analytical principles developed for the Nguni the most complex Sotho-Tswana settlement plan becomes quickly comprehensible.

The Pedi form a convenient bridge to the Sotho-Tswana. Like most Nguni they arrange their homesteads to reflect the ranking of wives. Mönnig (1967:212-13) explained:

> Ideally the Pedi consider that a polygamist should build the home-steads of his wives in a specified order according to rank. A man should build the *lapa* of his second wife on the left of that of the first wife, and immediately adjoining it, so that one outside wall serves for both homesteads. The third wife's *lapa* is then built on the right of the superior homestead. Subsequent wives then have their homestead alternately to the left and the right. This has the effect, due to the building pattern, of the homesteads forming a semi-circle, with the superior homesteads in the middle. (Cf. Harries, 1929:30-1, who opposes the senior 'leg' and junior 'arm' houses.)

The various Nguni people differed in the designation of 'right' and 'left' sections of the homestead, and the Pedi themselves are of two minds, Mönnig remarking a difference of opinion among the Pedi as to whether the superior or male arm is the left or the right arm. Some argue that the right arm is the superior arm, and that the arrange-ment of huts should be viewed from within the main household, looking towards the entrance.

> The more established view is, however, that the more important side is a man's left arm, the arm with which he shields his family . . . In any case, there is no difference of opinion as to where the various homesteads of a polygamist should be placed, and the difference of opinion is only on whether the superior or inferior sides are established by facing towards the unit or away from it. (1967:213)

There is also a lack of agreement as to whether the homestead should be divided into a principal homestead as well as superior and inferior wings, or simply into the two wings (*ibid.*). These ambiguities characterize the Nguni literature as well, and bear witness perhaps to the very fundamental similarity of the symbolic idioms being employed.

However, there are differences. Characteristically for many Sotho-Tswana, the Pedi homestead is focused not on a cattle-byre but on a male arena, which may include a byre within it. The displacement, or partial displacement, of the cattle-byre by the *kgotla* (or *kgoro*), the men's assembly place, reflects the political shift in many Sotho-Tswana communities to a larger-scale decision-making unit. As between the Nguni and Sotho-Tswana the change in spatial organization is not crucial, the area around the entrance of the cattle-byre, or between the cattle-byre and the great hut serving similarly as a public male arena among the Nguni. Shaw and van Warmelo note (1972:35) that the name for this space, *ikundla*, 'is etymologically the same word as *kgotla* found in the Sotho languages of the interior, meaning "courtyard, public or men's place in village" ... Not found in language clusters further north. Connected with the southern African layout of villages'. (Cf. H. Kuper, 1972.)

A superficially more significant difference is that the Pedi, again like many Sotho-Tswana, generally group homesteads into wards or villages. However, these larger agglomerations are based upon the same spatial principles as have been found to operate in the layout of the homestead. The Pedi homesteads, for example, are arranged in wards on the same basis as huts are grouped in homesteads. The homestead of the headman is placed in the centre, with that of the next senior family on his right, the third on his left, and so forth (Mönnig, 1967:222).

Even more striking is the fact that similar principles underlie the grouping of wards to make large towns, typically among the Tswana. Schapera has described how a generation ago Kanye, one of the Tswana capitals, was divided into three main sections into which wards were grouped. The first section, *fa gare* (in the centre) or *kgosing* (at the chief's place), incorporated the main council place and the chief's ward, which was beside it, as well as other affiliated wards. Then:

> On either side of the central division are the two divisions jointly termed *dintlha* (sing. *ntlha*) and more specifically *ntlha ya godimo* 'the upper (or right-hand) side', and *ntlha ya tlase*, 'the lower (or left-hand) side'.
>
> The 'upper side' is usually to the west, and the 'lower side' to the east, of the Chief's *kgotla*. (Schapera, 1943:70)

These are the same diametric oppositions as underlie the homestead layout of the Nguni; and here too a concentric arrangement is present as a counterpoint, for in each section the nobles live close to the central council place, while the commoners are ranged behind them, introducing an 'inner'/'outer' opposition.

I do not think it necessary to pursue the argument in detail. That even the Tswana, in whose towns tens of thousands of people live, think of residential space in the same symbolic terms as southeastern Nguni, who live in small scattered homesteads, is apparent enough from a consideration of the following passage. Written by the missionary scholar W. C. Willoughby, an authority on Tswana religious ideas, it relates the locational notions we have been discussing in a way which (given different vernacular terms) could equally apply to any Nguni people a generation ago:

> Godimo means 'above', 'high', and *legodimo* is their word for 'sky' . . . But *godimo* has other meanings. *Godimo* and *bophirimatsatsi* are convertible terms for 'west' . . . , and the former, denoting the quarter from which their streams flow, is oftener heard than the latter, which points to the place of the setting sun . . . the houses of a chief's sons are located according to their standing in the family, that of the heir being on his father's right hand, west of the chief's dwelling and consequently described by this word *godimo*, though it may not be on higher land . . . To sum up in a sentence, the meaning of this very wide term, *godimo*, may be 'overhead', or 'higher up', or 'west', or 'on the right-hand of the chief' – this last being a synonym for 'superior status'. (Willoughby, 1928:67-8)

Here, however, in contrast to the Nguni, the senior man occupies the easternmost location.

Transformations and other codes

The symbolical importance of homestead layout is naturally recognized, and consequently open to manipulation. Diviners often invert the layout of their homesteads as they reverse modes of dress and other conventions (e.g. Berglund, 1975:371). In 1957 two scholars visited the original and imaginative Zulu philosopher Laduma Madela, and particularly commented on the dramatic appearance of his homestead:

> Laduma's kraal was then without a cattle-pen. A dense ring of wattle trees completely screened the huts from view, whereas in the average kraal there is not even a fence to hide them. The path leading to Laduma's kraal approached it from above, unlike all other kraals which must be approached from below. The distribution of huts . . . was the very reverse of the normal pattern. Laduma's residence was at the bottom of the kraal, the visitor's hut at the top, while the women's huts . . . lay between them on various levels of the steep

site . . . Undoubtedly the set-up of the homestead would strike the ordinary Zulu caller with astonishment and awe. (Bodenstein and Raum, 1960:166)

Comparably systematic and thorough-going transformations of the underlying idiom may be anticipated even today, when there is a shift from the traditional Nguni pattern of round huts in a semi-circle or circle around a circular cattle-byre to straight rows of rectangular huts, perhaps facing a rectangular byre. It is suggestive, in this respect, that the traditional Swazi homestead may exhibit a linear transformation of the underlying system, if in a marginal fashion. An absorbing diagram of grain platforms belonging to different wives in a homestead is provided by Marwick (1940:24). Analysis reveals that these rectangular platforms, arranged in rows, are ordered by seniority along the axes right/left and front/back.

One finds not only transformations of the spatial code, but also quite complex relations between it and other symbolic codes. For example, social relations are typically expressed in these societies in terms of the distribution of the parts of a slaughtered cow or ox. A Zulu informant explicitly developed for Holleman the analogy between the symbolic use of the cow and the homestead:

[He] drew with his finger an incomplete oval in the sand, which stood for the trunk of a cow. Above, at the neck, he indicated the place of the homestead head. At breast height he indicated with his finger the *uyise wabantu*. At shoulder height, on the right side, he placed the heir, and on the right flank the junior right-hand son. The left-hand and junior left-hand sons were indicated on the left shoulder and flank. According to them the homestead thus presents itself, structurally, like a cow. (1940:69; cf. Cook, 1931:26)

How deep does this inter-penetration of symbolic codes go? The evidence now becomes less easily available, but some preliminary observations are worth making, certainly with reference to the comparatively rich Swazi material. Here one sees clearly the spatial expression of a variety of symbolic modes and relationship systems. There is, for example, a critical spatial dimension in the relation between the dead, the living, and the ancestors. The dead headman is buried beneath the cattle-byre. His spirit may be approached there by day, but at the end of the mourning period it is 'brought inside' the great hut, where it is approached particularly by night. Further, the spinal fluid of the corpse is said to turn into a white reptile, which then makes its way to the surface and as a pale green snake is allowed freely to come and go in the homestead (Marwick, 1940:232). Similar movements from east to west, down to up, and outside to inside are repeated in the marriage ceremony,[2] and in both cases east is clearly associated with liminality, 'outside' with the foreign and dangerous, west and 'inside' with the normal and domestic.

The preparation of food provides another level, or medium, in which the same locational elements recur.[3] Raw grain is stored initially on raised platforms outside the village (up/outside); is then threshed and buried in pits beneath the cattle-byre (down/east − that is, during its transitional or liminal phase); and finally brought to the hut where it is prepared for eating (up/west/inside).

This is, however, only one of several associations between food in various states, location, and other symbolic attributes. Thus grain may be boiled as porridge, a low-status dish associated particularly with domesticity and eaten in the hut; or fermented as beer, a high-status dish associated with public, masculine and ceremonial occasions, when it is drunk at the entrance to the cattle-byre. (Sorghum, the ancient grain crop, is used mainly for beer, while maize, the modern crop, is used mainly for porridge. The Zulu oppose these crops locationally: sorghum is threshed and winnowed outside the homestead, maize in the hut (Bryant, 1949:302–3).) Similarly, beef is roasted outside by men on ceremonial occasions, and eaten inside, boiled, by women. Here, then, in addition to the contrast between 'outside' and 'inside' we have a contrast between male and female, expressed, as Lévi-Strauss ([1968] 1978:471–96) has taught us to expect, in a contrast between the boiled (culturally transformed) and the roast or fermented (naturally transformed). Similar contrasts mark the treatment of milk. It is drunk raw, straight from the cow, outside the village, by boys; new wives, visitors and affines are not allowed to drink it; and it is drunk sour (naturally transformed) above all by men, in the village.

One could look at spatial elements of other symbolic codes, or at other spatial symbols, such as fences, or at the combination of colour coding and spatial arrangements, as in the opposition in the Swazi queen mother's homestead between the 'black' and 'white' *lusasa* (H. Kuper, 1947:236). However, without even attempting anything like an exhaustive inventory of the symbolic system, it may be worthwhile briefly to relate the four Swazi structures which have been discussed. Figure 16 summarizes schematically the main symbolic dimensions (a); the homestead model in which the wives and the mother are placed about the cattle-byre (b); that in which the headman and mother are

placed about the cattle-byre (c); the relations just discussed, between
the living, the dead and the ancestors (d); and raw grain, threshed grain
and beer (e).

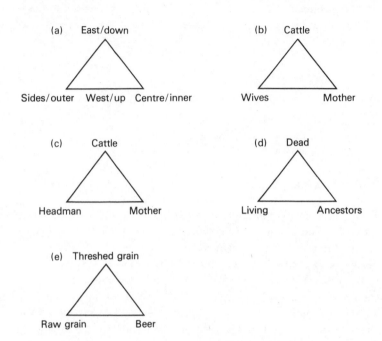

FIGURE 16 *A schematic summary of Swazi symbolic dimensions*

Because all the other triangles can be placed on the basic spatial
triangle (Figure 16a), they can obviously be directly related also to each
other. The interrelations are frequently quite explicit. Thus ancestors
are approached in the mother's hut and offered beer, which is indeed
often stored in the rear or inner part of the *indlunkulu*. Threshed grain
is buried below the cattle-byre, as are the dead.

Is there a deeper structure to be discerned, underlying all these
particular structures? One might be deduced from the five structures
summarized in Figure 16. This is represented in Figure 17. This triangle
may be read as representing a process which begins in the 'low-status'
corner and moves through a liminal phase to the 'high-status' corner.
It could be argued that this certainly applies to the movement from
living to dead to ancestor, or from raw grain to threshed grain to beer;

and that cattle in the form of bridewealth (and thus representing married-out sisters) might be said to occupy a comparably intermediary if not strictly liminal situation vis-à-vis the wives and the mother, or even the headman and his mother. (The mother represents the dead headman, the present headman's father, in some Swazi formulations. See, for example, Ziervogel, 1957:31–5.)

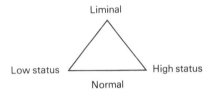

FIGURE 17 *A possible 'deep' Swazi structure*

There may be a yet deeper level to be plumbed, for there are slight indications in the data that one could superimpose yet another structure in which the poles of the triangle are defined by the oppositions nature/culture and sacred/profane, but this is perhaps to move too far beyond the available evidence. Even while admitting the sketchiness of some of the data, and the various relevant questions which remain to be posed, the point has surely been made that the spatial idiom interlocks with other symbolic codes in these cultures, and is therefore probably in turn ultimately defined with reference to a deeper underlying conceptual structure.

11 Transformation, persistence and adaptation

Transformations of a bridewealth system

This book is concerned with the varieties of bridewealth institutions among the Southern Bantu. I chose to concentrate on bridewealth institutions because of their significance in traditional Southern Bantu cultures, and my initial goal was to further the understanding of the Southern Bantu cultural tradition, rather than to contribute to the development of a general theory of bridewealth systems, a project about which I am in any case rather sceptical.[1] At the same time this is not a purely ethnographic exercise. The present analysis has implications for the understanding of cultural structures and processes everywhere. Specifically, it presents a model of the way in which any cultural tradition generates various local systems.

Cattle are exchanged for wives in all Southern Bantu communities. The same set of ideas underlies the transactions everywhere. Yet the organization of these transactions varies, local bridewealth systems adapting to local circumstances. These local adaptations are not rough and ready, *ad hoc*, solutions to particular problems. Nor are the local systems merely crude approximations to a purer grand tradition. The process by which modifications develop is regular and rule-bound. Folk models and actual marriage practices are systematically altered. In consequence the various local institutions represent highly constrained transformations of each other. This is the general theoretical conclusion which the present study supports.

Three sets of factors are responsible for the variations in the local bridewealth systems. These are (i) the relative importance of pastoralism and agriculture in the local economy; (ii) the kinship factor, specifically the different cousin marriage rules; and (iii) the political factor, especially the varying forms of political stratification.

(i) *Cattle and agriculture*
There is no simple relation between the number of cattle in a community

and the level of bridewealth payments. (Cf. Turton, 1980.) What matters, certainly in Southern Africa, is the relative importance of pastoralism and agriculture, agriculture depending largely on women. Where agriculture is the main subsistence activity bridewealth payments are high, both in comparison with other groups in the area and in relation to average livestock holdings. The Southern Sotho, Tsonga and Lovedu offer examples. Where agriculture is less significant, bridewealth payments are low, although there are usually more cattle per head of population. This is the case among the Tswana and Kgalagari, for example.

Where cattle are the main form of wealth, fathers are usually responsible for supplying their sons with bridewealth cattle. In the dominantly agricultural societies, men depend on their sisters to bring in bridewealth cattle which can be used to buy wives. This distinction applies also within societies, as between the cattle-rich, usually aristocratic families and the poorer mass of the population; and even within families, as between the heir of the great house, who inherits the bulk of the herd, and his brothers.

The Tsonga and Lovedu, on the one hand, and the Tswana and Kgalagari on the other, represent extreme cases. Among the Tsonga and Lovedu the main use of livestock is for bridewealth payments. Cattle holdings are largely in the form of bridewealth payments received for sisters, and they are rapidly paid out again to acquire wives. Among the Tswana and Kgalagari, in contrast, female labour is at a discount and cattle are highly productive. Bridewealth is provided in the first instance by fathers, it is relatively low, and it forms a minor element in the flow of cattle.

(ii) *Kin-marriage rules*

There are four types of alliance system among the Southern Bantu:

(a) *Ruling families marry close-kin.* This is the general pattern among the Sotho-Tswana and Venda, and even in Nguni and Tsonga communities there were traditionally tendencies towards elite endogamy. The extreme case is the preference of Tswana aristocratic families for father's younger brother's daughter marriage, a form of endogamy justified in the bridewealth idiom — 'The cattle will return to the byre.' Very commonly one or two families regularly provide the great wife of a particular line of rulers.

(b) *Preferential matrilateral cross-cousin marriage.* This is the general pattern among the Sotho-Tswana and Venda, though other forms of first-cousin marriage may also be favoured. The emphasis here is on the brother/sister tie, and as the Lovedu say, a woman 'follows the spoor of her cattle' and finds a wife for her son.

(c) *Second and third cousin marriage.* The Swazi have a system of preferential FMBSD marriage, which generates a repetitive but oscillating structure of alliance. Even more elaborate repetitive structures may exist elsewhere, based on alternative marriage rules, as I tried to show in the case of the Tsonga.

(d) *Non-kin marriage.* The literature on marriage rules among most Nguni groups is thin, but in general all first- and second-cousin marriages are apparently prohibited.

The distribution of these four modes of marriage alliance corresponds roughly to the cultural classification of the region. (a) is a Western and Southern Sotho aristocratic preference; (b) is a general Sotho-Tswana and Venda mode; (c) is characteristic of the Tsonga and Northern Nguni; and (d) is found among the Natal and Cape Nguni. Yet all four modes of alliance are linked to the same bridewealth ideology. Specifically, all invoke the debt a brother is felt to owe to his cattle-linked sister or to his father. In the Sotho-Tswana aristocratic model bridewealth is given by the father. The exchange is closed, or virtually so. The marriage is endogamous (FyBD), and bridewealth is paid and received by a man and his younger brother who ideally share one herd of cattle. In the commoner Sotho-Tswana and Venda systems the brother's debt is to his sister and it is discharged by the return of a daughter to marry a sister's son. In the Nguni and Tsonga systems the sister is provided with a co-wife, usually a younger sister or brother's daughter. These two formulae are mutually exclusive and may be described as 'Sotho' and 'Nguni' formulae, certainly given the Sotho influence on the Southern Transvaal Ndebele. Previous attempts to present the Venda and Swazi as intermediate cases were based on a misreading of their arrangements.

Each of these four modes of alliance can also be analysed as a specific formula for distributing bridewealth payments. Where alliances are repetitive and unilateral, for example, the structure of debts reinforces lines of stratification in the community.

(iii) *Social stratification*
Social stratification in the Bantu societies of Eastern and Southern Africa is largely a function of ethnic diversity. The Tsonga and Cape Nguni, on the whole more homogeneous, are less markedly stratified

than the Swazi or the conquest states formed by Zulu warrior leaders. The Sotho-Tswana and Venda chiefdoms are typically ethnically complex and stratified, both features becoming more significant in the larger chiefdoms.

The more complex and highly stratified communities tend also to be those with repetitive systems of marriage alliance. This relationship was predicted by Leach, who argued that in Kachin-type systems 'the asymmetrical relationship between wife-givers and wife-receivers tends always to push the ramifications of the system to wider and wider limits,' so leading to the inclusion of groupings differing widely in language and culture (Leach, 1961:103).

There seems, however, to be no way of predicting whether wife-takers or wife-receivers will be the superior party. These two possibilities occur without apparent pattern in the Southern Bantu systems, and they vary independently of the cousin marriage rules. I can offer no explanation for the contrast between Tswana, Lovedu and Xhosa hypergamy, and Swazi and Southern Sotho hypogamy, for example. In some cases perhaps the descriptive materials are inadequate to permit a satisfactory characterization.

Everywhere, however, hypergamous and hypogamous systems share a vital feature: the superior group is always advantaged by the operation of the bridewealth system. For example, Tswana men marry down, and bridewealth among the Tswana is low. Southern Sotho men marry up, and bridewealth in the Southern Sotho communities is high. When Swazi men marry down, bridewealth is below the average, when they marry up bridewealth is above the average. In the Lovedu case the bridewealth arrangements support the pivotal role of the queen in the allocation of wives among the more important families.

The local variations in marriage and bridewealth arrangements are reflected in ideological and symbolic shifts. I have dealt in particular with three. (a) The folk alliance models of the Lovedu, Swazi and Tsonga were shown to differ greatly, and yet to represent direct transformations of each other. They form an ordered series. Among the Lovedu a man married a MBD, and the alliance structure is replicated in each generation. Among the Swazi a woman claims a co-wife rather than a daughter-in-law from her brother, and marriage with a MBD (a 'mother') is favoured only if the 'mother' dies. The ideal marriage is with a FMBSD, a 'grandmother', and the alliance structure repeats itself every second generation. The Tsonga prohibit both the Lovedu and Swazi forms of cousin marriage, but there are indications that they have a model of an alliance structure which repeats itself every third generation, and which is based on marriage with a third cousin. (See Figure 18.)

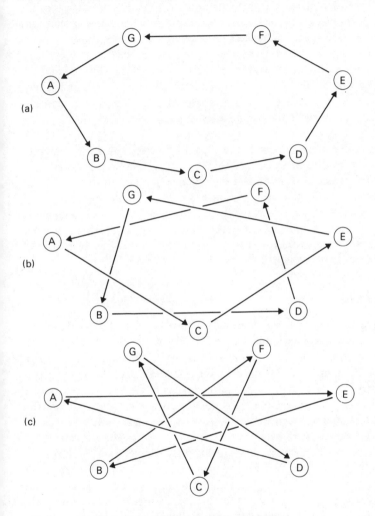

FIGURE 18 *Transformations of an alliance model*
(a) is the Lovedu model; (a) + (b) + (a) is the Swazi model;
(a) + (b) + (c) + (a) is the Tsonga model
I am grateful to Franklin Tjon Sie Fat for help in developing
this model. (See Tjon Sie Fat, 1981)

(b) The wedding ceremonies of the Sotho-Tswana and Nguni are direct transformations of each other, reflecting the fundamental distinction between the Sotho-Tswana assumption that marriage alliances are repetitive, and the Nguni assumption that they are not. As a secondary development the ceremonies also express local features of marriage, such as the presence of hypergamous or hypogamous tendencies.

(c) The layout of the homesteads also encodes local social and political arrangements, within an architectural idiom which is common to the whole culture area. The contrasts between the Nguni and Sotho-Tswana forms were again the most striking, and these reflect political differences between the two families of cultures.

To sum up, the Southern Bantu share a single formula of bridewealth, which is predicated upon a combination of pastoralism and agriculture. Within the cultural tradition a set of common ideas infuses bridewealth transactions. Despite these common features, the local organization of bridewealth varies, as does its detailed ideological and ceremonial articulation. Yet the local adaptations are not haphazard. I have specified some of the transformations, and indicated how at least in part local systems may be 'read off' from each other.

Persistence

There is little apparent continuity between the traditional Southern Bantu social systems and the rural African communities of modern South Africa. The rural population has been incorporated in a racially stratified industrial society. And yet bridewealth systems have proved remarkably persistent. Bridewealth payments are reported from the cities, and are common in the countryside. Although money is the usual medium of payment, some livestock may still be paid, and cattle remain the units of account (cf. Sansom, 1976). This persistence of bridewealth payments is an intriguing phenomenon, but unfortunately poorly documented. We must fall back on the excellent studies which have been made in neighbouring countries, especially Lesotho and Botswana, but developments in these countries are probably fairly typical of what is happening in parts of South Africa itself.

In Lesotho the custom of *bohali* has survived a century of sustained missionary assault and radical social change. Colin Murray has provided a detailed and sensitive analysis of how it works today.[2] Bridewealth remains relatively high — 'for nearly one fifth of households, annual *bohali* transfers (in or out) represent about one third of the median household income' (Murray, 1977:84). The payments are still calculated in livestock units, and cattle are usually included in the *bohali*. The traditional scale of payment is ideally still honoured. And yet the social context of the payment has changed radically. Chiefs no longer monopolize political and economic control; the active male population is engaged in migrant labour and not in pastoralism; and the broader family network is no longer the key resource that it was traditionally.

Murray explains that new conditions have arisen which serve to sustain the practice of *bohali*. The bridewealth payments represent a transfer of resources from young male migrants to the old and to the women and children upon whom the maintenance of the migrant's rural base depends. The migrant pays over a proportion of his earnings in the form of bridewealth, and in return he is granted the security of a rural subsistence base, acquiring a wife, children, and affines, upon whom he will be able to call in later life. Thus the fundamental conditions of the bridewealth system have been reconstituted: there is once again a dual economy, and as in the traditional system a man must invest his gains from one sphere in another in order to enhance his security. Bridewealth transfers are one mechanism by which this investment is made.

In Botswana pastoralism was relatively more important, agriculture less important than in Lesotho; and here the missionaries had greater success in their campaign against bridewealth.[3] The London Missionary Society ruled in 1875 that bridewealth payments were an infringement of church law. Some chiefs who had been converted to Christianity incorporated the prohibition in tribal law. A few (notably the Ngwato) maintained the prohibition into modern times, but elsewhere even Christian chiefs backtracked. Chief Lentswe paid bridewealth on behalf of his heir, and his successor prevailed on the church authorities to insist on the payment of bridewealth in all church marriages. Other chiefs also began actively to require the payment of bridewealth, at least from non-Christians.

But the churches were not the only instruments of change. Migrant labour and the decline of the regimental system weakened parental control of children, and in Botswana there was a rapid growth in the proportion of unmarried mothers.[4] Marriage became less formal, and bridewealth payments assumed a new function. They were made (sometimes late, even posthumously) above all to formalize a union in order to establish rights of inheritance and succession, and to institutionalize affinal relationships. The amount of play in these arrangements, and the role of bridewealth payments in reducing ambiguities, has been a central theme in the work of John Comaroff and Simon Roberts[5] (cf. A. Kuper, 1970b). There is continuity here with the traditional test of succession in a polygynous household, namely, which wife was paid for by the father of the headman?

Structural implications of bridewealth systems

An occupational hazard of field anthropology is the temptation to blow up a specific ethnographic case into a type. A particular bridewealth system, for example, is treated as the key to the analysis of all other bridewealth systems. The temptation is understandable, and type-cases are often extremely suggestive, but the structural relationships of bridewealth institutions are so diverse that this sort of simple generalization is hopeless. As in Southern Africa, bridewealth systems are adapted to various local economic conditions, kinship institutions and political circumstances.

The simplest possibility is an open market in which livestock, women and perhaps slaves and agricultural products are freely exchanged. This arrangement seems to be unusual, though examples have been described in East Africa, for example, by H. K. Schneider (1964) and Walter Goldschmidt (1974). More commonly bridewealth arrangements sustain a systematic bias in the allocation of wives, in favour of a privileged group. Various mechanisms give an advantage to particular classes of 'bidders'. Among the Lele (Douglas, 1963) and the Gouro (Meillassoux, 1964), for example, bridewealth arrangements protect the privileged access of the older men to wives. (Cf. Parkin, 1972.) In more complex stratified societies the bridewealth system often serves in a subtler way to sustain the influence and advantages of the powerful. I shall shortly discuss the example of the Kachin.

Every society also has its own kin-based model of alliance, and bridewealth institutions are found in combination with the whole gamut of alliance structures. This raises intriguing questions, since bridewealth payments have an independent effect on the allocation of wives. Both the bridewealth system and the alliance structure also have political and economic consequences. Any attempt to construct a type-case of a bridewealth system must take account of all these factors. The most interesting experiment of this type has concerned the Kachin peoples of Highland Burma.

The Kachin represent a classic instance of a marriage system based on a rule of preferential marriage with the 'mother's brother's daughter'. But the Kachin also have an elaborate system of bridewealth. Lévi-Strauss suggested that the rule of matrilateral cross-cousin marriage, although presupposing the equivalence of sisters and wives, nevertheless inevitably generated long-term inequalities. Women moved in one direction through the system, and some families successfully accumulated more than their fair share of wives through speculation and the development of secondary exchange cycles. The accumulation of women at certain points in the cycle in turn gave rise to social differentiation and to marriage between people of different status. It was at such a juncture that the Kachin bridewealth system had come into play, combating this erosion of the very basis of generalized exchange.

This analysis was unacceptable to Edmund Leach, who when Lévi-Strauss's study was first published in 1949 had already been working for many years on Kachin ethnography. To put the matter at its simplest, he rejected the radical analytical separation Lévi-Strauss imposed between the logical properties of the system of exchange and its political implications. Bridewealth was not something which had simply been added on to matrilateral cross-cousin marriage, and social stratification was not just an unfortunate consequence of the marriage rule. These institutions hung together, 'the whole organization is in political and economic balance.' The chief stood to the headman as feudal lord to freeholder, as landlord to tenant, and as father-in-law to son-in-law. By paying bridewealth in cattle to the chief's lineage, the lineage of the headman was at the same time rendering tribute and paying rent; and part of this payment was recycled in the form of feasts laid on by the chief for his followers (Leach [1951] 1961).

The 'Kachin-type' and its variants could be found in various parts of the world, and Leach identified one instance in Southern Africa, the Lovedu. They exemplified 'a Kachin system in reverse', women marrying up and patronage, including loans of cattle and bridewealth payments, passing down the hierarchy.

Eileeen Krige, the authority on Lovedu culture, criticized Leach's analysis on the grounds that Lovedu society was not genuinely stratified, an argument dealt with earlier in this book. (See Chapter 5, pp. 73–5). Jack Goody generalized her objection. He took the view that African bridewealth systems must indeed be understood in relation to African political economies, but that these were very different in form from Asian states like the Kachin. Goody constructed what was virtually an African counterpart to the classic type of 'Oriental despotism'. In these African systems, bridewealth played a role which contrasted sharply with the role of bridewealth in Kachin-type systems, at least as Leach understood it.[6]

Goody described an 'African' political economy which was based on shifting cultivation of poor soils. Land was plentiful, labour scarce, exploitation minimal. Economic differentiation and political stratification were undeveloped. These systems contrasted strongly with the 'Eurasian' states, where an advanced agricultural technology, more developed division of labour, and high level of exploitation gave rise to elaborate political institutions.

The organization of the family was also very different in 'Africa' and 'Eurasia'. Eurasian societies were characterized by differential access to land. Women could inherit, or else they were allocated part of the family property in the form of a dowry, and consequently there was a powerful incentive to marry kinswomen. In Africa rights in land were held by unilineal descent groups, which were roughly equivalent, and the incentive was to marry out, to create links between different corporations.

Whereas Leach attempted to propagate the 'Kachin-type' as a general paradigm, Goody's model was given a specifically regional identity. Bridewealth, itself a characteristically 'African' institution (Goody and Tanbiah, 1973:21-2), was to be understood in terms of an 'African' political economy. Yet Africanists seem to find the 'African' type defined by Goody more or less unacceptable. He underplays the importance of pastoralism, which is crucial in many African societies, including most of the Eastern and Southern Bantu. As I shall suggest, this is a grave omission. His attempt to characterize African political economies as generally egalitarian is crude, and moreover some studies have suggested that if there is a correlation between 'stratification' and bridewealth, then bridewealth institutions (and polygyny) are more likely to be found where social differentiation and hierarchy *are* present.[7] Finally, the Southern Bantu societies include several cases where a political hierarchy is systematically bolstered by a repetitive structure of marriage alliance. Despite Goody's assertion to the contrary, this conjunction is by no means exceptional in Africa.

Whatever their particular shortcomings, these and similar models are often helpful and suggestive. They provide more or less persuasive accounts of the local uses of bridewealth institutions, and are often relevant to what happens in unrelated societies which share certain significant features. Nevertheless, the most remarkable feature of bridewealth institutions is the vast range of social conditions with which they are associated. This is scarcely surprising, for substantial bridewealth payments are made in 38 per cent of the societies represented in the *Ethnographic Atlas*.

Precisely because of their number and variety, a typology of bridewealth systems might prove of value, and I shall tentatively attempt to define a class of cattle-bridewealth systems which includes the Southern Bantu cases. My starting-point is the thesis of Herskovits, although it is clearly unacceptable as it stands.

The value of cattle and the cost of wives

It will be recalled that Herskovits advanced an extremely idealist explanation of bridewealth payments in the 'cattle complex'. Cattle were sacred, and were used in economically irrational ways. Cattle were paid for wives not because they represented a direct equivalent to the value of a wife's services, but because they had a special ritual value. Later writers developed variants of the argument. J. D. Krige, for example, suggested that 'it is not primarily the sacredness of cattle which explains *munywalo* (bridewealth), but primarily *munywalo* which explains the sacredness of cattle' (1939:424). Bridewealth was a purely cultural phenomenon.

An alternative view is that cattle are used for bridewealth (and so become a subject of special ideological concern) because of their value as a productive resource. A generation of research has shown that herding practices in much of Africa are by no means irrational, given the technology and information available. If this is the case, then perhaps payments of cattle in bridewealth must also be understood as rational investments. One could even in principle try to explain fluctuations in the 'price' of wives by way of a cost-benefit analysis.[8]

In practice the detailed information needed to carry out such an analysis is seldom available. In most parts of Southern Africa the level of bridewealth remained fairly stable for several generations, at around ten head of cattle for the daughter of a commoner and a multiple of that for the daughter of an aristocrat. This represented a variable but generally high proportion of a family herd. In some areas the price was so high relative to the supply of cattle that bridewealth was a closed system, cattle becoming available for marriage payments only in exchange for daughters and sisters. Elsewhere, notably amongst the Tswana, bridewealth was very low in relation to average cattle holdings. This may have been because agriculture was poor in the arid Tswana country. The culturally very similar Southern Sotho, who lived in richer agricultural country, paid above average bridewealth prices. In such terms one may roughly estimate the costs and benefits, although not with any pretence at accuracy.

But if not much can be said about how the price of wives is determined in Southern Africa, it may be possible to identify more general economic functions of the cattle-bridewealth system. Perhaps Herskovits can even be stood on his head, for it may be argued that bridewealth payments in cattle are economically rational transfers in mixed pastoral-agricultural economies. It is worth sketching the form such a thesis might take.

The combination of pastoralism with agriculture is very common. The *Ethnographic Atlas* includes 125 societies which engage to a substantial degree in the herding of cattle, sheep or goats. Of these societies 115 also rely substantially on agriculture for subsistence.[9] The reason is that where technology is simple the yields on pastoral and agricultural work are seasonably variable, and both are vulnerable to the vagaries of climate and disease. Practised together each compensates to some extent for the risks presented by the other.

The combination need not be achieved by every family individually. In some cases there is a division of labour between groups in a community, often on ethnic lines. More commonly the division of labour is based rather on sex, but even then families may differ. Typically the richer families succeed in combining agriculture and pastoralism, while the poor have to depend more on agriculture, falling back where necessary on the patronage of the rich.

Jack Goody suggested that bridewealth payments and polygyny reduce economic differentiation. 'Not only do cattle pass in the opposite direction to brides, they also bring in additional children who will divide whatever remains. Even when differentiation occurs, polygyny dissipates' (Goody and Tambiah, 1973:12). If this were generally the case it would be economic folly for rich men to accumulate wives. In fact they are balancing their risks. Marriage payments represent a shift in investment, not a form of consumption; and although a man's sons will eventually divide his herd, this will be after many years, and in the meantime the herd itself will grow. In favourable conditions, even with the simplest technology, a cattle herd doubles in about 24 years, and sheep and goats reproduce even more rapidly.[10] Marriage payments and polygyny are not equalizing mechanisms. On the contrary, the rich rely on them to maintain their position.

This combination of agriculture and pastoralism is usually accompanied by the practice of patrilocal residence on marriage.[11] Consequently in-marrying wives and their children add to the agricultural labour force, while out-marrying sisters and daughters are lost to it.

Table 3 illustrates the strong tendency of mixed pastoral-agricultural societies to have bridewealth institutions. There are 76 societies in the *Ethnographic Atlas* which combine substantial reliance on pastoralism and agriculture with patrilocal residence at marriage. Eighty-two per cent of these societies are reported to have substantial bridewealth payments. These societies account for 17 per cent of the sample but for 42 per cent of the societies in which bridewealth is paid. They seem to represent a distinct category of bridewealth-paying societies, a category which surely includes most if not all of the societies in which bridewealth payments are made in livestock.

Table 3 Agro-pastoral societies and bridewealth payments

	Societies combining agriculture, pastoralism and patrilocal marriage	All other societies	Total
Bridewealth	62	86	148
No bridewealth	14	208	222
Total	76	294	370

(*34 missing observations*)

Societies of this type are particularly common in Africa, presumably because the combination of pastoralism and agriculture proved to be especially reliable on the African savannah. The adaptation is fairly general in Eastern Africa but it is also found in Western Africa, and it is not confined to any linguistic group.

My classification is tentative, and even if it can be more securely grounded it would only provide a preliminary orientation in the study of cattle-bridewealth systems. It cannot account for the variety of ways in which these bridewealth systems are organized.

Southern African bridewealth systems may serve as mechanisms for the transfer of resources from one sphere of production to another. This may even be their ultimate *raison d'être*. Yet to say that is to say very little about them. The Southern Bantu bridewealth systems incorporate transformations of a set of ideas shared even with non-pastoral Bantu peoples to the north and west. In action, each local bridewealth system is also precisely adjusted to specific political, social and economic conditions. I have tried to capture both the particularity of these systems and their more general features; and, above all, I have attempted to define the systematic character of the variations they exhibit.

Appendix: Kinship categories and preferential marriage

Kinship terminologies

Anthropologists who concern themselves with kin terminologies generally see their studies as a means to another end. If they were able to understand the principles by which kin are categorized this might tell them something about a more important subject, the sociology of kinship. Perhaps the principles regulating the classification of kin express underlying principles of kinship organization. Perhaps the kinship terminology plays an active part in the system of marriage exchange, either directly, by designating a category of preferred spouses, or indirectly, by sorting relatives into categories according to their exchange relationships.

For various reasons some anthropologists are sceptical of the fruitfulness of these lines of research, and they have been neglected by the British school and consequently little used in African anthropology. This is not the place to argue the pros and cons of the matter. I do not, in any case, propose to present a detailed technical discussion of various kinship terminologies. The concern of this chapter, restricted by the scope of the book as a whole, is with the ways in which the Southern Bantu marriage rules may find expression in the kinship terminologies of the region.[1]

Categories of kin

Any of the excellent Southern Bantu dictionaries will provide a vernacular translation for the term 'relative' or 'kinsman', but if one checks, the dictionary will usually show that the vernacular term may also be translated as 'friend'. Some dictionaries will indicate a further connection between the categories 'friend' and 'affine', and affinal terms of address are commonly used for school-friends and other intimate contemporaries.

None the less, the various categories are lexically distinguishable.

Among the Southern Sotho, for example, the verb stem *tswala*, to beget or to bear a child, is the root of *motswadi*, parent, *motswaduwa*, child, *seswalô*, family, *motswala*, cross-cousin, etc. A reciprocal verb form, *tswalana* means literally 'to beget one another' and also means 'to be related by a blood relationship'. It contrasts with a benefactive verb form, *tswallana*, 'to have children for one another', which yields the noun *motswallê*, 'friend' (Mabille and Dieterlen, revised edition, 1961).

According to Colenso (1884), a comparable distinction was made in Zulu by varying the noun class (marked by different prefixes). He distinguished:

> *Hlobo*   – (*isi* or *um*) n. Friend, acquaintance, relative in law, out of the immediate family circle.
> *Hlobo*   – (*u* for *ulu*) n. Sort, kind, species; race, breed, family; relative by blood.

A tripartite distinction between affines on the one hand and paternal and maternal kin on the other is also reported. Schapera (1950:143), for example, wrote that 'The Tswana themselves habitually group their closer relatives into three major categories: *ba ga etsho*, agnatic relatives; *ba ga etsho mogolo*, maternal relatives; and *bagwagadi* (man-speaking) or *bo-mmatsale* (woman-speaking), the kinsmen of one's spouse.' (Cf. H. Kuper, 1950:100, 107; Mönnig, 1967:237.)

All kinship terms belong to noun class la, a subdivision of the class in which all humans are placed. The specific feature of the sub-class is that the nouns in it (mainly kin terms and personal names) are normally used only in a possessive form, indicated by a suffixal possessive element.

Within the Southern Bantu language group the words used for kinsmen are fairly standard, and within the main dialect clusters virtually identical (cf. Van Warmelo, 1931). The classification of kin types varies, however. In many instances the variations seem very minor, but there are some contrasts which are clearly important. For example, the term *umZala* (corresponding to the Sotho-Tswana *motswala*, mentioned earlier) is found in all but one of the Nguni languages for which kin terminologies are available. It means 'cross-cousin'. The Bomvana, however, do not use the term, and classify cross-cousins with parallel cousins. In some early Zulu terminologies only mother's brother's children are referred to as *umZala*, father's sister's children being termed 'brother' and 'sister' (A. Kuper, 1979c).

Kin terms are 'extended' to more distant kin types. These extensions are regulated by genealogically formulated extension rules, and while minor variations are found in their formulation and application these rules correspond generally to the well-known 'Iroquois' type extension rules (see e.g. Buchler and Selby, 1968: ch. 10 and p. 257).

The fact that genealogically formulated extension rules may be applied to the classification of Southern Bantu kin types indicates that the native-speakers use genealogically defined categories; a conclusion which might also be drawn from the lexical marking of the category of 'blood relatives' discussed earlier. Informants also unhesitatingly apply explicit genealogical criteria when asked to distinguish between relatives in particular categories.

Cousin terms

The traditional typology of kinship terminologies is based upon the classification of cousins. Only seven or eight types are normally distinguished, and in Bantu Africa over 90 per cent of the terminologies belong to three types, the 'Iroquois', representing 59 per cent of the total, and the 'Hawaiian' and 'Omaha', each representing a further 16 per cent of the total.[2] The 'Iroquois' system distinguishes a special category of 'cross-cousin' (father's sister's child and mother's brother's child), other cousins being grouped together with siblings. The 'Omaha' systems also distinguish cross-cousins, but refer to mother's brother's children as 'mother', 'mother's brother' or 'grandparent' and father's sister's children reciprocally as 'child', 'sister's child' or 'grandchild'. 'Hawaiian' systems apply a simple generational criterion, all kin of one generation being grouped together. All cousins are consequently classified with siblings. There is a strong though not perfect association between these systems of classifying cousins and logically compatible classification of 'uncles', 'aunts' and 'nephews' and 'nieces'.

Various statistical studies have attempted to correlate the type of cousin classification with sociological factors, particularly descent rules and marriage rules. Of the three types common among the Bantu, the 'Omaha' is very strongly correlated with a system of patrilineal descent, while the others are not closely correlated with particular modes of descent. So far as marriage rules are concerned, the 'Hawaiian' and 'Omaha' systems are negatively associated with rules permitting cross-cousin marriage, while 'Iroquois' (or the similar and not always distinguished 'Dravidian') systems are positively associated with rules permitting cross-cousin marriage. Goody (1970), for example, found that cross-cousin marriage was prohibited in over 80 per cent of all 'Hawaiian' and 'Omaha' systems but in only 35 per cent of 'Iroquois' systems. Moreover, 70 per cent of the societies for which a preference for cross-cousin marriage was reported had an 'Iroquois' (or, apparently, 'Dravidian') terminology.

These associations are interesting, but one cannot assume that a particular terminology indicates the presence of a particular marriage rule, or the previous existence of such a rule. Among the Southern Bantu the majority of reported terminologies are 'Iroquois', and almost all the Nguni terminologies are 'Iroquois' even though most of the Nguni prohibit close-kin marriage. The Bomvana (Cook, 1931:ch. 3) have a 'Hawaiian' terminology, and some of the earlier recorded Zulu terminologies are also 'Hawaiian' (A. Kuper, 1979c). The Tsonga have an 'Omaha' terminology, as do the Shona from whom they originate.

Sibling terms

Less research has been done on the classification of siblings, but once again there is only a limited number of types of classification available (see Nerlove and Romney, 1967; Murdock, 1968). Three are represented among the Southern Bantu. The Nguni classify siblings more or less as do the English, as 'brother' and 'sister'. The Sotho-Tswana generally use a cross/parallel classification, distinguishing 'sibling of the same sex as the speaker' and 'sibling of the opposite sex to the speaker'. Some also use an alternative classification in which siblings are distinguished simply as 'senior to ego' or 'junior to ego'.

The Nguni systems are more or less elaborated, but the basic absolute sex distinction underlies all the varieties. The Xhosa system, for example, the most elaborate I have found recorded, is recognizably a subtler variant of the elementary *-fowa* ('brother') *-dade* ('sister') opposition sometimes reported.

Table 4 Xhosa classification of siblings and parallel cousins

Man-speaking		Woman-speaking	
-dadwethu	Z F BD MZD	*-dadewethu*	oZ FoBD MoZD
-khuluwa	oB FoBS	*-sakwethu*	yZ FyBD MyZD
-nnawe	yB FyBS	*-makwethu*	B MZS FBS
-kayise	FBS		
-kanina	MZS		

Source: Van Warmelo, 1931.

According to Murdock (1968:10) the Nguni system 'is exceptional among Bantu peoples and is not found elsewhere among them within a distance of less than 1,500 miles from the Nguni'. He suggested that the system might have been borrowed from the Bushmen.

The Sotho-Tswana and Venda systems are quite different. The commonest form is the cross-parallel classification. Three categories of sibling are distinguished: 'senior sibling of the same sex as ego', 'junior sibling of the same sex as ego', and 'sibling of opposite sex to ego'. Thus among the Tswana *mogolole* or *nkhunni* = a man's older brother or a woman's older sister; *nnake* = a man's younger brother or a woman's younger sister; and *kgantsadi* = a man's sister or a woman's brother. The alternative system drops the cross-parallel distinction, applying the first two terms simply to 'senior sibling (either sex)' and 'junior sibling (either sex)'.

Little work has been done on the relation of sibling classifications to social structure, but I have suggested (A. Kuper, 1978b: 254-5) a possible relation between the two forms of sibling terminology found among the Tswana and the two models of preferential marriage which they have developed. One of these models posits a preference for marriage with a mother's brother's daughter. As the reader will recall, this is based on the notion of an exchange between a brother and a sister. A woman's marriage brings her brother bridewealth cattle, which he uses for his own marriage. She has in this way provided him with a wife, and in return she must be given a wife to marry her son. When her son marries her brother's daughter the exchange is completed.

An alternative model posits a preference for marriage with a father's younger brother's daughter. The Tswana say, *ngwana rrangwane, nnyale, dikgomo di boele sakeng*, father's younger brother's daughter, marry me, that the cattle may return to the cattle-byre. The underlying idea here is that a man and his brother arrange a marriage among their children in order to avoid a marriage exchange in which bridewealth cattle really must be handed over. It is as it were a purely book-keeping transaction between brothers, who share a cattle-herd.

The hypothesis is that the marriage formula which assumes an exchange between brother and sister is related to the cross-parrallel classification of siblings, in which siblings of opposite sex are opposed. The marriage formula which assumes an exchange between older and younger brother simply opposes older and younger siblings. Mother's brother's daughter marriage is preferred by commoners, father's younger brother's daughter marriage by nobles, and the two models, and perhaps the two modes of classifying siblings, may be differentially employed by nobles and commoners.

The Nguni classification of siblings in terms of absolute rather than relative sex as 'brother' and 'sister' is clearly different from either of the Sotho-Tswana modes, as are the Nguni rules of exogamy.

The cross-parallel distinction

The classification of cousins and of siblings, and indeed of 'uncles', 'aunts', 'nephews' and 'nieces' may be viewed more holistically by abstracting the underlying classificatory principles which are being applied. An obvious criterion is the degree to which the cross-parallel distinction is being extended. Van Warmelo (1931:60, 118-19) identified the cross-parallel distinction as the fundamental principle underlying the Southern Bantu terminologies, but they vary in the degree to which it is applied.

There are difficulties in the formalization of the cross-parallel distinction (see, e.g., Scheffler, 1971), but for present purposes it may be defined simply as a principle of classification whereby siblings of opposite sex in each generation and (with certain reservations) their descendants in ego's generation and the generation of ego's children are systematically contrasted to siblings of the same sex and their descendants.

Table 5 The application of the cross-parallel distinction in some typical Southern Bantu kinship terminologies

		MB	MBC	FZC	♂ZC	FZ	♀B = ♂Z	♀BC
	BOMVANA	X	O	O	X⁺	O	O	O
ZULU {	Abraham	X	X	O	O	O	O	O
	Van Warmelo	X	X	X	O	O	O	O
	XHOSA	X	X	X	X	O	O	O
	S. Tvl. NDEBELE	X	X	X	X	O	O	O
	TSWANA	X	X	X	X	X	X	O
	VENDA	X	X	X	X	X	X	O
	KGALAGARI	X	X	X	X	X	X	X

Sources: Bomvana: Cook, 1931; Zulu: Abraham (cited in Morgan, 1871), Van Warmelo, 1931; Xhosa, Southern Transvaal Ndebele, Tswana and Venda can also be found in Van Warmelo, 1931. I collected the Kgalagari terms.
⁺ Optional.
A cross indicates the presence of a cross-parallel distinction, a circle its absence.

Table 5 reveals a continuum, some peoples applying the cross-parallel distinction to only a few kin types, others generalizing the distinction to a greater or lesser degree. The only cross-parallel distinction made in all the recorded systems is that between mother's sisters and father's brothers on the one hand and mother's brothers on the other. All the groups, including even the southern branch of the Tsonga, employ the term *malume*, literally 'mother male', for the mother's brother. Further distinctions are made in a definite order, as the table shows. Cross-cousins are very commonly distinguished, while at the extreme only the Kgalagari have been found to mark off a woman's brother's children from her sister's children.

Although there is a definite continuum, there is something of a break which marks the transition from the Nguni to the Sotho-Tswana and Venda systems. This suggests that the degree to which the cross-parallel distinction is applied may be correlated with the marriage rules. The assumption is that the cross-parallel distinction 'says' something about preferential cross-cousin marriage, perhaps even reflecting in the emphasis it is given the degree to which such a preference is developed. There is, however, no cross-cultural material known to me which could be readily used to test such an association.

Affinal terms

Preferential marriage rules may be expected particularly to influence the classification of affines, but again correlations are difficult to establish except perhaps in the (highly localized) Dravidian systems.

All Southern Bantu systems have a set of six or seven basic affinal terms which may be translated 'husband', 'wife' (and 'spouse'), and 'wife's parents and relatives' and 'son's wife or brother's wife' and their reciprocals. In Tswana for example (leaving aside the spouse terms) the basic categories are *matsale*, 'husband's relative', *ngwetsi*, 'kinsman's wife', *mogwagadi*, 'wife's relative', and *mogwe*, 'kinswoman's husband'. In addition there may be a number of specific terms which can be used of particular affines in the speaker's own generation. These distinguish 'spouse's sibling' and 'sibling's spouse', or even more particularly between siblings of different sex, seniority, etc. (e.g., A. Kuper, 1978b: 251–2).

An alternative 'descriptive' system may be used, in which one applies to an affine the kin term used by one's spouse with the modifier 'spouse of . . .' or '. . . of my spouse'. For example in Tswana a *rrakgadi* is 'father's sister', and one may refer to the husband of such a woman as *mogatsa-rrakgadi*, 'spouse of father's sister'.

Thirdly, particularly among the Sotho-Tswana and Venda, but in part also among the Tsonga, affines may be referred to by terms used in the first instance for consanguineal kin. To revert to the example of a father's sister's husband among the Tswana, he may be referred to by a purely affinal term as *mogwe*, by a descriptive term as *mogatsa-rrakgadi*, or by a consanguineal term, normally in this case *rrakgadi*, 'father's sister'.

Where consanguineal terms may be used for affines, a simple transformation rule is usually applied. This states that a spouse's relative is equivalent to the speaker's relative, and a relative's spouse is equivalent to that relative. (See A. Kuper, 1978b:249–51.) The Venda and Lovedu have a 'skewing rule', raising wife's kin a generation and lowering husband's kin a generation. (See above pp. 90–1, and A. Kuper, 1979b: 64–5.)

In a few instances affines must be referred to by consanguineal kin terms. The best-known example is the Venda and Lovedu equation of wife's parent and parent's parent. This equation has given rise to a certain amount of confusion, but it is less puzzling if it is taken together with the skewing rule already mentioned, whereby wife's kin are raised a generation. These rules are very likely connected with the Venda and Lovedu emphasis on unilateral cross-cousin marriage. (See above p. 90 and A. Kuper, 1979b:67–9.)

Reviewing these affinal classifications, some tentative conclusions suggest themselves. Some specific features – such as the Venda and Lovedu skewing rules – may plausibly be connected with specific kin marriage rules. More generally it is evident that the Nguni keep kin and affinal categories distinct while the Sotho-Tswana and Venda permit the use of consanguineal kin terms for affines, either through the use of a transformation rule or (in the case of a kinship marriage) by continuing to apply the premarital kin terms. This makes sense in terms of the Nguni bias against kin marriage and the Sotho-Tswana preference for kin marriage.

Taken together with the variations in the classification of cousins and siblings, and in the degree to which the cross-parallel distinction is applied, these variations in the classification of affines suggest that local differences in marriage rules do indeed influence the way in which the uniform Southern Bantu lexicon of kin terms is applied to social categories. One cannot, however, dismiss the alternative possibility that these are simply dialectical variants which purely fortuitously suggest some sociological correlations. This alternative hypothesis — though it must already appear rather implausible — can only be put to a conclusive test by pushing the comparisons further, to include other linguistically related peoples to the north.

Notes

Chapter 1 Introduction

1 I discuss regional comparison in African anthropology in more detail elsewhere (A. Kuper, 1979a), and the broader theoretical orientation is sketched in another recent paper (A. Kuper, 1980).

2 Van Warmelo (1974) has written an authoritative recent essay on the cultural classification of the Southern Bantu groups.

Chapter 2 'Cattle beget children'

1 My ideas on fertility were stimulated by conversations with Stephen Gudeman and by a reading of his highly suggestive manuscript paper on Gogo ideology. Maurice Bloch's lectures and writings on the relations between hierarchy and ritual were also a source of ideas. Finally, I have benefited greatly from the criticisms and suggestions of Kunnie Kooijman and Chris Uhlenbeck at Leiden.

2 Herskovits's thesis was set out in a series of papers published in 1926. The argument was subsequently revised on some points. His 1930 paper, 'The culture areas of Africa', provides a useful summary.

3 There are various critiques of Herskovits's argument. See, e.g. Schneider, 1957; and A. Kuper and Van Leynseele, 1978.

4 Brief but useful reviews may be found in Richards, 1932:91–7, and Shaw, 1974:94–7. Bigalke (1966) has some further details on the Cape Nguni, and Willoughby (1905) is a classic survey of Tswana customs with respect to cattle. Louw (1957) deals with the special cattle terminology.

5 Richards (1932:57) commented:

over a wide area of South and East Africa the women are definitely responsible for the supply of all vegetable produce. The role of cook is invariably associated with that of tiller of the soil. In fact, it might seem as though the one task gave the right to the performance of the other, since we read that the bride is not allowed to cook at her own fireplace for a year after marriage since she will not have sown and reaped her fields till then.

6 Richards (1932:106–9; 149–51) provides a useful summary of the material on hunting. Gathering is less well-documented (but see Shaw, 1974:99). However, a pointed story tells of the Zulu chief, Mpande, scorning a present of wild vegetables, the narrator concluding: 'a man who resorted to eating wild vegetables was a man in a position of need, one who had been driven from his country by war' (Webb and Wright, 1979:188).

7 The principles of exchange are discussed in Goodfellow, 1939, *passim*.

8 For a survey of ancestor beliefs see Hammond-Tooke, 1974:324–36.

9 The duties of the ruler and the expectations of the people are surveyed in Schapera, 1956.

10 See Schapera, 1978b, 1979; E. J. Krige, 1954: 68-9; Junod, 1910 and 1927; Berglund, 1975, *passim*; and Ngubane, 1977, especially chapter 5.
11 The literature on theories of conception is scattered and bitty. The best account is Schapera, 1978b. See also Stayt, 1931:260-1; Hunter, 1936:145; H. Kuper, 1947:109; Bryant, 1949:621; Ashton, 1952:26 and Murray, 1980b.
12 See, e.g., Junod, 1927, I:275-6; Hunter, 1936:190; Bryant, 1949:591; Mönnig, 1967:132.
13 For the relevant general characteristics of Central Bantu cultures see Richards, 1939:17-21, 342, 381-3; Richards, 1950; and Vansina, 1966:19-36.

Chapter 3 The bridewealth account

1 For an extended statement of these rules, in the language, at once precise and subtly misleading, of 'customary law', see, e.g., Seymour, 1970:92-119, 142-203.
2 See, e.g., E. J. Krige, 1936:179, for the Zulu, and Schapera, 1950:142-3 for the Sotho-Tswana.
3 Earning bridewealth was from the start, in the last third of the nineteenth century, an important motive for migrant labourers. A traditional way of earning bridewealth was described by a Zulu informant of Callaway (1868:258):

The husband gains such a cow in this way, – he cultivates a garden by himself, and the resulting produce is not mixed with the produce of the chief house, but is kept by itself, and he buys a cow with it. Such, then, is the distinction between that cow and the cattle of the hereditary estate. Or he may cultivate tobacco; he does not say that tobacco-field is the chief wife's, but he says, 'It is my field,' and he does not call the field by the chief wife's house, for a chief wife can put in a claim if a thing is called hers, when it has been taken away again. The husband acts thus that no claim may be made to such a thing.

When that cow, then, has increased, and he has taken another wife by it, it is known that that wife does not belong to the chief wife's house, nor to the hereditary estate of the husband; for nothing has been derived from either for the purchase of the cow.

4 A number of textbooks are devoted substantially to the house-property system and associated issues. Seymour (1970) is probably the best. Some valuable specialist studies in this area of customary law are Van Tromp, 1948; Kerr, 1961; Hamnett, 1975; and Poulter, 1976. Gluckman made the system better known to anthropologists under the label of the 'house-property complex' (1950:194-6).
5 See e.g., Seymour, 1970:128-9.
6 Among the Sotho-Tswana a man could marry his wife's sister during his wife's lifetime, but he had no particular claim on her unless his wife was barren.
7 Luc de Heusch has suggested that the joking and obscene demands of the sister's son amongst the Tsonga reflected a recognized but unrequitable claim to the mother's brother's daughter. He pointed out that among the neighbouring Lovedu a man had a recognized claim to his mother's brother's daughter, and there men joked not with their mother's brothers but with their cross-cousins (de Heusch, 1974). But joking did not appear – in the same general circumstances – among the Nguni. More importantly, the model takes no account of the idiom in which the joking claims are made, namely the claim of the nephew on a return for his mother's bridewealth, which financed his uncle's marriage. These points are taken up again in chapter 8 which deals with the Tsonga.

Chapter 4 States, clans, lineages and ruling lines

1 The Swazi (e.g., H. Kuper, 1947:113) had some totemic features, while the Southern Transvaal Ndebele had the same totem system as the Sotho-Tswana (Fourie, 1921:106–9). Some Sotho groupings lacked totems but employed Nguni-style patronymics (e.g., Ashton, 1952:13).

2 For the definition of Nguni marriage prohibitions see inter alios Alberti, 1968; Shooter, 1857:45–6; MacLean, 1906:65; Hunter, 1936:184–5; Cook, 1931:72; Hammond-Tooke, 1962:97. The Swazi case is dealt with in detail in chapter 7. For the Thembu see A. Kuper, 1981.

3 See e.g., Willoughby, 1905:300–1; Schapera, 1952: *passim*; Mönnig, 1967:16, 17, 18, 234–5.

4 See e.g., H. Kuper, 1952:20; Hughes, 1956:36–45; Hammond-Tooke, 1962: 58; Preston-Whyte, 1974:195–6.

5 For example, Hughes, 1956:35ff.; Bothma, 1962; Reader, 1966; Wilson, 1969:116–7.

6 See, e.g., Schapera, 1963b; Hammond-Tooke, 1965.

7 See, e.g., Holleman, 1941; H. Kuper, 1947:57; Schapera, 1940:61–2.

8 Schapera, 1950, 1957, 1963a, 1963b.

Chapter 5 The Lovedu: marrying in

1 Apart from some notes by missionaries (e.g. Reuter, 1907) and some texts (e.g., Eiselen, 1928a and b; Kruger, 1936) the only full ethnography of the Lovedu which has been available until recently was E. J. and J. D. Krige's *The Realm of a Rain-Queen*. Important additional information on some aspects of the social organization was published separately (J. D. Krige, 1939; E. J. Krige, 1941) and in E. J. Krige's contribution to Gray and Gullivers's *The Family Estate in Africa* in 1964. Mönnig (1963) also published a useful independent account. Now, however, in three recent papers (1974, 1975a and b) E. J. Krige has added extremely important information, drawing also on additional fieldwork. These papers permit a more complex appreciation of the Lovedu social system than was possible earlier (e.g., Leach [1951] 1961:95–99; A. Kuper, 1975a:139–43). Finally, a draft of this chapter was exhaustively criticized by Eileen Krige, who also sent me fresh material. My debt to her is very great indeed.

2 For good outlines of the culture area see J. D. Krige, 1937 and E. J. Krige, 1938. A comparison of Lovedu and Venda kinship terminologies is to be found in A. Kuper, 1979b.

3 Jaques (1934:377) notes that:

> The facts regarding the succession and filiation of these chiefs are secrets jealously guarded by the members of the royal family, and anyone disclosing them would, in olden times, have been poisoned. Even today, I have had to promise not to publish the exact name of the tribe and of the individuals concerned, in order to safeguard my informants against the ill-feelings which this disclosure would provoke.

4 The main sources I have found are E. J. Krige, 1975b:69–72, and Mönnig, 1963. Each is clearly favourable to a particular faction. There is some interesting material in Grimsehl, 1955. In a personal communication to me (1980) Professor Krige has corrected some crucial details in her account.

5 Leach (1961:96) has made familiar the description of the wife-giver/wife-taker relationship in vernacular Lovedu terms as *vamakhulu-vaduhulu*. This is based on E. J. and J. D. Krige's (1943:144) opposition between 'the brides or

parents-in-law (*vamakhulu*)': and 'the group supplying bridegrooms (*vatsezi*) or sons-in-law (*vaduhulu*). The *vamakhulu* give brides and receive cattle; the *vaduhulu* give cattle and receive brides.'

These category terms are the plural form of kin terms most readily translated as 'grandparents' and 'grandchildren' or '(man-speaking) sisters' children'. (The term for 'mother's brothers' is also sometimes used for bride-givers.)

The problems involved in sorting out the usages involved here are complex. I have discussed the matter elsewhere (A. Kuper, 1979b:63–8; cf. Mönnig, 1961), but would suggest that rather than use a complex vernacular phrase it is better to attempt English glosses adapted to the particular context.

6 A detailed case-study of succession in a Southern Sotho chieftaincy displays many of the mechanisms and conflicts found among the Khaha and Lovedu, including woman-marriage and the issue of genitor/levir identification (Hamnett, 1975:116–36). Cf. also Schapera, 1971:26–31.

Chapter 6 The Venda variant

1 This is a very bald summary of a complex argument. I shall be treating the issue again in the chapter on the Tsonga.

2 The five volumes of Venda Law were published over a long period, but the paragraphs are numbered consecutively and they are intended to be read as one book. The basic material is texts dictated by Venda experts, translated and annotated by the authors. I refer to them as *Venda Law*, giving page and volume.

3 WBD marriage is also permitted among the Lovedu.

4 The full set of reduction rules needed to analyse the terminology is provided in A. Kuper, 1979b:63–8.

5 See Kruger, 1936; Lestrade, 1930. Van Warmelo's standard Venda dictionary has been out of print for many years, but a new edition is almost ready.

6 In one reference Stayt (1931:174) seems to suggest that the sister's contribution is direct, but this conflicts with his other discussions (e.g., p. 167), and with other sources, including Junod (1927, I:304–5), Lestrade, 1930, and the detailed first volume of *Venda Law*.

Chapter 7 The Swazi: marrying up

1 The hypothesis that the preferential marriage rules are of Sotho origin begs a number of questions. First of all, the rules are very different from the Sotho-Tswana rules. Second, even if it is simply the idea of preferential cousin marriage which is being borrowed, why should a conquering aristocracy borrow the marriage customs of a minority group of different ethnic origin and low status? Finally, of course, even if the rules could be shown to be of foreign origin, they are now certainly characteristic Swazi customs and must be understood as such. (See, e.g., H. Kuper, 1947:95n.1; 1950:103; Derman, 1977:120.)

2 Derman has reported that in recent times in one part of the country informants were unanimously in favour of marriage with genealogical MBD, and in a sample of 67 marriages 17 were with women classified as MBD, including at least three with genealogical first maternal cross-cousins. (Derman, 1977: 129 n.12.)

3 The Swazi refer to these wives as 'grandmother', but there are no grounds for suspecting the presence of Omaha classification rules. First, the paternal and maternal grandmothers are classified together. Second, both cross-cousins

are classed together as *mzala*, a dialectical variant of the term for 'cross-cousin' in most Southern Bantu societies. Unfortunately, however, the single available Swazi kinship terminology (H. Kuper, 1950:101) deals only with first cousins.

4 In his forthcoming reanalysis of Swazi royal ritual, Luc de Heusch provides a fascinating analysis of the ritual position of the queen mother.

Chapter 8 The Tsonga: marrying out

1 Junod's first general Tsonga ethnography was published in French in 1898. In 1912–13 a two-volume English version was published, much revised and expanded, and then in 1927 Junod published a new and again revised edition. A French translation was published posthumously. Junod also published a number of extremely important articles, and collections of Tsonga folk-tales; and he contributed significantly to the ethnography of the Venda and Pedi. The famous passage in which he describes his encounter with Lord Bryce is quoted from the introduction to the English version of the monograph.

2 See Clerc, 1938:103; Gluckman, 1950:198–9; Harris, 1959:55; Junod, 1927, I:331.

3 See Clerc, 1938:85; Junod, 1912, I:261; 1927, I:276n.; Ramsay, 1946:148.

4 See Harris, 1959:57; Junod, 1927, II:147; Schapera, 1947:140, 160.

5 Clerc, 1938:85. Cf. Harris, 1959:57; Ramsay, 1946:144.

6 De Heusch (1978) has published a fascinating analysis of Tsonga sacrifice, which opens up a number of suggestive lines of research.

7 I have discussed elsewhere the hypotheses of Radcliffe-Brown and Junod, and the debate amongst the Tsonga ethnographers (A. Kuper, 1976).

8 The main sources on the marriage rules are Junod, 1927, I:254–6 and Clerc, 1938. Junod's presentation of these rules lacks his usual clarity, partly because the rules from several areas are given together. It is an open question how much variation was to be found in 'Tsonga' marriage rules.

9 See, e.g., Lévi-Strauss, 1966; Héritier, 1981; Ackerman, 1976; and Tjon Sie Fat, 1981.

10 The reduction rules are set out by Lounsbury (1964:372–5), who classifies the system as 'Omaha Type III', citing the Tsonga as an example of the type. The citations from Jaques are to his essay on Tsonga kinship terminology (1929).

11 See Junod, 1927, I:376–7, 381.

Chapter 9 Wedding ceremonies

1 The large number of sources which provide descriptions of Nguni wedding ceremonies reflects, of course, the importance of these ceremonies in the lives of the people. The following references are a selection:

Cape Nguni: Dugmore, 1906:47–56; Soga, 1931:225–43; Cook, 1931:72–88; Hunter, 1936:186–202; Laubscher, 1937:154–85; Hammond-Tooke, 1962:99–121; De Jager, 1971:160–75.

Zulu-speakers: E. J. Krige, 1936:120–55 collates a number of important sources. Particularly interesting are perhaps Braatvedt, 1927; Bryant, 1949:533–604; and Fuze, 1979:32–9.

Swazi: Engelbrecht, 1930:14–18; Marwick, 1940:101–23; Ziervogel, 1944:24–35; 49–56; H. Kuper, 1945.

Southern Transvaal Ndebele: Fourie, 1921:109–20; Van Warmelo, 1930: 35–46; A. Kuper, 1978a:114–16.

2 Linguistically among the Nguni-speakers a woman courts, marries, etc., a man is courted, married, etc., or causes a woman to court, marry, etc. (See, e.g.,

Fuze, 1979:162n.) Cf. p. 139 below.

3 Among the Swazi the ten head of the bridewealth cattle are exactly matched by ten pots of beer. An eleventh, corresponding to the extra *lugege* beast, is split in the cattle-byre just as the *lugege* beast is slaughtered (Engelbrecht, 1930:19; Marwick, 1940:120).

4 The descriptions of Sotho-Tswana and Venda ceremonies are generally less rich than for the Nguni, presumably because the payment of the bridewealth is less spectacular than the Nguni wedding. Consult the usual authorities for a variety of descriptions. Jacottet, 1896:112–20 is also worthwhile.

5 There are, of course, many symbolic features of these ceremonies which cry out for analysis – to name only one, completely ignored here, the use of the spear by the new bride and by her father.

6 Some of the Nguni sources suggest that only among aristocrats does the girl or her father normally take the initiative, but more commonly this is taken to be the traditional mode of procedure.

7 A man also avoids his mother-in-law and sometimes other affines in the early stages of the marriage, but is not made to pass through a stage of liminality and subordination. (See, e.g., J. D. Krige, 1934:142–3.) While *hlonipha* is very clearly an Nguni custom it is occasionally recorded (in a less extreme form) among the Southern Sotho. Thus Jacottet (1896:114n) writes that immediately she is engaged the young woman must not enter her future in-law's hut, and above all must not eat there. Once married she must not pronounce her husband's father's name. This he says, is originally a Cape Nguni custom 'qui est, depuis quelques années, entrée dans les moeurs des Ba-Souto'.

8 The evidence for this statement was discussed in the course of the case-study of the Swazi in Chapter 7 (pp. 101–3).

9 The introduction of Christian marriage, and of registry office ceremonies, has increased the significance attached by the Sotho-Tswana to the public delivery of the bride. Today the two phases of the ceremony (often occurring on successive days), balance each other more than in the past.

Chapter 10 The system on the ground: the homestead layout

1 The more recent contributions include a survey and brief summary of the main settlement patterns (De Jager, 1964); Hilder Kuper's study (1972) of the political implications (among the Swazi) of where a decision is made or announced; and Shaw and Van Warmelo's invaluable compilation of materials on Cape Nguni homesteads (1972). This is an area where cultural anthropology and archaeology join hands, and there is much of interest in the archaeological record. A particularly suggestive recent study is Maggs, 1976.

2 See Beidelman (1966) for a suggestive discussion of some Swazi symbolic ideas in ritual, including right/left and east/west.

3 For rich ethnographic materials on Swazi food customs see Beemer, 1939; S. Jones, 1963; and Marwick, 1940.

Chapter 11 Transformation, persistence and adaptation

1 A number of general theories of bridewealth are critically reviewed by Comaroff (1980b).

2 The description given is based on the writings of Colin Murray. See especially Murray, 1976, 1977, 1978, 1980a. Cf. Poulter, 1976:318–22.

3 The changes in bridewealth arrangements introduced as a consequence of

missionary pressure are detailed in Schapera, 1970, especially pp. 138-9, and Schapera, 1978a.

4 See Schapera, 1933, 1947, 1970: ch. 7. Excellent descriptions of contemporary conditions are to be found in Kooijman, 1978, and Kocken and Uhlenbeck, 1980.

5 See Comaroff and Roberts, 1977; Roberts, 1977; and Comaroff 1980b.

6 Goody's thesis is sketched in a long essay, *Bridewealth* (1973), and developed more fully in *Production and Reproduction* (1976).

7 See, e.g., Divale, 1977; Clignet, 1970; Grossbard, 1980.

8 My thinking on these points owes much to discussions with Amyra Grossbard-Schechtman. See Grossbard, 1976, 1980.

9 The definitions are derived from the *Ethnographic Atlas*. 'Pastoral societies' are those defined by the symbols 'B' and 'S' in column 39. 'B' refers to the keeping of 'bovine animals', including cattle, mithun, water buffaloes and yaks. 'S' refers to sheep and goat husbandry where larger domestic animals are not present or are much less important. I have excluded societies in which pastoralism or agriculture are marginal. Specifically, I excluded societies scoring below 2 on the scale given in columns 10 and 11.

10 On these points the reader should consult the splendid study by Dahl and Hjort (1976). A project dealing specifically with the agro-pastoral societies of eastern Africa is being carried on at the University of Gothenburg. See Brandström, Hultin and Lindström, 1979.

11 Agriculture and pastoralism are defined as in note 9 above. Patrilocal residence is coded in column 16.

Appendix

1 The basic source on Southern Bantu kinship terminologies is Van Warmelo's excellent compilation (1931). Junod (1927, I:496-503) provides a useful list of Tsonga, Chopi, Zulu, Xhosa, Southern Sotho, Pedi and Venda terms. I have tabulated and analysed the Venda and Lovedu terms (1979b:60-1), and also a series of Zulu terminologies (1979c), in both cases using and listing various sources, and I have analysed in great detail seven Tswana terminologies (1978b). A fine analysis of the Shona system is provided by Borland (1979). There are basic terminologies in most of the standard monographs, the data provided in Ashton (1952), Cook (1931) and Stayt (1931) being particularly good. Jaques (1929) is an outstanding source for the Tsonga. Dictionaries and grammars are helpful, the Zulu dictionaries of Bryant (1905) and Doke and Vilikazi (1948) and the Southern Sotho dictionary of Mabille and Dieterlen being particularly useful in this field.

2 This figure is based on the run of Bantu societies included in Murdock's *Ethnographic Atlas* (1967).

References

ACKERMAN, C. (1976), Omaha and 'Omaha'. *American Ethnologist*, pp. 555-72.
ADLER, A. (1976), Avunculat et marriage matrilatéral en Afrique noire. *L'Homme*, XVI (4):7-27.
ALBERTI, LUDWIG (1968), *Account of the Tribal Life and Customs of the Xhosa in 1807*. (English translation) Cape Town: Balkema.
ASHTON, H. (1952), *The Basuto*. London: Oxford University Press for the International African Institute.
BEEMER, H. (1939), Notes on the diet of the Swazi in the Protectorate. *Bantu Studies*, 13:199-236.
BEIDELMAN, T. O. (1966), Swazi royal ritual. *Africa*, 36:373-405.
BERGLUND, A. I. (1976), *Zulu Thought-Patterns and Symbolism*. London: Hurst.
BIGALKE, E. H. (1966), Notes on the place of domestic and indigenous animals in Cape Nguni life. *Annals of the Cape Provincial Museums*, 6 (1):1-16.
BLOCH, M. (1978), Marriage amongst equals: An analysis of the marriage ceremony of the Merina of Madagascar. *Man* (n.s.), 12 (1):21-33.
BODENSTEIN, W. and RAUM, O. F. (1960), A present-day Zulu philosopher. *Africa*, 30:166-81.
BORLAND, C. H. (1979), Kinship term grammar: A review. *Anthropos*, 74: 326-52.
BOTHMA, C. V. (1962), *Ntshabeleng Social Structure: A Study of a Northern Transvaal Sotho Tribe*. Pretoria: Department of Bantu Administration and Development. Ethnological Publications no. 48.
BRAATVEDT, H. P. (1927), Zulu marriage customs and ceremonies. *South African Journal of Science*, XXIV:553-65.
BRANDSTRÖM, P., HULTIN, J. and LINDSTRÖM, J. (1979), *Aspects of Agro-pastoralism in East Africa*. Research report no. 51. Scandinavian Institute of African Studies, Uppsala.
BROWN, J. T. (1926), *Among the Bantu Nomads*. London: Seeley, Service.
BRYANT, A. T. (1905), *A Zulu-English Dictionary*. Pinetown, Natal: Mariannhill Mission Press.
BRYANT, A. T. (1923), The Zulu family and state organisation. *Bantu Studies*, 2 (1):47-51.
BRYANT, A. T. (1929), *Olden Times in Zululand and Natal*. London: Longmans.
BRYANT, A. T. (1949), *The Zulu People As They Were Before the White Man Came*. Pietermaritzburg: Shuter & Shooter.
BUCHLER, I. and SELBY, H. (1968), *Kinship and Social Organization*. New York: Macmillan.
CALLAWAY, REV. CANON (1868), *Nursery Tales, Traditions and Histories of the Zulus*. London: Trübner.
CALLAWAY, REV. CANON (1870), *The Religious System of the Amazulu*.

Springvale, Natal: J. A. Blair.

CASALIS, E. (1861), *The Basutos*. London: James Nisbet.

CLERC, ANDRÉ (1938), The marriage law of the Ronga tribe (especially the clans of the Maputo District, south of the Espirito Santo, Portuguese East Africa). *Bantu Studies*, XII:75-104.

CLIGNET, R. (1970), *Many Wives, Many Powers*. Evanston: Northwestern University Press.

COLE, D. T. (1955), *An Introduction to Tswana Grammar*. Cape Town: Longmans.

COLENSO, J. W. (1884), *Zulu-English Dictionary*. Pietermaritzburg: P. Davis (Revised edition).

COMAROFF, J. (with COHEN, A. P.) (1976), The management of meaning: On the phenomenology of political transactions. In Bruce Kapferer (ed.) *Transaction and Meaning*. Philadelphia: ISHI.

COMAROFF, J. (1978), Rules and rulers: Political processes in a Tswana chiefdom. *Man*, 12 (1):1-20.

COMAROFF, J. (1980a), Introduction, in J. L. Comaroff (ed.) *The Meaning of Marriage Payments*, London and New York: Academic Press.

COMAROFF, J. (1980b), Bridewealth and the control of ambiguity in a Tswana chiefdom. In J. L. Comaroff (ed.) *The Meaning of Marriage Payments*, London and New York: Academic Press.

COMAROFF, J. L. and ROBERTS, S. (1977), Marriage and extra-marital sexuality: The dialectics of legal change among the Kgatla. *Journal of African Law*, 21 (1):97-123.

COOK, P. A. W. (1931), *Social Organisation and Ceremonial Institutions of the Bomvana*. Cape Town: Juta.

DAHL, G. and HJORT, A. (1976), *Having Herds: Pastoral Herd Growth and Household Economy*. Stockholm Studies in Social Anthropology 2. University of Stockholm, Department of Social Anthropology.

DANIEL, J. B. McI. (1964), The Swazi rural economy. In J. F. Holleman (ed.) *Experiment in Swaziland*. Cape Town: Oxford University Press.

DERMAN, P. J. (1977), Stock and aristocracy: The political implications of Swazi marriage. *African Studies*, 36:119-29.

DIVALE, W. (1977), Comment on Kressel, 'Bride-price reconsidered'. *Current Anthropology*, 183:451-3.

DOKE, C. M. and COLE, D. T. (1961), *Contributions to the History of Bantu Linguistics*. Johannesburg: Witwatersrand University Press.

DOKE, C. M. and VILAKAZI, B. W. (1948), *Zulu-English Dictionary*. Johannesburg: Witwatersrand University Press.

DOUGLAS, M. (1963), *The Lele of the Kasai*. London: Oxford University Press.

DUGMORE, H. H. (1906), Rev. H. H. Dugmore's Papers. In Col. MacLean (ed.) *Compendium of Kafir Laws and Customs*. Grahamstown: J. Slater.

EARTHY, E. DORA (1933), *Valenge Women*. London: Oxford University Press.

EISELEN, W. (1928a), *Nuwe Sesoeto Tekste van Volkekundige Belang*. Annale van die Universiteit van Stellenbosch, VI, B.3.

EISELEN, W. (1928b), Zur Erforschung des Lovelu-Dialektes. *Zeitschrift für Eingeborenen-Sprachen*, XIX:98-116.

EISELEN, W. (1928c), Preferential marriage: Correlation of the various modes among the Bantu tribes of the Union of South Africa. *Africa*, I (4):413-28. London.

ELAM, Y. (1973), *The Social and Sexual Roles of Hima Women*. Manchester University Press.

ELLENBERGER, D. F. and MACGREGOR, J. C. (1912), *History of the Basuto: Ancient and Modern*. London: Caxton.

ENGELBRECHT, J. A. (1930), *Swazi customs relating to marriage.* Annals University Stellenbosch, 8 B, 3.

FAYE, C. (1923), *Zulu References.* Pietermaritzburg: City Printing Works.

FORTES, M. (1953), The structure of unilineal descent groups. *American Anthropologist,* LV:17–41.

FORTES, M. (1970), *Kinship and the Social Order: The Legacy of Lewis Henry Morgan.* London: Routledge & Kegan Paul.

FORTES, M. and EVANS-PRITCHARD, E. E. (ed.) (1940), *African Political Systems.* London: Oxford University Press.

FOURIE, H. C. M. (1921), *Amandebele van Fene Mahlangu en hun Religieus-Sociaal Leven.* Zwolle: La Riviere & Voorhoeve.

FUZE, MAGEMA, M. (1979), *The Black People and Whence They Came.* Translated by H. C. Lugg and edited by A. T. Cope. Pietermaritzburg: University of Natal Press (First Zulu edition, 1922).

GERMOND, R. C. (1967), *Chronicles of Basutoland.* Morija: Morija Sesuto Book Depot.

GLUCKMAN, M. (1940), The kingdom of the Zulu of South Africa. In M. Fortes and E. E. Evans-Pritchard (eds) *African Political Systems.* London: Oxford University Press.

GLUCKMAN, M. (1950), Kinship and marriage among the Lozi of Northern Rhodesia and the Zulu of Natal. In A. R. Radcliffe and D. Forde (eds) *African Systems of Kinship and Marriage.* London: Oxford University Press for the International African Institute.

GLUCKMAN, M. (1954), *Rituals of Rebellion in Southeast Africa.* Manchester: Manchester University Press.

GOLDSCHMIDT, W. (1974), The economics of brideprice among the Sebei and in East Africa. *Ethnology,* 13 (4):311–31.

GOODFELLOW, D. (1939), *Principles of Economic Sociology: The Economics of Primitive Life as Illustrated from the Bantu Peoples of South and East Africa.* London: Routledge.

GOODY, J. (1970), Cousin terms. *Southwestern Journal of Anthropology,* 26: 125–42.

GOODY, J. (1976), *Production and Reproduction: A Comparative Study of the Domestic Domain.* Cambridge University Press.

GOODY, J. and TAMBIAH, S. J. (1973), *Bridewealth and Dowry.* Cambridge University Press.

GRIMSEHL, H. W. (1955), Onluste in Modjadjiland, 1890–1894. *Argiefjaarboek vir Suid-Afrikaanse Geskiedenis,* II.

GROSSBARD, A. (1976), An economic analysis of polygyny: The case of Maiduguri. *Current Anthropology,* 17:701–7.

GROSSBARD, A. (1980), The economics of polygamy. *Research in Population Economics,* 2:321–50.

HAMMOND-TOOKE, W. D. (1962), *Bhaca Society.* Cape Town: Oxford University Press.

HAMMOND-TOOKE, W. D. (1965), Segmentation and fission in Cape Nguni political units. *Africa,* 35 (2):143–67.

HAMMOND-TOOKE, W. D. (1968), The morphology of Mpondomise descent groups. *Africa,* 38:26–45.

HAMMOND-TOOKE, W. D. (1974), World-view. In W. D. Hammond-Tooke (ed.) *The Bantu-Speaking Peoples of Southern Africa.* London: Routledge & Kegan Paul.

HAMNETT, I. (1975), *Chieftainship and Legitimacy: An Anthropological Study of Executive Law in Lesotho.* London: Routledge & Kegan Paul.

HANSON, F. and MILLER, F. (1977), The wife's brother's wife and the marriage contract: A structural analysis. *Bijdragen tot de Taal-, Land- en Volkenkunde*, 133 (1):11-22.

HARRIES, C. L. (1929), *The Laws and Customs of the Bapedi and Cognate Tribes of the Transvaal*. Johannesburg: Hortors Ltd.

HARRIS, MARVIN (1959), Labour migration among the Mocambique Thonga: Cultural and political factors. *Africa*, XXIX:50-65.

HÉRITIER, F. (1981), *L'Exercise de la parenté*. Paris: Editions du Seuil.

HERSKOVITS, M. J. (1926), The cattle complex in East Africa. *American Anthropologist*, 28:230-72, 361-80, 494-528, 633-44.

HERSKOVITS, M. J. (1930), The culture areas of Africa. *Africa*, 3:59-77.

HEUSCH, L. DE (1974), The debt of the maternal uncle. *Man*, 9 (4):609-19.

HEUSCH, L. DE (1976), Parenté et historie en Afrique australe (réponse à Alfred Adler). *L'Homme*, XVI (4):29-47.

HEUSCH, L. DE (1978), Le sacrifice, le marriage, la mort et la folie chez les Thonga. In *Systèmes de Pensée en Afrique noire*. Vol. 3, *Le Sacrifice*. Paris: CNRS.

HEUSCH, L. DE (1982), *Rois nés d'un coeur de vache*. Mythes et rites Bantous, vol. 2. Paris: Gallimard.

HOERNLÉ, A. W. (1925), The importance of the sib in the marriage ceremonies of the S. E. Bantu. *South African Journal of Science*, 22:484-92.

HOERNLÉ, A. W. (1931), Introduction to H. Stayt, *The Bavenda*.

HOERNLÉ, A. W. (1937), Social organisation. In I. Schapera (ed.) *The Bantu-Speaking Tribes of South Africa: An Ethnographical Survey*. London: Routledge & Kegan Paul.

HOFFMANN, C. (1913), Verlöbnis und Heirat bei den Basutho in Holzbuschgebirge Transvaals. *Zeitschrift für Kolonialsprachen*, III (12):4-139.

HOLLEMAN, J. F. (1940), Die twee-eenheidsbeginsel in die sosiale en politieke samelewing van die Zulu. *Bantu Studies*, 14:31-75.

HOLLEMAN, J. F. (1941), Die Zulu isigodi. *Bantu Studies*, 15:91-118, 245-76.

HUGHES, A. J. B. (1956), *Kin, Caste and Nation among the Rhodesian Ndebele*. Rhodes-Livingstone Papers. Manchester University Press.

HUGHES, A. J. B. (1962), Some Swazi views on land tenure. *Africa*, 32:253-78.

HUGHES, A. J. B. (1972), *Land Tenure, Land Rights and Land Communities on Swazi National Land*. University of Natal: Institute of Social Research.

HUNTER, M. (1932), Results of culture contact on the Pondo and Xosa Family. *South African Journal of Science*, 29:681-6.

HUNTER, M. (1936), *Reaction to Conquest: Effects of Contact with Europeans on the Pondo of South Africa*. London: Oxford University Press.

JACOBSON-WIDDING, A. (1979), *Red-White-Black as a Mode of Thought*. Uppsala Studies in Cultural Anthropology No. 1. Stockholm: Almquist & Wiksell.

JACOTTET, E. (1896), Moeurs, coutumes et superstitions des Ba-Souto. *Bulletin de la Société Neuchâteloise de Géographie*, IX:107-51.

JAGER, E. J. DE (1964), *Settlement Types of the Nguni and Sotho tribes*. Fort Hare Papers.

JAGER, E. J. DE (1971), 'Traditional' Xhose marriage in the rural areas of the Ciskei, South Africa. In E. J. de Jager (ed.) *Man, Anthropological Essays Presented to O. F. Raum*. Cape Town: Struik.

JAQUES, A. A. (1929), Terms of kinship and corresponding patterns of behaviour among the Thonga. *Bantu Studies*, 3:327-48.

JAQUES, A. A. (1934), Genealogy of male and female chiefs of a Sotho tribe. *Bantu Studies*, 8 (4):377-82.

JEFFREYS, M. D. W. (1951), Lobolo is child-price. *African Studies* 10:148–84.
JENKINSON, T. (1882), *Amazulu*. London: W. H. Allen.
JONES, G. I. (1951), *Basutoland Medicine Murder*. London: HMSO.
JONES, G. I. (1966), Chiefly succession in Basutoland. In J. Goody (ed.) *Succession to High Office*. Cambridge Papers in Social Anthropology, no. 4. Cambridge University Press.
JONES, H. M. (1968), *Report of the 1966 Swazi Population Census*. Mbabane: Government of Swaziland.
JONES, S. M. (1963), *A Study of Swazi Nutrition*. Durban: Institute of Social Research, University of Natal.
JUNOD, H. A. (1910), Les conceptions physiologiques des Bantous sud-africains et leur tabous. *Revue d'Ethnographie et de Sociologie*, 1:126–69.
JUNOD, H. A. (1927), *The Life of a South African Tribe*. (2 vols, 2nd edition) London: Macmillan (1st edition, 1912).
KERR, A. J. (1961), *The Native Law of Succession in South Africa: With Special Reference to the Nguni Tribes of the Ciskeian and Transkeian Territories and Natal*. London: Butterworth.
KIDD, D. (1906), *Savage Childhood: A Study of Kafir Children*. London: A. P. C. Black.
KOCKEN, E. M. and UHLENBECK, G. C. (1980), *Tlokweng, A Village Near Town*. Institute of Cultural and Social Studies, Leiden University, Leiden.
KOHLER, M. (1933), *Marriage Customs in Southern Natal*. Pretoria: Department of Native Affairs, Ethnological Publications, vol. IV.
KOOIJMAN, K. F. M. (1978), *Social and Economic Change in a Tswana Village*. Leiden: Afrika Studie Centrum.
KOTZÉ, J. C. (1978), Die moedersbroer: Institusioneel en konseptueel. *South African Journal of Ethnology*, 1 (2):21–9.
KRIGE, E. J. (1936), *The Social System of the Zulus*. London: Longmans.
KRIGE, E. J. (1937), Note on the Phalaborwa and their Morula complex. *Bantu Studies*, XI:357–67.
KRIGE, E. J. (1938), The place of the North-Eastern Transvaal Sotho in the South Bantu complex. *Africa*, XI (3):265–93.
KRIGE, E. J. (1941), Economics of exchange in a primitive society. *South African Journal of Economics*, 9 (1):1–21.
KRIGE, E. J. (1954), The Lovedu of the Transvaal. In C. D. Forde (ed.) *African Worlds*. London: Oxford University Press.
KRIGE, E. J. (1964), Property, cross-cousin marriage and the family cycle among the Lovedu. In R. Gray and P. Gulliver *The Family Estate in Africa*. London: Routledge & Kegan Paul.
KRIGE, E. J. (1968), Girls' puberty songs and their relation to fertility, health, morality and religion among the Zulu. *Africa*, 38 (2):173–97.
KRIGE, E. J. (1974), Woman-marriage, with special reference to the Lovedu – Its significance for the definition of marriage. *Africa*, XLIV (1):11–37.
KRIGE, E. J. (1975a), Asymmetrical matrilateral cross-cousin marriage. The Lovedu case. *African Studies*, 34 (4):231–7.
KRIGE, E. J. (1975b), Divine kingship, change and development. In Meyer Fortes and Sheila Patterson (eds) *Studies in African Social Anthropology*. London: Academic Press.
KRIGE, E. J. and KRIGE, J. D. (1943), *The Realm of a Rain Queen: A Study of the Pattern of Lovedu Society*. Oxford University Press for the International African Institute.
KRIGE, J. D. (1934), Bridewealth in Balobedu marriage ceremonies. *Bantu Studies*, 8:135–49.

KRIGE, J. D. (1937), Traditional origins and tribal relationships of the Sotho of the Northern Transvaal. *Bantu Studies*, 11:321-57.

KRIGE, J. D. (1939), The significance of cattle exchanges in Lovedu social structure. *Africa*, XII (4):393-424.

KROPF, A. (1848), Verfassung und Gesetzgebung im Kafferlande. *Berliner Missionsberichte*, 11:171-88.

KRUGER, F. (1936), The Lovedu. *Bantu Studies*, 10:89-105.

KUPER, A. (1969), The kinship factor in Ngologa politics. *Cahiers d'études Africaines*, IX:290-305.

KUPER, A. (1970a), *Kalahari Village Politics: An African Democracy*. Cambridge University Press.

KUPER, A. (1970b), The Kgalagari and the jural consequences of marriage. *Man*, (n.s.) 5 (3):355-81.

KUPER, A. (1970c), The Kagalagadi in the nineteenth century. *Botswana Notes and Records*, II:45-51.

KUPER, A. (1975a), The social structure of the Sotho-speaking peoples of Southern Africa. *Africa*, 54 (1):67-81; (2):139-49.

KUPER, A. (1975b), Preferential marriage and polygyny among the Tswana. In Meyer Fortes and Sheila Patterson (eds) *Studies in African Social Anthropology*. London: Academic Press.

KUPER, A. (1976), Radcliffe-Brown, Junod and the mother's brother in South Africa. *Man*, 11 (1):111-15.

KUPER, A. (1978a), Fourie and the southern Transvaal Ndebele. *African Studies*, 37:107-23.

KUPER, A. (1978b), Determinants of form in seven Tswana kinship terminologies. *Ethnology*, XVII (3):239-86.

KUPER, A. (1979a), Regional comparison in African anthropology. *African Affairs*, 78 (310):103-13.

KUPER, A. (1979b), How peculiar are the Venda? *L'Homme*, XIX:49-72.

KUPER, A. (1979c), Zulu kinship terminology over a century. *Journal of Anthropological Research*, 35 (3):373-83.

KUPER, A. (1980), The man in the field and the man in the study: Ethnography, theory and comparison in social anthropology. *European Journal of Sociology*, 21:14-39.

KUPER, A. (1981), Cousin marriage among the Thembu? *African Studies*, 40(1): 41-2.

KUPER, A. (1982), Lineage Theory: A Critical Retrospect. *Annual Review of Anthropology for 1982*.

KUPER, A. and VAN LEYNSEELE, P. (1978), Social anthropology and the 'Bantu expansion'. *Africa*, 48 (4):335-52.

KUPER, H. (1945), The marriage of a Swazi princess. *Africa*, 15 (3):145-55.

KUPER, H. (1947), *An African Aristocracy*. London: Oxford University Press.

KUPER, H. (1950), Kinship among the Swazi. In A. R. Radcliffe-Brown and C. D. Forde (eds) *African Systems of Kinship and Marriage*. London: Oxford University Press.

KUPER, H. (1952), *The Swazi*. (Ethnographic Survey of Africa) London: International African Institute.

KUPER, H. (1963), *The Swazi: A South African Kingdom*. New York: Holt, Rinehart.

KUPER, H. (1972), The language of sites in the politics of space. *American Anthropologist*, 74 (3):411-25.

KUPER, H. (1978), *Sobhuza II, Ngwenyama and King of Swaziland*. London: Duckworth.

LAUBSCHER, B. J. F. (1937), *Sex, Custom and Psychopathology*. London: Routledge & Kegan Paul.

LEACH, E. R. (1951), The structural implications of matrilateral cross-cousin marriage. *Journal of the Royal Anthropological Institute*, LXXXI:23–55.

LEACH, E. R. (1961), *Rethinking Anthropology*. London: Athlone Press (includes Leach, 1951).

LESTRADE, G. P. (1926), Some notes on the bogadi system of the Bahurutshe. *South African Journal of Science*, XXIII:937–42.

LESTRADE, G. P. (1927), Some notes on the ethnic history of the VhaVenda and their Rhodesia affinities. *South African Journal of Science*, XXIV:486–95.

LESTRADE, G. P. (1930), The 'mala' system of the Venda-speaking tribes. *Bantu Studies*, 4:193–204.

LÉVI-STRAUSS, C. (1956), Les organisations dualistes, existent-elles? *Bijdragen tot de Taal-, Land- en Volkenkunde* 112:99–128. Trans. and reprinted in *Structural Anthropology* (New York: Basic Books, 1963).

LÉVI-STRAUSS, C. (1966), The future of kinship studies. *Proceedings of the Royal Anthropological Institute for 1965*, pp. 13–22.

LÉVI-STRAUSS, C. (1969), *The Elementary Structures of Kinship*. London: Eyre & Spottiswoode. (First French edition, 1949.)

LÉVI-STRAUSS, C. (1978), *The Origin of Table Manners*. London: Jonathan Cape. (First French edition, 1968.)

LOUNSBURY, F. G. (1964), A formal account of the Crow- and Omaha type kinship terminology. In W. Goodenough (ed.) *Explorations in Cultural Anthropology*. New York: McGraw-Hill.

LOUW, J. A. (1957), *The Nomenclature of Cattle in the South-Eastern Bantu Languages*. Pretoria: Communications of the University of South Africa, C, 2.

MABILLE, A. and DIETERLEN, H. (1961), *Southern Sotho-English Dictionary*. (revised by R. A. Paroz) Morija Sesuto Book Depot.

MACLEAN, J. B. (1906), *Compendium of Kafir Laws and Customs*. Grahamstown: J. Slater.

MAGGS, T. N. O'C. (1976), *Iron Age Communities of the Southern Highveld*. Pietermaritzburg: The Natal Museum.

MARWICK, B. A. (1940), *The Swazi*. Cambridge University Press.

MATSEBULA, J. S. M. (1972), *A History of Swaziland*. Cape Town: Longman.

MATTHEWS, Z. K. (1940), Marriage customs among the Barolong. *Africa*, 13 (1):1–23.

MAYR, F. (1906), The Zulu Kafirs of Natal. *Anthropos*, 1:453–71.

MEILLASSOUX, C. (1964), *Anthropologie Économique des Gouro de Côte d'Ivoire*. The Hague: Mouton.

MIDDLETON, J. and TAIT, D. (eds) (1958), *Tribes Without Rulers*. London: Routledge & Kegan Paul.

MÖNNIG, H. (1961), Lovedu kinship terminology. *African Studies*, XX (4): 226–36.

MÖNNIG, H. (1963), The structure of Lovedu social and political organisation. *African Studies*, XXII (2):49–64.

MÖNNIG, H. (1967), *The Pedi*. Pretoria: van Schaik.

MORGAN, L. H. (1870), *Systems of Consanguinity and Affinity of the Human Family*. Washington: Smithsonian Contributions to Knowledge.

MORGAN, L. H. (1878), *Ancient Society*. New York: Henry Holt.

MURDOCK, G. P. (1949), *Social Structure*. New York: Macmillan.

MURDOCK, G. P. (1959), *Africa: Its Peoples and Their Culture History*. New York: McGraw Hill.

MURDOCK, G. P. (1967), Ethnographic atlas: A summary. *Ethnology*, 6:109–236.

MURDOCK, G. P. (1968), Patterns of sibling terminology. *Ethnology*, 7:1–24.
MURDOCK, G. P. (1970), Kin term patterns and their distribution. *Ethnology*, 9:165–208.
MURRAY, C. (1976), Marital strategy in Lesotho: the redistribution of migrant earnings. *African Studies*, 35(2):99–121.
MURRAY, C. (1977), High bridewealth, migrant labour and the position of women in Lesotho. *Journal of African Law*, 21 (1):79–96.
MURRAY, C. (1978), Migration, differentiation and the developmental cycle in Lesotho. In W. van Binsbergen and H. Meilink (eds) *Migration and the Transformation of Modern African Society*. Leiden: Afrika-studiecentrum.
MURRAY, C. (1980a), Migrant labour and changing family structure in the rural periphery of Southern Africa. *Journal of Southern African Studies*, 6 (2): 139–56.
MURRAY, C. (1980b), Sotho fertility symbolism. *African Studies*, 39 (1):64–76.
NERLOVE, S. and ROMNEY, A. K. (1967), Sibling terminology and cross-sex behaviour. *American Anthropologist*, 69:179–87.
NGUBANE, H. (1977), *Body and Mind in Zulu Medicine*. London: Academic Press.
NICHOLSON, B. (1888), Heirship of the youngest among the Kafirs of Africa. *Archaeological Review*, 2 (3):163–6.
Notes and Queries on Anthropology (1951). 6th edition. London: Routledge & Kegan Paul.
PARKIN, D. J. (1972), *Palms, Wine and Witnesses*. New York: Chandler.
PEIRES, J. B. (1975), The rise of the 'Right-Hand House' in the history and historiography of the Xhosa. *History in Africa*, 2:113–26.
POULTER, S. (1976), *Family Law and Litigation in Basotho Society*. Oxford: Clarendon Press.
PRESTON-WHYTE, E. (1974), Kinship and marriage. In W. D. Hammond-Tooke (ed.) *The Bantu-Speaking Peoples of Southern Africa*. London: Routledge & Kegan Paul.
RADCLIFFE-BROWN, A. R. (1924), The mother's brother in South Africa. *South African Journal of Science*, 22:542–55.
RADCLIFFE-BROWN, A. R. (1940), On joking relationships. *Africa*, XIII: 195–210.
RAMSAY, T. D. (1946), Tsonga law in the Transvaal. *African Studies*, 9 (3): 143–56.
READER, D. H. (1966), *Zulu Tribe in Transition*. Manchester University Press.
Report and Proceedings with Appendices of the Government Commission on Native Law and Customs (1883). Cape Town: Government Printer. Cape of Good Hope Blue Book: Nr. G 4, 1883.
REUTER, F. (1907), Modjadje, a native queen in Northern Transvaal: An ethnological study. *South African Journal of Science*, 3:242–50.
RICHARDS, A. I. (1932), *Hunger and Work in a Savage Tribe: A Functional Study of Nutrition among the Southern Bantu*. London: Routledge & Kegan Paul.
RICHARDS, A. I. (1939), *Land, Labour and Diet in Northern Rhodesia*. London: Oxford University Press.
RICHARDS, A. I. (1950), Some types of family structure amongst the Central Bantu. In A. R. Radcliffe-Brown and C. D. Forde (eds) *African Systems of Kinship and Marriage*. London: Oxford University Press.
ROBERTS, S. (1977), The Kgatla marriage: Concepts of validity. In S. Roberts (ed.) *Law and the Family in Africa*. The Hague: Mouton.

ROUMEGUÈRE-EBERHARDT, J. (1963), *Pensée et Société Africaines. Essais sur une Dialectique de Complémentarité Antagoniste chez les Bantu de Sud-Est.* Paris-La Haye, Mouton (Cahiers de L'Homme, n.s., 111).

SAMUELSON, L. H. (1930), *Zululand: Its Traditions, Legends, Customs and Folklore.* Natal: Mariannhill Mission Press.

SANSOM, B. (1976), A signal transaction and its currency. In Bruce Kapferer (ed.) *Transaction and Meaning.* Philadelphia: ISHI.

SCHAPERA, I. (1933), Premarital pregnancy and native opinion. *Africa,* 6: 59–89.

SCHAPERA, I. (1938), *A Handbook of Tswana Law and Custom.* London: Oxford University Press for the International African Institute.

SCHAPERA, I. (1940), *Married Life in an African Tribe.* London: Faber & Faber.

SCHAPERA, I. (1943), *Native Land Tenure in the Bechuanaland Protectorate.* Alice: Lovedale Press.

SCHAPERA, I. (1947), *Migrant Labour and Tribal Life: A Study of Conditions in the Bechuanaland Protectorate.* London: Oxford University Press.

SCHAPERA, I. (1949), The Tswana conception of incest. In M. Fortes (ed.) *Social Structure.* London: Oxford University Press.

SCHAPERA, I. (1950), Kinship and marriage among the Tswana. In A. R. Radcliffe-Brown and C. D. Forde (eds) *African Systems of Kinship and Marriage.* London: Oxford University Press.

SCHAPERA, I. (1952), *The Ethnic Composition of Tswana Tribes.* London School of Economics Monographs on Social Anthropology. No. 11.

SCHAPERA, I. (1953), *The Tswana.* London: International African Institute.

SCHAPERA, I. (1956), *Government and Politics in Tribal Society.* London: Watts.

SCHAPERA, I. (1957), Marriage of near kin among the Tswana. *Africa,* 27 (2): 139–59.

SCHAPERA, I. (1963a), Agnatic marriage in Tswana royal families. In I. Schapera (ed.) *Studies in Kinship and Marriage.* London: Royal Anthropological Institute. Occasional Paper, no. 16.

SCHAPERA, I. (1963b), Kinship and politics in Tswana history. *Journal of the Royal Anthropological Institute,* 93:159–73.

SCHAPERA, I. (1970), *Tribal Innovators: Tswana Chiefs and Social Change 1795-1940.* London: Athlone Press.

SCHAPERA, I. (1971), *Rainmaking Rites of Tswana Tribes.* Leiden: Africa Study Centre.

SCHAPERA, I. (1978a), Some notes on Tswana bogadi. *Journal of African Law,* 22 (2):112–24.

SCHAPERA, I. (1978b), Some Kgatla theories of procreation. In John Argyle and Eleanor Preston Whyte (eds) *Social System and Tradition in Southern Africa.* Cape Town: Oxford University Press.

SCHAPERA, I. (1979), Kgatla notions of ritual impurity. *African Studies,* 38 (1): 3–15.

SCHAPERA, I. (ed.) (1937), *The Bantu-Speaking Tribes of South Africa: An Ethnographical Survey.* London: Routledge.

SCHEFFLER, H. (1971), Dravidian-Iroquois: The Melanesian evidence. In C. Jayawardena and R. L. Hiatt (eds) *Anthropology in Oceania.* Sydney: Angus & Robertson.

SCHNEIDER, H. K. (1957), The subsistence role of cattle among the Pakot and in East Africa. *American Anthropologist,* 59:278–300.

SCHNEIDER, H. K. (1964), A model of African indigenous economy and society. *Comparative Studies in Society and History,* 7 (1):37–55.

SEYMOUR, S. M. (1970), *Bantu Law in South Africa.* Cape Town: Juta & Co.

SHAW, E. M. and VAN WARMELO, N. J. (1972), *The Material Culture of the Cape Nguni: Part 1: Settlement.* Annals of the South African Museum 58 (1).

SHAW, E. M. (1974), Material culture. In W. Hammond-Tooke (ed.) *The Bantu-Speaking Peoples of Southern Africa.* London: Routledge & Kegan Paul.

SHEDDICK, V. G. J. (1953), *The Southern Sotho.* Ethnographic Survey of Africa. London: International African Institute.

SHOOTER, J. (1857), *The Kafirs of Natal and the Zulu Country.* London: Stanford.

SOGA, J. H. (1931), *The Ama-Xosa: Life and Customs.* Lovedale: Lovedale Press.

STAYT, H. (1931), *The Bavenda.* London: Oxford University Press.

TJON SIE FAT, F. (1981), More complex formulae of generalized exchange. *Current Anthropology,* 22 (4):377–99.

TURTON, DAVID (1980), The economics of Mursi bridewealth: A comparative perspective. In J. L. Comaroff (ed.) *The Meaning of Marriage Payments.* London and New York: Academic Press.

VANSINA, JAN (1966), *Kingdoms of the Savanna.* Madison: University of Wisconsin Press.

VAN TROMP, J. (1948), *Xhosa Law of Persons: A Treatise on the Legal Principles of Family Relations among the Amaxhosa.* Cape Town: Juta & Co.

VAN WARMELO, N. J. (1930), *Transvaal Ndebele Texts.* Pretoria: Dept. of Native Affairs.

VAN WARMELO, N. J. (1931), *Kinship Terminology of the South African Bantu.* Pretoria: Dept. of Native Affairs. Ethnological Publications, vol. 2.

VAN WARMELO, N. J. (1935), *A Preliminary Survey of the Bantu.* Pretoria: Dept. of Native Affairs. Ethnological Publications, vol. 5.

VAN WARMELO, N. J. (1944), *The Bakoni ba Maake.* Pretoria: Government Ethnological Publications no. 12.

VAN WARMELO, N. J. (1953), *Die Tlokwa en Birwa van Noord Transvaal.* Pretoria: Dept. of Bantu Affairs. Ethnological Publications, no. 29.

VAN WARMELO, N. J. (1974), The classification of cultural groups. In Hammond-Tooke, W. (ed.) *The Bantu Speaking Peoples of Southern Africa.* London: Routledge & Kegan Paul.

VAN WARMELO, N. J. (1977), *Anthropology of Southern Africa in Periodicals to 1950.* Johannesburg: Witwatersrand University Press.

VAN WARMELO, N. J. and PHOPHI, W. M. D. (1948–67), *Venda Law.* Pretoria, Government Printer.

I: Betrothal. Thakka, Wedding, 1948 (Ethnological Publications no. 23);

II: Married Life, 1948 (Ethnological Publications no. 23);

III: Divorce, 1948 (Ethnological Publications no. 23);

IV: Inheritance, 1949 (Ethnological Publications no. 23);

V: Property, 1967 (Ethnological Publications no. 50).

WALTON, J. (1956), *African Village.* Pretoria: Van Schaik.

WEBB, C. and WRIGHT, J. (1979), *The James Stuart Archive* vol. 2. Pietermaritz-burg: University of Natal Press.

WEBSTER, D. (1977), Spreading the risk: The principles of laterality among the Chopi. *Africa,* 47 (2):192–207.

WHITFIELD, G. M. B. (1948), *South African Native Law.* Cape Town: Juta.

WILLOUGHBY, W. C. (1905), Totemism of the Becwana. *Journal of the Royal Anthropological Institute,* 35:295–314.

WILLOUGHBY, W. C. (1923), *Race Problems in the New Africa.* Oxford: Claren-don Press.

WILLOUGHBY, W. C. (1928), *The Soul of the Bantu*. New York: Doubleday, Doran.

WILSON, M. (1969), The Nguni people. In Monica Wilson and Leonard Thompson (eds) *The Oxford History of South Africa*. vol. 1. Oxford: Clarendon Press.

WILSON, M. (1969), The Sotho, Venda and Tsonga. In M. Wilson and L. Thompson (eds) *The Oxford History of South Africa*. vol. 1. Oxford: Clarendon Press.

ZIERVOGEL, D. (1944), *Swazi-Gebruike vanaf Geboorte tot Huwelik*. University of Pretoria, Dept. van Bantoe-tale en volkekunde, reeks A, I.

ZIERVOGEL, D. (1954), *The Eastern Sotho: A Tribal, Historical and Linguistic Survey*. Pretoria: Van Schaik.

ZIERVOGEL, D. (1957), *Swazi Texts*. Pretoria: Van Schaik.

Index

Routledge Social Science Series

Routledge & Kegan Paul   London, Henley and Boston

39 Store Street,
London WC1E 7DD
Broadway House,
Newtown Road,
Henley-on-Thames,
Oxon RG9 1EN
9 Park Street,
Boston, Mass. 02108

Contents

*Authors wishing to submit manuscripts for any series
in this catalogue should send them to the Social Science Editor,
Routledge & Kegan Paul Ltd, 39 Store Street,
London WC1E 7DD.*
● *Books so marked are available in paperback.*
○ *Books so marked are available in paperback only.*
*All books are in metric Demy 8vo format (216 × 138mm approx.)
unless otherwise stated.*

International Library of Sociology
General Editor John Rex

GENERAL SOCIOLOGY

Barnsley, J. H. The Social Reality of Ethics. *464 pp.*
Brown, Robert. Explanation in Social Science. *208 pp.*
● Rules and Laws in Sociology. *192 pp.*
Bruford, W. H. Chekhov and His Russia. *A Sociological Study. 244 pp.*
Burton, F. and **Carlen, P.** Official Discourse. *On Discourse Analysis, Government Publications, Ideology. About 140 pp.*
Cain, Maureen E. Society and the Policeman's Role. *326 pp.*
● **Fletcher, Colin.** Beneath the Surface. *An Account of Three Styles of Sociological Research. 221 pp.*
Gibson, Quentin. The Logic of Social Enquiry. *240 pp.*
Glassner, B. Essential Interactionism. *208 pp.*
Glucksmann, M. Structuralist Analysis in Contemporary Social Thought. *212 pp.*
Gurvitch, Georges. Sociology of Law. *Foreword by Roscoe Pound. 264 pp.*
Hinkle, R. Founding Theory of American Sociology 1881–1913. *About 350 pp.*
Homans, George C. Sentiments and Activities. *336 pp.*
Johnson, Harry M. Sociology: *A Systematic Introduction. Foreword by Robert K. Merton. 710 pp.*
● **Keat, Russell** and **Urry, John.** Social Theory as Science. *278 pp.*
Mannheim, Karl. Essays on Sociology and Social Psychology. *Edited by Paul Keckskemeti. With Editorial Note by Adolph Lowe. 344 pp.*
Martindale, Don. The Nature and Types of Sociological Theory. *292 pp.*
● **Maus, Heinz.** A Short History of Sociology. *234 pp.*
Myrdal, Gunnar. Value in Social Theory: *A Collection of Essays on Methodology. Edited by Paul Streeten. 332 pp.*
Ogburn, William F. and **Nimkoff, Meyer F.** A Handbook of Sociology. *Preface by Karl Mannheim. 656 pp. 46 figures. 35 tables.*
Parsons, Talcott and **Smelser, Neil J.** Economy and Society: *A Study in the Integration of Economic and Social Theory. 362 pp.*
Payne, G., Dingwall, R., Payne, J. and **Carter, M.** Sociology and Social Research. *About 250 pp.*
Podgórecki, A. Practical Social Sciences. *About 200 pp.*
Podgórecki, A. and **Łos, M.** Multidimensional Sociology. *268 pp.*
Raffel, S. Matters of Fact. *A Sociological Inquiry. 152 pp.*
● **Rex, John.** Key Problems of Sociological Theory. *220 pp.*
    Sociology and the Demystification of the Modern World. *282 pp.*
● **Rex, John.** (Ed.) Approaches to Sociology. *Contributions by Peter Abell, Frank Bechhofer, Basil Bernstein, Ronald Fletcher, David Frisby, Miriam Glucksmann, Peter Lassman, Herminio Martins, John Rex, Roland Robertson, John Westergaard and Jock Young. 302 pp.*
Rigby, A. Alternative Realities. *352 pp.*
Roche, M. Phenomenology, Language and the Social Sciences. *374 pp.*
Sahay, A. Sociological Analysis. *220 pp.*
Strasser, Hermann. The Normative Structure of Sociology. *Conservative and Emancipatory Themes in Social Thought. About 340 pp.*
Strong, P. Ceremonial Order of the Clinic. *267 pp.*
Urry, John. Reference Groups and the Theory of Revolution. *244 pp.*
Weinberg, E. Development of Sociology in the Soviet Union. *173 pp.*

FOREIGN CLASSICS OF SOCIOLOGY

● **Gerth, H. H.** and **Mills, C. Wright.** From Max Weber: *Essays in Sociology. 502 pp.*

● **Tönnies, Ferdinand.** Community and Association *(Gemeinschaft und Gesell-schaft).\Translated and Supplemented by Charles P. Loomis. Foreword by Pitirim A. Sorokin. 334 pp.*

SOCIAL STRUCTURE

Andreski, Stanislav. Military Organization and Society. *Foreword by Professor A. R. Radcliffe-Brown. 226 pp. 1 folder.*

Broom, L., Lancaster Jones, F., McDonnell, P. and Williams, T. The Inheritance of Inequality. *About 180 pp.*

Carlton, Eric. Ideology and Social Order. *Foreword by Professor Philip Abrahams. About 320 pp.*

Clegg, S. and Dunkerley, D. Organization, Class and Control. *614 pp.*

Coontz, Sydney H. Population Theories and the Economic Interpretation. *202 pp.*

Coser, Lewis. The Functions of Social Conflict. *204 pp.*

Crook, I. and D. The First Years of the Yangyi Commune. *304 pp., illustrated.*

Dickie-Clark, H. F. Marginal Situation: *A Sociological Study of a Coloured Group. 240 pp. 11 tables.*

Giner, S. and Archer, M. S. (Eds) Contemporary Europe: *Social Structures and Cultural Patterns, 336 pp.*

● **Glaser, Barney and Strauss, Anselm L.** Status Passage: *A Formal Theory. 212 pp.*

Glass, D. V. (Ed.) Social Mobility in Britain. *Contributions by J. Berent, T. Bottomore, R. C. Chambers, J. Floud, D. V. Glass, J. R. Hall, H. T. Himmelweit, R. K. Kelsall, F. M. Martin, C. A. Moser, R. Mukherjee and W. Ziegel. 420 pp.*

Kelsall, R. K. Higher Civil Servants in Britain: *From 1870 to the Present Day. 268 pp. 31 tables.*

● **Lawton, Denis.** Social Class, Language and Education. *192 pp.*

McLeish, John. The Theory of Social Change: *Four Views Considered. 128 pp.*

● **Marsh, David C.** The Changing Social Structure of England and Wales, 1871–1961. *Revised edition. 288 pp.*

Menzies, Ken. Talcott Parsons and the Social Image of Man. *About 208 pp.*

● **Mouzelis, Nicos.** Organization and Bureaucracy. *An Analysis of Modern Theories. 240 pp.*

● **Ossowski, Stanislaw.** Class Structure in the Social Consciousness. *210 pp.*

● **Podgórecki, Adam.** Law and Society. *302 pp.*

Renner, Karl. Institutions of Private Law and Their Social Functions. *Edited, with an Introduction and Notes, by O. Kahn-Freud. Translated by Agnes Schwarzschild. 316 pp.*

Rex, J. and Tomlinson, S. Colonial Immigrants in a British City. *A Class Analysis. 368 pp.*

Smooha, S. Israel: Pluralism and Conflict. *472 pp.*

Wesolowski, W. Class, Strata and Power. *Trans. and with Introduction by G. Kolankiewicz. 160 pp.*

Zureik, E. Palestinians in Israel. *A Study in Internal Colonialism. 264 pp.*

SOCIOLOGY AND POLITICS

Acton, T. A. Gypsy Politics and Social Change. *316 pp.*

Burton, F. Politics of Legitimacy. *Struggles in a Belfast Community. 250 pp.*

Crook, I. and D. Revolution in a Chinese Village. *Ten Mile Inn. 216 pp., illustrated.*

Etzioni-Halevy, E. Political Manipulation and Administrative Power. *A Comparative Study. About 200 pp.*

Fielding, N. The National Front. *About 250 pp.*

● **Hechter, Michael.** Internal Colonialism. *The Celtic Fringe in British National Development, 1536–1966. 380 pp.*

Kornhauser, William. The Politics of Mass Society. *272 pp. 20 tables.*

Korpi, W. The Working Class in Welfare Capitalism. *Work, Unions and Politics in Sweden. 472 pp.*

Kroes, R. Soldiers and Students. *A Study of Right- and Left-wing Students. 174 pp.*

Martin, Roderick. Sociology of Power. *About 272 pp.*

Merquior, J. G. Rousseau and Weber. *A Study in the Theory of Legitimacy. About 288 pp.*

Myrdal, Gunnar. The Political Element in the Development of Economic Theory. *Translated from the German by Paul Streeten. 282 pp.*

Varma, B. N. The Sociology and Politics of Development. *A Theoretical Study. 236 pp.*

Wong, S.-L. Sociology and Socialism in Contemporary China. *160 pp.*

Wootton, Graham. Workers, Unions and the State. *188 pp.*

CRIMINOLOGY

Ancel, Marc. Social Defence: *A Modern Approach to Criminal Problems. Foreword by Leon Radzinowicz. 240 pp.*

Athens, L. Violent Criminal Acts and Actors. *104 pp.*

Cain, Maureen E. Society and the Policeman's Role. *326 pp.*

Cloward, Richard A. and **Ohlin, Lloyd E.** Delinquency and Opportunity: *A Theory of Delinquent Gangs. 248 pp.*

Downes, David M. The Delinquent Solution. *A Study in Subcultural Theory. 296 pp.*

Friedlander, Kate. The Psycho-Analytical Approach to Juvenile Delinquency: *Theory, Case Studies, Treatment. 320 pp.*

Gleuck, Sheldon and **Eleanor.** Family Environment and Delinquency. *With the statistical assistance of Rose W. Kneznek. 340 pp.*

Lopez-Rey, Manuel. Crime. *An Analytical Appraisal. 288 pp.*

Mannheim, Hermann. Comparative Criminology: *A Text Book. Two volumes. 442 pp. and 380 pp.*

Morris, Terence. The Criminal Area: *A Study in Social Ecology. Foreword by Hermann Mannheim. 232 pp. 25 tables. 4 maps.*

Rock, Paul. Making People Pay. *338 pp.*

● **Taylor, Ian, Walton, Paul** and **Young, Jock.** The New Criminology. *For a Social Theory of Deviance. 325 pp.*

● **Taylor, Ian, Walton, Paul** and **Young, Jock.** (Eds) Critical Criminology. *268 pp.*

SOCIAL PSYCHOLOGY

Bagley, Christopher. The Social Psychology of the Epileptic Child. *320 pp.*

Brittan, Arthur. Meanings and Situations. *224 pp.*

Carroll, J. Break-Out from the Crystal Palace. *200 pp.*

● **Fleming, C. M.** Adolescence: Its Social Psychology. *With an Introduction to recent findings from the fields of Anthropology, Physiology, Medicine, Psychometrics and Sociometry. 288 pp.*

● The Social Psychology of Education: *An Introduction and Guide to Its Study. 136 pp.*

Linton, Ralph. The Cultural Background of Personality. *132 pp.*

● **Mayo, Elton.** The Social Problems of an Industrial Civilization. *With an Appendix on the Political Problem. 180 pp.*

Ottaway, A. K. C. Learning Through Group Experience. *176 pp.*

Plummer, Ken. Sexual Stigma. *An Interactionist Account. 254 pp.*

● **Rose, Arnold M.** (Ed.) Human Behaviour and Social Processes: *an Interactionist Approach. Contributions by Arnold M. Rose, Ralph H. Turner, Anselm Strauss, Everett C. Hughes, E. Franklin Frazier, Howard S. Becker et al. 696 pp.*

Smelser, Neil J. Theory of Collective Behaviour. *448 pp.*

Stephenson, Geoffrey M. The Development of Conscience. *128 pp.*

Young, Kimball. Handbook of Social Psychology. *658 pp. 16 figures. 10 tables.*

SOCIOLOGY OF THE FAMILY

Bell, Colin R. Middle Class Families: *Social and Geographical Mobility. 224 pp.*
Burton, Lindy. Vulnerable Children. *272 pp.*
Gavron, Hannah. The Captive Wife: *Conflicts of Household Mothers. 190 pp.*
George, Victor and **Wilding, Paul.** Motherless Families. *248 pp.*
Klein, Josephine. Samples from English Cultures.
    1. Three Preliminary Studies and Aspects of Adult Life in England. *447 pp.*
    2. Child-Rearing Practices and Index. *247 pp.*
Klein, Viola. The Feminine Character. *History of an Ideology. 244 pp.*
McWhinnie, Alexina M. Adopted Children. *How They Grow Up. 304 pp.*
● **Morgan, D. H. J.** Social Theory and the Family. *About 320 pp.*
● **Myrdal, Alva** and **Klein, Viola.** Women's Two Roles: *Home and Work. 238 pp.*
    27 tables.
Parsons, Talcott and **Bales, Robert F.** Family: Socialization and Interaction Process.
    In collaboration with James Olds, Morris Zelditch and Philip E. Slater. 456 pp.
    50 figures and tables.

SOCIAL SERVICES

Bastide, Roger. The Sociology of Mental Disorder. *Translated from the French by*
    Jean McNeil. 260 pp.
Carlebach, Julius. Caring For Children in Trouble. *266 pp.*
George, Victor. Foster Care. *Theory and Practice. 234 pp.*
    Social Security: *Beveridge and After. 258 pp.*
George, V. and **Wilding, P.** Motherless Families. *248 pp.*
● **Goetschius, George W.** Working with Community Groups. *256 pp.*
Goetschius, George W. and **Tash, Joan.** Working with Unattached Youth. *416 pp.*
Heywood, Jean S. Children in Care. *The Development of the Service for the Deprived*
    Child. Third revised edition. 284 pp.
King, Roy D., Ranes, Norma V. and **Tizard, Jack.** Patterns of Residential Care.
    356 pp.
Leigh, John. Young People and Leisure. *256 pp.*
● **Mays, John.** (Ed.) Penelope Hall's Social Services of England and Wales.
    368 pp.
Morris, Mary. Voluntary Work and the Welfare State. *300 pp.*
Nokes, P. L. The Professional Task in Welfare Practice. *152 pp.*
Timms, Noel. Psychiatric Social Work in Great Britain (1939–1962). *280 pp.*
●   Social Casework: *Principles and Practice. 256 pp.*

SOCIOLOGY OF EDUCATION

Banks, Olive. Parity and Prestige in English Secondary Education: a Study in
    Educational Sociology. *272 pp.*
● **Blyth, W. A. L.** English Primary Education. *A Sociological Description.*
    2. Background. *168 pp.*
Collier, K. G. The Social Purposes of Education: *Personal and Social Values in*
    Education. 268 pp.
Evans, K. M. Sociometry and Education. *158 pp.*
● **Ford, Julienne.** Social Class and the Comprehensive School. *192 pp.*
Foster, P. J. Education and Social Change in Ghana. *336 pp. 3 maps.*
Fraser, W. R. Education and Society in Modern France. *150 pp.*
Grace, Gerald R. Role Conflict and the Teacher. *150 pp.*
Hans, Nicholas. New Trends in Education in the Eighteenth Century. *278 pp.*
    19 tables.
●   Comparative Education: *A Study of Educational Factors and Traditions. 360 pp.*
● **Hargreaves, David.** Interpersonal Relations and Education. *432 pp.*
●   Social Relations in a Secondary School. *240 pp.*
    School Organization and Pupil Involvement. *A Study of Secondary Schools.*

● **Mannheim, Karl** and **Stewart, W. A. C.** An Introduction to the Sociology of
Education. *206 pp.*
● **Musgrove, F.** Youth and the Social Order. *176 pp.*
● **Ottaway, A. K. C.** Education and Society: An Introduction to the Sociology of
Education. *With an Introduction by W. O. Lester Smith. 212 pp.*
Peers, Robert. Adult Education: *A Comparative Study. Revised edition. 398 pp.*
Stratta, Erica. The Education of Borstal Boys. *A Study of their Educational
Experiences prior to, and during, Borstal Training. 256 pp.*
● **Taylor, P. H., Reid, W. A.** and **Holley, B. J.** The English Sixth Form. *A Case Study in
Curriculum Research. 198 pp.*

SOCIOLOGY OF CULTURE

Eppel, E. M. and **M.** Adolescents and Morality: *A Study of some Moral Values and
Dilemmas of Working Adolescents in the Context of a changing Climate of
Opinion. Foreword by W. J. H. Sprott. 268 pp. 39 tables.*
● **Fromm, Erich.** The Fear of Freedom. *286 pp.*
● The Sane Society. *400 pp.*
Johnson, L. The Cultural Critics. *From Matthew Arnold to Raymond Williams.
233 pp.*
Mannheim, Karl. Essays on the Sociology of Culture. *Edited by Ernst Mannheim in
co-operation with Paul Kecskemeti. Editorial Note by Adolph Lowe. 280 pp.*
Merquior, J. G. The Veil and the Mask. *Essays on Culture and Ideology. Foreword
by Ernest Gellner. 140 pp.*
Zijderfeld, A. C. On Clichés. *The Supersedure of Meaning by Function in Modernity.
150 pp.*

SOCIOLOGY OF RELIGION

Argyle, Michael and **Beit-Hallahmi, Benjamin.** The Social Psychology of Religion.
256 pp.
Glasner, Peter E. The Sociology of Secularisation. *A Critique of a Concept.
146 pp.*
Hall, J. R. The Ways Out. *Utopian Communal Groups in an Age of Babylon. 280 pp.*
Ranson, S., Hinings, B. and **Bryman, A.** Clergy, Ministers and Priests. *216 pp.*
Stark, Werner. The Sociology of Religion. *A Study of Christendom.*
Volume II. *Sectarian Religion. 368 pp.*
Volume III. *The Universal Church. 464 pp.*
Volume IV. *Types of Religious Man. 352 pp.*
Volume V. *Types of Religious Culture. 464 pp.*
Turner, B. S. Weber and Islam. *216 pp.*
Watt, W. Montgomery. Islam and the Integration of Society. *320 pp.*

SOCIOLOGY OF ART AND LITERATURE

Jarvie, Ian C. Towards a Sociology of the Cinema. *A Comparative Essay on the
Structure and Functioning of a Major Entertainment Industry. 405 pp.*
Rust, Frances S. Dance in Society. *An Analysis of the Relationships between the Social
Dance and Society in England from the Middle Ages to the Present Day. 256 pp.
8 pp. of plates.*
Schücking, L. L. The Sociology of Literary Taste. *112 pp.*
Wolff, Janet. Hermeneutic Philosophy and the Sociology of Art. *150 pp.*

SOCIOLOGY OF KNOWLEDGE

Diesing, P. Patterns of Discovery in the Social Sciences. *262 pp.*

● **Douglas, J. D.** (Ed.) Understanding Everyday Life. *370 pp.*
● **Hamilton, P.** Knowledge and Social Structure. *174 pp.*
  Jarvie, I. C. Concepts and Society. *232 pp.*
  Mannheim, Karl. Essays on the Sociology of Knowledge. *Edited by Paul Kecskemeti.*
    Editorial Note by Adolph Lowe. 353 pp.
  Remmling, Gunter W. The Sociology of Karl Mannheim. *With a Bibliographical*
    Guide to the Sociology of Knowledge, Ideological Analysis, and Social Planning.
    255 pp.
  Remmling, Gunter W. (Ed.) Towards the Sociology of Knowledge. *Origin and*
    Development of a Sociological Thought Style. 463 pp.
  Scheler, M. Problems of a Sociology of Knowledge. *Trans. by M. S. Frings. Edited*
    and with an Introduction by K. Stikkers. 232 pp.

URBAN SOCIOLOGY

  Aldridge, M. The British New Towns. *A Programme Without a Policy. 232 pp.*
  Ashworth, William. The Genesis of Modern British Town Planning: *A Study in*
    Economic and Social History of the Nineteenth and Twentieth Centuries. 288 pp.
  Brittan, A. The Privatised World. *196 pp.*
  Cullingworth, J. B. Housing Needs and Planning Policy: *A Restatement of the*
    Problems of Housing Need and 'Overspill' in England and Wales. 232 pp. 44
    tables. 8 maps.
  Dickinson, Robert E. City and Region: *A Geographical Interpretation. 608 pp. 125*
    figures.
    The West European City: *A Geographical Interpretation. 600 pp. 129 maps.*
    29 plates.
  Humphreys, Alexander J. New Dubliners: *Urbanization and the Irish Family.*
    Foreword by George C. Homans. 304 pp.
  Jackson, Brian. Working Class Community: *Some General Notions raised by a Series*
    of Studies in Northern England. 192 pp.
● **Mann, P. H.** An Approach to Urban Sociology. *240 pp.*
  Mellor, J. R. Urban Sociology in an Urbanized Society. *326 pp.*
  Morris, R. N. and **Mogey, J.** The Sociology of Housing. *Studies at Berinsfield. 232 pp.*
    4 pp. plates.
  Mullan, R. Stevenage Ltd. *About 250 pp.*
  Rex, J. and **Tomlinson, S.** Colonial Immigrants in a British City. *A Class Analysis.*
    368 pp.
  Rosser, C. and **Harris, C.** The Family and Social Change. *A Study of Family and*
    Kinship in a South Wales Town. 352 pp. 8 maps.
● **Stacey, Margaret, Batsone, Eric, Bell, Colin** and **Thurcott, Anne.** Power, Persistence
    and Change. *A Second Study of Banbury. 196 pp.*

RURAL SOCIOLOGY

  Mayer, Adrian C. Peasants in the Pacific. *A Study of Fiji Indian Rural Society. 248 pp.*
    20 plates.
  Williams, W. M. The Sociology of an English Village: *Gosforth. 272 pp. 12 figures.*
    13 tables.

SOCIOLOGY OF INDUSTRY AND DISTRIBUTION

  Dunkerley, David. The Foreman. *Aspects of Task and Structure. 192 pp.*
  Eldridge, J. E. T. Industrial Disputes. *Essays in the Sociology of Industrial Relations.*
    288 pp.
  Hollowell, Peter G. The Lorry Driver. *272 pp.*
● **Oxaal, I., Barnett, T.** and **Booth, D.** (Eds) Beyond the Sociology of Development.

Economy and Society in Latin America and Africa. 295 pp.

Smelser, Neil J. Social Change in the Industrial Revolution: *An Application of Theory to the Lancashire Cotton Industry, 1770–1840. 468 pp. 12 figures. 14 tables.*

Watson, T. J. The Personnel Managers. *A Study in the Sociology of Work and Employment, 262 pp.*

ANTHROPOLOGY

Brandel-Syrier, Mia. Reeftown Elite. *A Study of Social Mobility in a Modern African Community on the Reef. 376 pp.*

Dickie-Clark, H. F. The Marginal Situation. *A Sociological Study of a Coloured Group. 236 pp.*

Dube, S. C. Indian Village. *Foreword by Morris Edward Opler. 276 pp. 4 plates.*
India's Changing Villages: *Human Factors in Community Development. 260 pp. 8 plates. 1 map.*

Fei, H.-T. Peasant Life in China. *A Field Study of Country Life in the Yangtze Valley. With a foreword by Bronislaw Malinowski. 328 pp. 16 pp. plates.*

Firth, Raymond. Malay Fishermen. *Their Peasant Economy. 420 pp. 17 pp. plates.*

Gulliver, P. H. Social Control in an African Society: a Study of the Arusha, Agricultural Masai of Northern Tanganyika. *320 pp. 8 plates. 10 figures.*
Family Herds. *288 pp.*

Jarvie, Ian C. The Revolution in Anthropology. *268 pp.*

Little, Kenneth L. Mende of Sierra Leone. *308 pp. and folder.*
Negroes in Britain. *With a New Introduction and Contemporary Study by Leonard Bloom. 320 pp.*

Tambs-Lyche, H. London Patidars. *About 180 pp.*

Madan, G. R. Western Sociologists on Indian Society. *Marx, Spencer, Weber, Durkheim, Pareto. 384 pp.*

Mayer, A. C. Peasants in the Pacific. *A Study of Fiji Indian Rural Society. 248 pp.*

Meer, Fatima. Race and Suicide in South Africa. *325 pp.*

Smith, Raymond T. The Negro Family in British Guiana: *Family Structure and Social Status in the Villages. With a Foreword by Meyer Fortes. 314 pp. 8 plates. 1 figure. 4 maps.*

SOCIOLOGY AND PHILOSOPHY

Adriaansens, H. Talcott Parsons and the Conceptual Dilemma. *About 224 pp.*

Barnsley, John H. The Social Reality of Ethics. *A Comparative Analysis of Moral Codes. 448 pp.*

Diesing, Paul. Patterns of Discovery in the Social Sciences. *362 pp.*

● **Douglas, Jack D.** (Ed.) Understanding Everyday Life. *Toward the Reconstruction of Sociological Knowledge. Contributions by Alan F. Blum, Aaron W. Cicourel, Norman K. Denzin, Jack D. Douglas, John Heeren, Peter McHugh, Peter K. Manning, Melvin Power, Matthew Speier, Roy Turner, D. Lawrence Wieder, Thomas P. Wilson and Don H. Zimmerman. 370 pp.*

Gorman, Robert A. The Dual Vision. *Alfred Schutz and the Myth of Phenomenological Social Science. 240 pp.*

Jarvie, Ian C. Concepts and Society. *216 pp.*

Kilminster, R. Praxis and Method. *A Sociological Dialogue with Lukács, Gramsci and the Early Frankfurt School. 334 pp.*

● **Pelz, Werner.** The Scope of Understanding in Sociology. *Towards a More Radical Reorientation in the Social Humanistic Sciences. 283 pp.*

Roche, Maurice. Phenomenology, Language and the Social Sciences. *371 pp.*

Sahay, Arun. Sociological Analysis. *212 pp.*

● **Slater, P.** Origin and Significance of the Frankfurt School. *A Marxist Perspective. 185 pp.*

Spurling, L. Phenomenology and the Social World. *The Philosophy of Merleau-Ponty and its Relation to the Social Sciences. 222 pp.*

Wilson, H. T. The American Ideology. *Science, Technology and Organization as Modes of Rationality. 368 pp.*

International Library of Anthropology
General Editor Adam Kuper

● **Ahmed, A. S.** Millennium and Charisma Among Pathans. *A Critical Essay in Social Anthropology. 192 pp.*
Pukhtun Economy and Society. *Traditional Structure and Economic Development. About 360 pp.*

Barth, F. Selected Essays. *Volume I. About 250 pp.* Selected Essays. *Volume II. About 250 pp.*

Brown, Paula. The Chimbu. *A Study of Change in the New Guinea Highlands. 151 pp.*

Foner, N. Jamaica Farewell. *200 pp.*

Gudeman, Stephen. Relationships, Residence and the Individual. *A Rural Panamanian Community. 288 pp. 11 plates, 5 figures, 2 maps, 10 tables.*
The Demise of a Rural Economy. *From Subsistence to Capitalism in a Latin American Village. 160 pp.*

Hamnett, Ian. Chieftainship and Legitimacy. *An Anthropological Study of Executive Law in Lesotho. 163 pp.*

Hanson, F. Allan. Meaning in Culture. *127 pp.*

Hazan, H. The Limbo People. *A Study of the Constitution of the Time Universe Among the Aged. About 192 pp.*

Humphreys, S. C. Anthropology and the Greeks. *288 pp.*

Karp, I. Fields of Change Among the Iteso of Kenya. *140 pp.*

Lloyd, P. C. Power and Independence. *Urban Africans' Perception of Social Inequality. 264 pp.*

Parry, J. P. Caste and Kinship in Kangra. *352 pp. Illustrated.*

Pettigrew, Joyce. Robber Noblemen. *A Study of the Political System of the Sikh Jats. 284 pp.*

Street, Brian V. The Savage in Literature. *Representations of 'Primitive' Society in English Fiction, 1858–1920. 207 pp.*

Van Den Berghe, Pierre L. Power and Privilege at an African University. *278 pp.*

International Library of Phenomenology and Moral Sciences
General Editor John O'Neill

Apel, K.-O. Towards a Transformation of Philosophy. *308 pp.*

Bologh, R. W. Dialectical Phenomenology. *Marx's Method. 287 pp.*

Fekete, J. The Critical Twilight. *Explorations in the Ideology of Anglo-American Literary Theory from Eliot to McLuhan. 300 pp.*

Medina, A. Reflection, Time and the Novel. *Towards a Communicative Theory of Literature. 143 pp.*

International Library of Social Policy
General Editor Kathleen Jones

Bayley, M. Mental Handicap and Community Care. *426 pp.*

Bottoms, A. E. and **McClean, J. D.** Defendants in the Criminal Process. *284 pp.*

Bradshaw, J. The Family Fund. *An Initiative in Social Policy. About 224 pp.*

Butler, J. R. Family Doctors and Public Policy. *208 pp.*

Davies, Martin. Prisoners of Society. *Attitudes and Aftercare. 204 pp.*

Gittus, Elizabeth. Flats, Families and the Under-Fives. *285 pp.*

Holman, Robert. Trading in Children. *A Study of Private Fostering. 355 pp.*

Jeffs, A. Young People and the Youth Service. *160 pp.*

Jones, Howard and Cornes, Paul. Open Prisons. *288 pp.*

Jones, Kathleen. History of the Mental Health Service. *428 pp.*

Jones, Kathleen with **Brown, John, Cunningham, W. J., Roberts, Julian** and **Williams, Peter.** Opening the Door. *A Study of New Policies for the Mentally Handicapped. 278 pp.*

Karn, Valerie. Retiring to the Seaside. *400 pp. 2 maps. Numerous tables.*

King, R. D. and **Elliot, K. W.** Albany: Birth of a Prison—End of an Era. *394 pp.*

Thomas, J. E. The English Prison Officer since 1850: *A Study in Conflict. 258 pp.*

Walton, R. G. Women in Social Work. *303 pp.*

● **Woodward, J.** To Do the Sick No Harm. *A Study of the British Voluntary Hospital System to 1875. 234 pp.*

International Library of Welfare and Philosophy
General Editors   Noel Timms and David Watson

● **McDermott, F. E.** (Ed.) Self-Determination in Social Work. *A Collection of Essays on Self-determination and Related Concepts by Philosophers and Social Work Theorists. Contributors: F. P. Biestek, S. Bernstein, A. Keith-Lucas, D. Sayer, H. H. Perelman, C. Whittington, R. F. Stalley, F. E. McDermott, I. Berlin, H. J. McCloskey, H. L. A. Hart, J. Wilson, A. I. Melden, S. I. Benn. 254 pp.*

● **Plant, Raymond.** Community and Ideology. *104 pp.*

Ragg, Nicholas M. People Not Cases. *A Philosophical Approach to Social Work. 168 pp.*

● **Timms, Noel** and **Watson, David.** (Eds) Talking About Welfare. *Readings in Philosophy and Social Policy. Contributors: T. H. Marshall, R. B. Brandt, G. H. von Wright, K. Nielsen, M. Cranston, R. M. Titmuss, R. S. Downie, E. Telfer, D. Donnison, J. Benson, P. Leonard, A. Keith-Lucas, D. Walsh, I. T. Ramsey. 320 pp.*

● Philosophy in Social Work. *250 pp.*

● **Weale, A.** Equality and Social Policy. *164 pp.*

Library of Social Work
General Editor   Noel Timms

● **Baldock, Peter.** Community Work and Social Work. *140 pp.*

○ **Beedell, Christopher.** Residential Life with Children. *210 pp. Crown 8vo.*

● **Berry, Juliet.** Daily Experience in Residential Life. *A Study of Children and their Care-givers. 202 pp.*

○ Social Work with Children. *190 pp. Crown 8vo.*

● **Brearley, C. Paul.** Residential Work with the Elderly. *116 pp.*

● Social Work, Ageing and Society. *126 pp.*

● **Cheetham, Juliet.** Social Work with Immigrants. *240 pp. Crown 8vo.*

● **Cross, Crispin P.** (Ed.) Interviewing and Communication in Social Work. *Contributions by C. P. Cross, D. Laurenson, B. Strutt, S. Raven. 192 pp. Crown 8vo.*

● **Curnock, Kathleen** and **Hardiker, Pauline.** Towards Practice Theory. *Skills and Methods in Social Assessments. 208 pp.*

● **Davies, Bernard.** The Use of Groups in Social Work Practice. *158 pp.*

● **Davies, Martin.** Support Systems in Social Work. *144 pp.*

Ellis, June. (Ed.) West African Families in Britain. *A Meeting of Two Cultures. Contributions by Pat Stapleton, Vivien Biggs. 150 pp. 1 Map.*

● **Hart, John.** Social Work and Sexual Conduct. *230 pp.*

● **Hutten, Joan M.** Short-Term Contracts in Social Work. *Contributions by Stella M. Hall, Elsie Osborne, Mannie Sher, Eva Sternberg, Elizabeth Tuters. 134 pp.*

Jackson, Michael P. and **Valencia, B. Michael.** Financial Aid Through Social Work. *140 pp.*

● **Jones, Howard.** The Residential Community. *A Setting for Social Work. 150 pp.*

● (Ed.) Towards a New Social Work. *Contributions by Howard Jones, D. A. Fowler, J. R. Cypher, R. G. Walton, Geoffrey Mungham, Philip Priestley, Ian Shaw, M. Bartley, R. Deacon, Irwin Epstein, Geoffrey Pearson. 184 pp.*

Jones, Ray and **Pritchard, Colin.** (Eds) Social Work With Adolescents. *Contributions by Ray Jones, Colin Pritchard, Jack Dunham, Florence Rossetti, Andrew Kerslake, John Burns, William Gregory, Graham Templeman, Kenneth E. Reid, Audrey Taylor. About 170 pp.*

○ **Jordon, William.** The Social Worker in Family Situations. *160 pp. Crown 8vo.*

● **Laycock, A. L.** Adolescents and Social Work. *128 pp. Crown 8vo.*

● **Lees, Ray.** Politics and Social Work. *128 pp. Crown 8vo.*

● Research Strategies for Social Welfare. *112 pp. Tables.*

○ **McCullough, M. K.** and **Ely, Peter J.** Social Work with Groups. *127 pp. Crown 8vo.*

● **Moffett, Jonathan.** Concepts in Casework Treatment. *128 pp. Crown 8vo.*

Parsloe, Phyllida. Juvenile Justice in Britain and the United States. *The Balance of Needs and Rights. 336 pp.*

● **Plant, Raymond.** Social and Moral Theory in Casework. *112 pp. Crown 8vo.*

Priestley, Philip, Fears, Denise and **Fuller, Roger.** Justice for Juveniles. *The 1969 Children and Young Persons Act: A Case for Reform? 128 pp.*

● **Pritchard, Colin** and **Taylor, Richard.** Social Work: Reform or Revolution? *170 pp.*

○ **Pugh, Elisabeth.** Social Work in Child Care. *128 pp. Crown 8vo.*

● **Robinson, Margaret.** Schools and Social Work. *282 pp.*

○ **Ruddock, Ralph.** Roles and Relationships. *128 pp. Crown 8vo.*

● **Sainsbury, Eric.** Social Diagnosis in Casework. *118 pp. Crown 8vo.*

● Social Work with Families. *Perceptions of Social Casework among Clients of a Family Service. 188 pp.*

Seed, Philip. The Expansion of Social Work in Britain. *128 pp. Crown 8vo.*

● **Shaw, John.** The Self in Social Work. *124 pp.*

Smale, Gerald G. Prophecy, Behaviour and Change. *An Examination of Self-fulfilling Prophecies in Helping Relationships. 116 pp. Crown 8vo.*

Smith, Gilbert. Social Need. *Policy, Practice and Research. 155 pp.*

● Social Work and the Sociology of Organisations. *124 pp. Revised edition.*

● **Sutton, Carole.** Psychology for Social Workers and Counsellors. *An Introduction. 248 pp.*

● **Timms, Noel.** Language of Social Casework. *122 pp. Crown 8vo.*

● Recording in Social Work. *124 pp. Crown 8vo.*

● **Todd, F. Joan.** Social Work with the Mentally Subnormal. *96 pp. Crown 8vo.*

● **Walrond-Skinner, Sue.** Family Therapy. *The Treatment of Natural Systems. 172 pp.*

● **Warham, Joyce.** An Introduction to Administration for Social Workers. *Revised edition. 112 pp.*

● An Open Case. *The Organisational Context of Social Work. 172 pp.*

○ **Wittenberg, Isca Salzberger.** Psycho-Analytic Insight and Relationships. *A Kleinian Approach. 196 pp. Crown 8vo.*

Primary Socialization, Language and Education
General Editor Basil Bernstein

Adlam, Diana S., *with the assistance of Geoffrey Turner and Lesley Lineker.* Code in Context. *272 pp.*
Bernstein, Basil. Class, Codes and Control. *3 volumes.*
● 1. *Theoretical Studies Towards a Sociology of Language. 254 pp.*
2. *Applied Studies Towards a Sociology of Language. 377 pp.*
● 3. *Towards a Theory of Educational Transmission. 167 pp.*
Brandis, W. and **Bernstein, B.** Selection and Control. *176 pp.*
Brandis, Walter and **Henderson, Dorothy.** Social Class, Language and Communication. *288 pp.*
Cook-Gumperz, Jenny. Social Control and Socialization. *A Study of Class Differences in the Language of Maternal Control. 290 pp.*
● **Gahagan, D. M.** and **G. A.** Talk Reform. *Exploration in Language for Infant School Children. 160 pp.*
Hawkins, P. R. Social Class, the Nominal Group and Verbal Strategies. *About 220 pp.*
Robinson, W. P. and **Rackstraw, Susan D. A.** A Question of Answers. *2 volumes. 192 pp. and 180 pp.*
Turner, Geoffrey J. and **Mohan, Bernard A.** A Linguistic Description and Computer Programme for Children's Speech. *208 pp.*

Reports of the Institute of Community Studies

Baker, J. The Neighbourhood Advice Centre. A Community Project in Camden. *320 pp.*
● **Cartwright, Ann.** Patients and their Doctors. *A Study of General Practice. 304 pp.*
Dench, Geoff. Maltese in London. *A Case-study in the Erosion of Ethnic Consciousness. 302 pp.*
Jackson, Brian and **Marsden, Dennis.** Education and the Working Class: *Some General Themes Raised by a Study of 88 Working-class Children in a Northern Industrial City. 268 pp. 2 folders.*
Marris, Peter. The Experience of Higher Education. *232 pp. 27 tables.*
● Loss and Change. *192 pp.*
Marris, Peter and **Rein, Martin.** Dilemmas of Social Reform. *Poverty and Community Action in the United States. 256 pp.*
Marris, Peter and **Somerset, Anthony.** African Businessmen. *A Study of Entrepreneurship and Development in Kenya. 256 pp.*
Mills, Richard. Young Outsiders: *a Study in Alternative Communities. 216 pp.*
Runciman, W. G. Relative Deprivation and Social Justice. *A Study of Attitudes to Social Inequality in Twentieth-Century England. 352 pp.*
Willmott, Peter. Adolescent Boys in East London. *230 pp.*
Willmott, Peter and **Young, Michael.** Family and Class in a London Suburb. *202 pp. 47 tables.*
Young, Michael and **McGeeney, Patrick.** Learning Begins at Home. *A Study of a Junior School and its Parents. 128 pp.*
Young, Michael and **Willmott, Peter.** Family and Kinship in East London. *Foreword by Richard M. Titmuss. 252 pp. 39 tables.*
The Symmetrical Family. *410 pp.*

Reports of the Institute for Social Studies in Medical Care

Cartwright, Ann, Hockey, Lisbeth and **Anderson, John J.** Life Before Death. *310 pp.*
Dunnell, Karen and **Cartwright, Ann.** Medicine Takers, Prescribers and Hoarders. *190 pp.*
Farrell, C. My Mother Said. . . *A Study of the Way Young People Learned About Sex and Birth Control. 288 pp.*

Medicine, Illness and Society
General Editor W. M. Williams

Hall, David J. Social Relations & Innovation. *Changing the State of Play in Hospitals. 232 pp.*
Hall, David J. and **Stacey, M.** (Eds) Beyond Separation. *234 pp.*
Robinson, David. The Process of Becoming Ill. *142 pp.*
Stacey, Margaret *et al.* Hospitals, Children and Their Families. *The Report of a Pilot Study. 202 pp.*
Stimson, G. V. and **Webb, B.** Going to See the Doctor. *The Consultation Process in General Practice. 155 pp.*

Monographs in Social Theory
General Editor Arthur Brittan

● **Barnes, B.** Scientific Knowledge and Sociological Theory. *192 pp.*
Bauman, Zygmunt. Culture as Praxis. *204 pp.*
● **Dixon, Keith.** Sociological Theory. *Pretence and Possibility. 142 pp.*
  The Sociology of Belief. *Fallacy and Foundation. About 160 pp.*
Goff, T. W. Marx and Mead. *Contributions to a Sociology of Knowledge. 176 pp.*
Meltzer, B. N., Petras, J. W. and **Reynolds, L. T.** Symbolic Interactionism. *Genesis, Varieties and Criticisms. 144 pp.*
● **Smith, Anthony D.** The Concept of Social Change. *A Critique of the Functionalist Theory of Social Change. 208 pp.*

Routledge Social Science Journals

The British Journal of Sociology. *Editor – Angus Stewart; Associate Editor – Leslie Sklair. Vol. 1, No. 1 – March 1950 and Quarterly. Roy. 8vo. All back issues available. An international journal publishing original papers in the field of sociology and related areas.*
Community Work. *Edited by David Jones and Marjorie Mayo. 1973. Published annually.*
Economy and Society. *Vol. 1, No. 1. February 1972 and Quarterly. Metric Roy. 8vo. A journal for all social scientists covering sociology, philosophy, anthropology, economics and history. All back numbers available.*

Ethnic and Racial Studies. *Editor – John Stone. Vol. 1 – 1978. Published quarterly.*
Religion. Journal of Religion and Religions. *Chairman of Editorial Board, Ninian Smart. Vol. 1, No. 1, Spring 1971. A journal with an inter-disciplinary approach to the study of the phenomena of religion. All back numbers available.*
Sociology of Health and Illness. *A Journal of Medical Sociology. Editor – Alan Davies; Associate Editor – Ray Jobling. Vol. 1, Spring 1979. Published 3 times per annum.*
Year Book of Social Policy in Britain. *Edited by Kathleen Jones. 1971. Published annually.*

Social and Psychological Aspects of Medical Practice
Editor Trevor Silverstone

Lader, Malcolm. Psychophysiology of Mental Illness. *280 pp.*
● **Silverstone, Trevor** and **Turner, Paul.** Drug Treatment in Psychiatry. *Revised edition. 256 pp.*
Whiteley, J. S. and **Gordon, J.** Group Approaches in Psychiatry. *240 pp.*

Printed and bound in Great Britain by
Redwood Burn Limited, Trowbridge & Esher